D1216240

Incompatible with God's Design

A History of the Women's Ordination Movement in the U.S. Roman Catholic Church

Mary Jeremy Daigler

ROWMAN & LITTLEFIELD
Lanham • Boulder • New York • London

MORRILL MEMORIAL LIBRARY
NORWOOD, MASS 02062

262.14
Daigler

Published by Rowman & Littlefield
A wholly owned subsidiary of The Rowman & Littlefield Publishing Group, Inc.
4501 Forbes Boulevard, Suite 200, Lanham, Maryland 20706
www.rowman.com

Unit A, Whitacre Mews, 26-34 Stannery Street, London SE11 4AB

Copyright © 2012 by Mary Jeremy Daigler
First paperback edition 2015

All rights reserved. No part of this book may be reproduced in any form or by any electronic or mechanical means, including information storage and retrieval systems, without written permission from the publisher, except by a reviewer who may quote passages in a review.

British Library Cataloguing in Publication Information Available

Library of Congress Cataloging-in-Publication Data
The hardback edition of this book was previously catalogued by the Library of Congress as follows:

Daigler, Mary Jeremy, 1938–
Incompatible with God's design : a history of the women's ordination movement in the U.S. Roman Catholic Church / Mary Jeremy Daigler.
p. cm.
Includes bibliographical references and index.
1. Ordination of women—Catholic Church. 2. Women in the Catholic Church—History. 3. Women clergy. I. Title.
BX1912.2.D35 2012
262'.14273082—dc23
2012019292

ISBN 978-0-8108-8479-3 (cloth : alk. paper)
ISBN 978-1-4422-4582-2 (pbk : alk. paper)
ISBN 978-0-8108-8480-9 (ebook)

♾™ The paper used in this publication meets the minimum requirements of American National Standard for Information Sciences Permanence of Paper for Printed Library Materials, ANSI/NISO Z39.48-1992.

Printed in the United States of America

Dedicated in gratitude to the memory of
Gustave Weigel, SJ

Every form of social or cultural discrimination in fundamental personal rights on the grounds of sex, race, color, social conditions, language or religion must be curbed and eradicated as incompatible with God's design.

—Documents of Vatican II, *Gaudium et Spes*, article 29, English translation, 2nd edition, translated by Austin P. Flannery and promulgated by Pope John Paul II, September 8, 1997

Contents

Preface

This book contains the first comprehensive history of the Roman Catholic women's ordination movement in the United States. While it is true that individuals have written brief histories of their respective regions or organizations, the one-hundred-year history of the movement, as a whole, has been left undone until now.

In addition, scholars have thoroughly studied and published every other aspect of the issue except its history: sacramental theology, pastoral implications, canon law, scriptural exegesis, church history, statistics regarding the male priest shortage, and opinion surveys of church members.

The defining elements of this volume are clear in its title. It is a *history*, not a polemic or an apologia; its subject is *ordination*, not merely "increased participation" in the life and ministries of the church; it describes a broad *movement*, not merely the one organization called "WOC"; its focus is on the *Roman Catholic* movement only; and its setting is the *United States*, providing a national picture while including international and local groups insofar as they relate to the U.S. story. You will find stories of engaging human beings and inspirational ones.

My goal has been to offer materials that will be of general interest, as well as of responsible scholarship (hence, the abundant notes to each chapter). Still, no historical research can be taken as "proof" of how things happened. Even authentic documents of the time or the lived experience of the reader all are subject to the hermeneutic of suspicion. A historian must acknowledge that archival materials have been preselected (either by the person who is the subject or by the executor of her estate) and must try to imagine why these particular documents were saved and what documents might have been accidentally lost or deliberately purged.

The unfolding of the history here is not strictly chronological but traces a classic Greek meander line, simultaneously folding back and moving forward because hints of the future are discernible in events that have already occurred. The story is partial as well, especially because of limitations in using the names of some individuals (particularly in chapters 4 and 5) who are at risk of disciplinary action by the hierarchy if their words or actions become public. The incompleteness and indirection remain for more thorough exploration, which I leave to historians and doctoral students to come.

At the foundation of my writing were countless hours of very enjoyable sleuthing in archives, somewhat less enjoyable months at the computer, interviews with the famous and the infamous, informal conversations, and decades of listening as a Roman Catholic woman. The task lengthened during the years I spent pondering the great mass of material and trying to prune it to best effect.

Direct influences on my work have been the scholarship of Mary Henold, Susan Lindley Hill, and John Wijngaards, each of whom came to my awareness by accident, so to speak. I hope to contribute to the discussion of women's ordination only a fraction of the insight I received from their work. Indirect influences are listed among the theologians and other scholars whose names appear in the bibliography. They have profoundly affected my understanding of and response to the Roman Catholic Church.

It is a joy for me to acknowledge the Sisters of Mercy, particularly of the South Central Regional Community, who have provided me with time, material resources, moral support, and patient listening for decades. To Mary Aquin O'Neill and the Mount Saint Agnes Theological Center for Women, I am deeply grateful for intellectual stimulation, opportunities to float "trial balloons," and dialogue events with their participative students. Anthony Berret has for many years been a quietly reassuring sounding board and most recently contributed his critical professorial eye to reviewing the manuscript for this book. Wendy Hefter, who worked wonders with the technical aspects of formatting and polishing the text, provided a single-minded focus and kept me on deadline when I languished.

Matthew Blessing and Phillip Runkel at Marquette University will stand as representative of the several archivists whom I gratefully encountered in various institutions along the way. They hold with care, respect, and professionalism the records of history and share them with gladness and encouragement. Lastly, I acknowledge my deep and humble gratitude to friends and acquaintances who urged me on and energized me with the simplest of questions: "How's the book coming?"

Introduction

Before building a house, there is much literal groundwork to be done, such as sampling the soil, studying the infrastructure capabilities, noting the proximity to public utilities, and assessing the location's desirability. There is groundwork too before building an understanding of the controversial women's ordination movement in the U.S. Roman Catholic Church. The following paragraphs may provide some preliminary tools for that endeavor.

CONTEMPORARY POINTS OF CONTROVERSY REGARDING WOMEN'S ORDINATION

From the point of view of the current pope and of his predecessor, expressed in their writings, the reason women cannot be ordained is because they do not bear a physical resemblance to Jesus, whom they would be representing. This is called the *in persona Christi* argument, first advanced officially by Paul VI in 1976. From the point of view of most scholars of ancient languages, *persona* does not refer to the human body but to the human spirit; therefore, they hold that women are qualified to be ordained. Another reason given by the hierarchy favoring the current law is that church polity must flow from the Scriptures, and those sources contain no evidence that Jesus ordained any women. Taking the opposite stand are Scripture scholars who hold that Jesus did not ordain anyone at all—male or female. They say that because of this, both male and female are eligible.

Broader than the specifically Roman Catholic debates noted above are three additional challenges that give rise to controversy. Contemporary societies in most Western countries and elsewhere understand women to be equal to men. There may be *de facto* discrimination against women in those places, but the civil laws generally do not endorse it as do the church's laws. Secondly, there is a Scripture-based theology in Christianity that flows from the explicit statement of the apostle Paul that "There does not exist among you Jew or Greek, slave or free, male or female. All are one in Christ Jesus" (Gal. 3:28). Thirdly, within the Roman Catholic Church much is made of its role as a witnessing, teaching community, as seen in the documents of Vatican II and the talks and writings of popes and bishops. Yet their actions do not match their words regarding women in the church. These three contradictions color the controversy surrounding women's ordination and are difficult to reconcile.

EARLY CHRISTIAN COMMUNITIES AND THE ISSUE

Beginning with Paul's letter to the Galatians, written in about AD 54, the foundational attitude of the early Christian community was egalitarian. Elsewhere (Rom. 16) Paul specifically mentions Phoebe who was serving as a deacon, and he described her with that term, a Greek word with broad application, meaning "someone who serves." It is very difficult to know for certain if Paul used the term in its secular sense, or in a specifically religious sense. Even if he was using it regarding a religious role, such a role must not be understood in the same way that it is implemented today. To think that the diaconate of AD 54 was the same as what we see today is to paint the past with a very frayed brush. Not only the diaconate but the priesthood itself has changed over two millennia in ways that many moderns find unimaginable. One cannot impose the patterns of the present on the practices of the past.

In addition to Paul's writings, there is archaeological evidence that until the sixth century several Christian Mediterranean communities specified on tombstones and in frescoes that the deceased woman was a deacon, presbyter, or bishop. Tombstones inscribed in this way have been found in Palestine/Israel, Greece, Asia Minor, Macedonia, Italy, Sicily, and France. Some classicists point out that frescoes of women fulfilling priestly functions can be seen in catacombs in and near Rome. Skeptics remind their readers the tombstone inscriptions merely indicate that the deceased woman was the wife of a man holding the office mentioned. The variety in these findings reinforces the Scripture scholars' observation that what we today call "the early church" was really a very diverse cluster of regional, decentralized faith communities that implemented various practices in many matters.

SUBSEQUENT CENTURIES

As time went on Christianity grew in numbers, in locations, and in diversity of practices. Inevitably there arose a simultaneous impulse toward uniformity, found in admonitions and exhortations from theologians and pious men wanting to reform what they perceived as errors. Several of these writers specifically condemned certain forms of women's service to the communities, especially the services of teaching and liturgical ministries. Yet the very fact that these condemnations were written suggests that women of that time were, indeed, serving in the sanctuary in visible liturgical ministries. If they were not, there would have been no need for the exhortations. The dating and content of such documents of opposition proves that women's roles were multiple and controversial until at least the early ninth century.

Ecclesiastical writings preserved from subsequent centuries, the Middle Ages, continued the pattern of attempted control of women as lay persons (sexual matters) and as members of religious communities (cloister, obedience, finances). During those times, however, there was a veritable explosion of new religious communities of women, who may have seen in these groups the possibility for a preferable sort of control over their own lives. The nuns of Hildegarde of Bingen, the non-cloistered communities of Beguines, and individuals like Jeanne d'Arc are but a very few exemplars of the sorts of freedom available to Catholic women of the Middle Ages if they chose. It may be that the women who felt called to the ordained ministries of the church were willing to transfer the energy of that call into a communal religious life as nuns and Sisters. In addition, each passing century led the church farther away from the charisms and practices of the early church, until the ordination of women had become a fantasy or the dream of one or another eccentric woman.

MODERN TIMES

The outlook of the medieval church spilled over smoothly into the next centuries, but by the 1800s women's roles in society were changing significantly, especially in the Western world. Catholics were, perhaps, slower than others to embrace such changes, imbued as they were by the acute traditionalism and the tightly hierarchical nature of their church. Eventually, in 1911 the first recorded Catholic organization advocating women's ordination came into being in London as the St. Joan's Alliance. Its earliest task was to gain the right to vote for women in the United Kingdom and, having accomplished that goal, they expanded their work to secure rights for women in the Roman Catholic Church. The organization had established itself under the banner of civil rights, and they approached their second goal in the same spirit: for them the ordination issue was one of justice.

In the middle of the twentieth century, the Catholic hierarchy began to acknowledge women in ways similar to the secular society of the times, periodically writing statements and documents concerning their importance to church and society. The ordination issue was studiously avoided, or never even entered their minds. Women, though, were beginning to think about it themselves in ever-increasing numbers. They deepened and broadened their education, including scriptural and theological studies at the doctoral level. Catholic institutions of secondary and higher education of the 1950s unintentionally equipped their students to later critique the church, just as they were taught to critique academic questions of philosophy, literature, and economics. Thus, U.S. Catholics began to raise questions even about their own church, its rules, and its regulations, including the prohibition against ordaining women.

After translation, dissemination, and discussion of the documents of Vatican II (1962–1965), many Catholic women envisioned a changed role for themselves in church and society. As with any threat to traditions, ideological sides emerged, either for or against each new idea. The points of controversy among them regarding women's ordination can be observed still today in varying degrees.

1. Among the Catholic Churches there are different practices regarding women's ordination. In recent years some of the Eastern Orthodox Churches (the Armenian and the Greek) have made a public recommitment to ordaining women to the diaconate. Roman Catholic tradition prohibits these ordinations, and these realities will no doubt be the source of future tensions among the groups.
2. In the wider arena it is still the case that those who interpret the Scriptures literally are at odds with those who understand their various roots and applications differently. One controversy that arises, among many others, is the issue of unquestioned papal authority. The former group derives its belief from the New Testament, whereas the latter points out that there was no papacy in those times.
3. Within the ordination movement itself there is a wide divergence of theologies, so far coexisting in relative amity. The most challenging position comes from profoundly Catholic feminist theologians and their followers: A true community (even a church) must show no discrimination among its members; all must be perfectly equal, with no hints of class or caste in their structure or practices. Proponents of this theory speak against the worth of pursuing ordination in the current incarnation of the Roman Catholic Church.
4. Differing goals define two other groups within the movement: those whose primary goal is that the church reinstitute the ordination of women to the diaconate; and those who will settle for nothing less than ordination to the priesthood.
5. An unspoken tension in the movement is the one between the women who remain committed to the reform of the church and those who

despair of that possibility and have walked away from the church altogether.

SOME POINTS OF CONFLICT

- Every time a woman chaplain in a hospital is faced with a patient request for the sacrament of the sick and she cannot oblige . . .
- Every time a female staff member prepares an individual or group for sacraments and is banned from baptizing, confirming, or reconciling a person with God . . .
- Every time a woman campus minister is not allowed to officially witness alumnae/i marriages, or to celebrate Eucharist for student groups, or to preach at campus liturgies . . .
- Every time students who are scriptural literalists refuse to accept their female professor's teaching authority . . .
- Every time a more-than-competent female theologian is denied a seminary position in teaching or administration or student counseling . . .
- Every time a young girl is denied the right to assist the priest as an altar server . . .
- Every time a new pope is elected without a woman's vote . . .
- Every time changes in canon law or diocesan polity are passed without a woman's vote . . .
- Every time a bishop or pastor is appointed without a woman's equal voice in the process . . .
- Every time a Catholic woman meets an ordained woman from another faith . . .

These are some of the times and places when the current realities conflict.

Chapter One

Illuminating a Design

EARLY AMERICAN PERIOD TO VATICAN II

The word "illuminating" stirs up at least two meanings in the modern mind: the literal meaning of bringing a source of light into a dark place—a spotlight onto a stage, for example—and the figurative meaning of painting a visual picture in order to facilitate understanding, such as a miniature scene painted on a medieval manuscript page. In exploring any period of history, a third meaning is applicable as well: the bringing to the light of public view the stories of individuals and groups that have been in the relative darkness of attics, basements, closets, and bottom desk-drawers.

The following pages will illuminate their topics in each of those ways: by casting a spotlight onto an unacknowledged corner of Roman Catholic Church history (the work of many Catholics over a long period of time to promote the ordination of women to the diaconate and priesthood), and by providing miniature verbal paintings of women and men whose lives raise the question of what it means to be "compatible with God's design."

The term "design," too, has multiple meanings and connotations in contemporary English—especially when invoked in a religious context. Designs can be understood as humanly devised, such as fashion design, architectural design, or media design, for which there are even academic programs of preparation. Yet another use of the word reflects the conviction that natural energies were originally set in motion by their creator and according to their composition spin out into what humans consider to be matter and design. And for many persons, the term means that every aspect and moment of human and nonhuman creation is actively, specifically, and individually designed by the deity. In the document of Vatican II called *Gaudium et Spes*, there is an underlying theological presumption that the human mind can by

1

life experience, or in prayer or by study of Scripture and of human nature, discern what is "God's design" for all peoples and planets. Even though it is, in fact, not possible for humans to know that design indisputably, believers and faiths through all ages and cultures have struggled to overcome that inherent uncertainty.

It is shortsighted to claim, as many do, that the women's ordination movement reached its visible intensity in the 1970s solely because of the women's liberation movement that pervaded the U.S. culture at that time. In human history, very few social movements, cultural trends, religious creeds, intellectual concepts, or legal codes are generated completely spontaneously and independently of previously existing influences. Instead they come about slowly, either in harmony with the human realities preceding and surrounding them or in resistance against those realities. The artist, the politician, the scholar, the scientist, and the revolutionary in any field may want to deny this fact, but the truth is that there is nothing completely new under the sun. This truism is evident in the millennia-long movement of women to resist being treated as unequal to men in society, in the home, and in religion.

The internalization of outside influences is most often a subtle process. For example, the debate about whether or not violence in the media increases the likelihood of the viewer, listener, or reader becoming violent in their own thoughts or actions turns on acceptance or rejection of this principle. Likewise, the stories told in history classes or heard in religious education programs may never afterward be consciously alluded to, but they do create the raw material out of which future "Aha!" moments are created. So while the main focus of this book is specifically the Roman Catholic Church in the United States, it is realistic to glance at a few of the "secular" and non–Roman Catholic elements that predated and contributed to the start of the explicit women's ordination movement in this country.

The Seventeenth Century

Indigenous Spirituality

Early American events and persons had at least an unconscious influence on their contemporaries and on those who came later; and they form the background out of which the current women's ordination movements emerge.[1] For example, as early as the 1600s the constitution of the early Iroquois Nations assigned to the women of the tribe the right to declare war and to forge peace agreements. The Iroquois women also enjoyed the equivalent of what the United States did not accept until three hundred years later: women's suffrage. These responsibilities of the Iroquois women were known and visible to the explorers and colonizers coming into the land but surely did not figure in the western movies on which many later Americans were raised. Nonetheless, their "energy field" or "Great Spirit" or "collective unconscious" has been present and at work across the centuries.

Early Colonial Religion

Native American spirituality, religion, and daily life are and were inseparable, and the Puritan colonizers who arrived from England in 1630 were unknowingly similar to them in that respect—or wanted to be. The Puritans' voyage across the ocean was for them a pilgrimage to a sort of utopia where they could live and worship in freedom, union, and harmony. Their religious beliefs would expressly infuse their daily activities at home and in the community. All held the same religious faith, or claimed that they did. But Anne Marbury Hutchinson's arrival in the Massachusetts Bay Colony in 1634 shone a light on the darker side of utopia, and the content of her spiritual guidance and public teaching resulted in conflict and controversy, as the introduction of new ideas can so easily do in a tight-knit community. In 1637 she, her family, and her followers were ejected from the Massachusetts Bay Colony and found welcome in Rhode Island, which had been settled by Roger Williams to provide a free place for those whose beliefs were not acceptable to their surrounding faiths or cultures.[2]

Hutchinson's story has been told and taught in elementary and secondary schools in the United States since long before the women's liberation movement of the 1970s, and its subtext of the persecution of a woman for her religious beliefs and her leadership has strengthened many in similar circumstances. On the other hand, to ponder her fate and that of the slightly later women who were tried and hanged for witchery might move some women and men to be less risk-taking precisely in areas of faith.

Roman Catholic Visibility

Like Hutchinson, Margaret Brent was not typical of the women of her time and place (1601–1671). She was a Roman Catholic who lived and worked in the Maryland colony. An unmarried woman of considerable wealth, Margaret Brent argued law before the civil courts for eight years (1642–1650) with great success; and in 1648 she was the first person in the colonies to petition that voting rights be granted to women. The petition was denied, but Brent's intelligence, wealth, skill, and public persona kept her in the forefront of the colony and of the legal profession. So esteemed was she that Governor Leonard Calvert appointed her to manage his material assets, and yet, despite his support of her, she was eventually penalized by the colony because of her strong expression of views that differed from those of the local leaders. Margaret Brent and her relatives were ejected from Maryland, and they resettled in Virginia. Her life is not widely well known today, even in Maryland, but it was nonetheless part of the gathering mass of energy mentioned above.

Quakers Arrive from England

Some eight years after the Brents' crisis, there arrived from England in 1656 the first Quakers in this land, including Mary Fisher and Ann Austin. The Quaker belief in the fundamental equality of women and men gravely threatened the colonies' leaders. That women and men shared the public religious teaching function, that they were involved as equals in public business life, and that they abhorred interior as well as exterior violence was perceived as a threat to the surrounding culture. How could their neighbors be secure if the pacifist Quakers would not fight off enemies? How could they look forward to financial survival and material prosperity if any of the town's business life rested in women's hands? How could husbands continue to expect compliance and tranquility in the home if their wives began to imitate the more outspoken ways of the Quaker wives? These fears and the atmosphere they poisoned led to the hanging four years later of Mary Barrett Dyer in Boston. The charge was based on the fact that she had rejected the Puritan belief system and converted to Quakerism.

"Consorting with the devil" would be a charge laughed out of court today in U.S. civil law, but the murky mingling of secular laws and religious values in 1692 Salem had anything but frivolous outcomes: 180 women and men of the settlement were accused of the crime of witchcraft. But in the notorious one year of the trials, "only" nineteen persons were executed: thirteen women and six men.[3] Execution was the tragic and disproportionate price exacted for behavior that exceeded the bounds of what their community could absorb, and even more extremely than with Margaret Brent, the community forcibly cut off the guilty from its life.

Even today the pervasive image of a witch is that of a woman, and our culture still associates women with witchery and fails to examine the significance of the Salem lives and deaths. On the surface the witches' executions were about magic, fortune-telling, or disobedience, but the underlying cause was but one: their violent rejection by their own faith community because of their behaviors or beliefs.

The Eighteenth Century

Deadly as the Salem trials often were, they marked a turning point of some sort, for after them there was never again a trial for witchcraft in the colonies, and executions for heresy declined dramatically. In 1704 the public practice of Catholicism was banned, churches were locked, priests dispersed, and Catholic families began to rely on their women as spiritual guides, prayer leaders, and organizers of the very rare services of underground priests. The development of such Catholic female pastoral leadership can be considered one positive, though small, outcome of the discriminatory laws against the Roman Catholic Church.

The period beginning shortly after the banning of Roman Catholic religious practice is known as the period of the Great Awakenings, which were campaigns to renew the religious and spiritual lives of the people in the colonies. Tangential to the Awakenings movement, the first Catholic Sisters arrived in the colonies in 1727: the Sisters of St. Ursula, who came to New Orleans from France to undertake the teaching of young girls. And at the very end of the century, in 1790 there came from Holland to Port Tobacco, Maryland, a small community of contemplative Carmelite nuns. The original colonial settlers would have been familiar, to greater and lesser degrees, with Catholic vowed religious life in their various countries of origin; but by 1727 American society at large had probably lost awareness of that life's nature and purpose. Both of these communities have been in continuous, lively existence from those days to our own as visible reminders of an "alternative" way of life for female Catholics.

An abundance of individual "firsts" arose in the North American Colonies during the eighteenth century, some secular and some related to religions: the first woman newspaper publisher, the first woman book publisher, the first published black female poet, the first North American Shaker community; the first woman to fight in the army, and the first two colonies (New Jersey and Virginia) to grant women their right to vote (later rescinded).

During this period of time, transatlantic communications depended solely on months-long crossings, but news eventually reached the colonists on paper or in conversations with women and men who arrived in person. By these means, stories of France's *citoyennes* barricading the roads and storming the Bastille in 1789 alongside their male counterparts gave the colonists pause regarding women's roles in society. Three years later Mary Wollstonecraft published in England her widely circulated manifesto, "A Vindication of the Rights of Women." Its text made its way across the ocean and even today is sometimes used to fortify contemporary women's struggle for equality.

The Nineteenth Century

A typical listing of women's advancements in the nineteenth century[4] indicates an explosion of "firsts," so many that a reader might lose sight of the tremendous significance of each individual woman mentioned on the roster. The great number of women leaders may create a second challenge as well: the reader can forget that for each name on the list, thousands upon thousands of "ordinary" women, not in the public eye, were simultaneously making small changes in their daily lives and communities that laid the foundations upon which the more publicly charismatic individual women could stand. One of these hidden women may have simply decided to send her daughter to secondary school. Or another may have taken a job on the line in a textile mill and asked one or two questions about employees' rights. Another woman overheard the questions and pressed forward with the same ones, but among a different group of employees. And so it spread.

One thread weaving through the burgeoning of women's leadership during this period is its broad geographical spread. Lest one dismiss the claim as merely an East Coast phenomenon, the following data will reveal how widespread this development really was. In addition to the states in the east, the sometimes surprising workplaces of these women included California, Idaho, Illinois, Iowa, Kansas, Kentucky, Louisiana, Michigan, Minnesota, Nebraska, New Mexico, North Dakota, Ohio, Oklahoma, South Dakota, Tennessee, Texas, Utah, and Washington.

Another thread is the gradually increasing ethnic and racial diversification of the pool of women themselves. Abolition of slavery was one of three great goals of many women of the middle and upper classes of the time, along with temperance and suffrage. Immigration rapidly changed the workplace between 1815 and 1860, as large numbers of women from other lands moved as quickly as possible into the workforce outside their homes.

To grasp even a portion of the volume of women's achievements in the nineteenth century, it can be helpful to cluster them into four major arenas in our nation's life in which the continual increase in women's leadership was evident: education, employment, political life, and religion.

Education

Late in the nineteenth century, the Roman Catholic bishops became aware that large numbers of the new immigrants were Roman Catholic and were lacking in employment and learning opportunities. Realizing that education would lead to employment, they developed within their parishes and dioceses a focus on education for all Catholic children: girls as well as boys. An additional benefit, the bishops believed, was that the faith of the young would not be subject to the secular influence of the public schools. It was in this period that the bishops stepped up their requests of religious communities across the Atlantic to send missionaries to North America. This emphasis on education had two unforeseen outcomes: the children grew up equipped to question the religious practices of their ancestors, and their teachers—the Sisters—gradually emerged from the fairly cloistered life they had formerly lived in Europe.

As elementary education became well established, either in the home or in the school, an upward funnel developed in the nineteenth century, advancing students to whatever level of education they sought. The lack of opportunity for girls and women was clear. So in 1821, the first secondary school for girls opened in Troy, New York. Shortly thereafter, Mt. Holyoke Seminary (College) opened in order to provide for women the type of education that would be of the same high quality as men's colleges. During this same period Vassar, Wellesley, and Smith Colleges were founded for women students only. In the midst of the openings of all-female colleges, several formerly all-male ones began to open their doors to women: first Oberlin and then Geneva Medical College. The University of Michigan and Cornell University also eventually opened their doors to women students in the 1800s.

Each of these advancements in education represents the dogged persistence of individual girls and women to achieve recognition of their abilities as equal to boys' and men's. Their rising levels of education sharpened their awareness of the areas of life in which they were not recognized as equal to males. This insight spilled over into the churches and synagogues, which gradually had to deal with the critiques of women seeking equality with men in their faith communities.

Employment

The large number of women in the labor force during the 1800s gave rise to a shared hope that they could improve their harsh and abusive lot by banding together. The first known strike of U.S. women workers occurred in Dover, New Hampshire, in 1828 over the issues of wages and working conditions and subsequently ignited a conflagration of similar walkouts elsewhere in New England; notably, in Lowell, Massachusetts, and in Lawrence, Massachusetts. One of the banners in Lawrence read "Give Us Bread and Give Us Roses" and was later versified, set to music, and embraced as the laborers' rallying song. In the final decade of the century a woman, Mary Kenny O'Sullivan, became the first female organizer in the American Federation of Labor.

Some sixty years after the strikes by the female laborers in New England, Mary Harris "Mother" Jones took on the coal mining industry in Pennsylvania and West Virginia, fighting for the rights of the men and young boys who labored for little compensation in a slave-like system of total enforced dependence on the companies. She crossed the country many times to support and advocate for laboring children, women, and men who worked in intolerable conditions.

By mid-century, women's employment in diverse fields of work continued to increase: local and state courts of law, organized social services, research science, journalism, medicine, eco-activism, and management and ownership of newspapers. Education and training gave the early women the tools needed to learn of these and other fields, and to design their futures according to their skills and passions, rather than according to tradition.

Legal Systems

A third arena in which women made their presence felt in the nineteenth century was that of securing a place within the legal systems in the country so that their human rights would be ensured. They sought to be freed from dependence on the personal whim of spouses, fathers, clergy, town elders, male-protecting laws, or chance. The women who engaged in these struggles were audacious, astute, and strong in choosing and implementing their strategies. Since women had no legal status themselves, they often succeeded by personal persuasion of male friends or family members, as demonstrated in their documented success at getting property laws changed by the official, all-male lawmakers. Once women were property owners, other legal rights accrued to them, and they began to gradually develop ever-larger spheres of influence in their own locale and beyond. Those who chose a different sort of activism used the psychology of numbers in their demonstrations. They used their own eloquence whenever and wherever they could find an ear, even an unlikely or unwilling one. And upon occasion they showed rage.

It is a common belief that power is never given over freely; that it must always be wrested from the hands of the powerful by some sort of force, not necessarily physical. And in the case of justice toward women, the scale was pervasively and heavily imbalanced against them. They had no legal toehold, except the words of the nation's Constitution; the guardians and interpreters had failed to apply them to women. Many women were killed, jailed, physically abused, verbally humiliated, ostracized, and materially penalized; and yet, all across the country women really believed that if they worked hard enough, they would be able to change the systems, both secular and religious. And they did, to a great degree—even without the right to vote.

In mid-century (1848), Lucretia Coffin Mott and Elizabeth Cady Stanton organized and led an initial gathering at Seneca Falls, New York, which focused on the suffrage rights issue as the main plank of their platform and ignited the women's rights movement in the United States. Twelve years later, they held another National Convention for Women's Rights in Rochester, New York, at which the main action items concerned wages, the marriage vow of obedience, and gaining the vote. Not letting up for a moment, Elizabeth Cady Stanton entered her name in candidacy for a seat in Congress, before women could even vote. And two years later, in 1868, the first proposal for a women's suffrage amendment was introduced in the Senate, but failed passage. Year by year from then on, the issue never went away, due partly to two organizations that were almost identical in purpose and name: the National Women Suffrage Association, and the American Suffrage Association. Eleven years later, Belva Bennett Lockwood won passage of the law granting women the right to practice law before the U.S. Supreme Court. Victoria Claflin Woodhull declared herself a candidate in the race for the

U.S. presidency. Meanwhile, the state of Wyoming went its own way and allowed women to vote (1869) and to serve on juries (1871) far ahead of the rest of the nation, which did not grant women the right to vote in all states until 1920.

Simultaneously, Frances Willard of Illinois found the courage to publicly address the issue of alcohol abuse as a destroyer of family life and of the social fabric. She led the Women's Christian Temperance Union (WCTU), which became the largest women's organization in the nation at that time. Though the WCTU's strategies were ridiculed, cartooned, caricatured, and satirized, the purpose of the union found resonance across gender lines, economic lines, and religious lines. For example, of the three social movements of the day, temperance, abolition, and women's suffrage, temperance was the only one to receive widespread support from the Catholic bishops. This was rooted in their avowed desire to improve family dynamics and ensure decent housing and steady income for their people.

The women who fought to alter laws and attitudes that both caused and flowed from the secular legal systems not only changed them but modeled successful strategies, behaviors, and attitudes for the women who have come after them and have sought to change any disempowering system—even religion.

Religion

It is time now to meet some women of the nineteenth century who put their attention not primarily to education, nor to employment issues, nor to a discriminatory legal system, but to the arena that is often affected by all of the aforementioned: religion. There were, during that century, many women who implicitly or explicitly challenged their religion's teachings, attitudes, or behaviors regarding women.

Very early in the century Elizabeth Bayley Seton, a widow with children, converted from the Episcopalian to the Roman Catholic Church and founded in Maryland the first U.S. community of Roman Catholic Sisters. The model she established was based on Catholic children's educational needs and was very different from the monastic style of life familiar to the European immigrants, Catholics and non-Catholics, and laity and clergy, who were pouring into this country. In 1975 Seton was officially declared a saint by Pope Paul VI. Some thirty years after Seton's main works another founder, Ellen Harmon White, and her followers broke off from the Adventists in New York State and established the Seventh Day Adventists in New England, Michigan, Europe, and Australia. She was a committed abolitionist and activist for the temperance movement and was thus a very public person who presented a new and unfamiliar image of church leadership in herself as she traveled across the country and the globe.

Other women who traveled extensively for their ministries were the German Lutheran "deaconesses" who first arrived in Pittsburgh in1849 to minister at the city infirmary. Perhaps their uniform lifestyle and dress conveyed an image too close to Roman Catholic nuns, who were not yet widely known or accepted in the United States, but they were not well received, and their small community disappeared in a few years. Still, three decades later seven deaconesses moved from Germany to Philadelphia, and others from Norway to Brooklyn, from Brooklyn to Minneapolis, and thence to Chicago as the order continued to spread.

In mid-century, Antoinette Brown Blackwell was the first woman ordained a Congregationalist minister in the United States, having graduated from Oberlin College and Seminary. The Unitarians ordained their first woman minister, Olympia Brown Willis, shortly thereafter; and several years later Mary Morse Baker Eddy founded the Church of Christ, Scientist. Hannah Greenbaum Solomon founded the National Council of Jewish Women in 1893, giving a new strength to women's public leadership in a culture where they had been spiritual leaders in the home only.

Toward the end of the nineteenth century, two significant church-related events occurred among black women. First, they began to openly organize by states and to develop their leadership for the good of their churches. Just as with their white sisters before them, the strengths they developed during the waiting time qualified and prepared them for the next step—ordination. Second, Julia A. J. Foote and Mary Small—both black—were the first women to be ordained deacons in the Methodist Episcopal Zion Church, though as women they were not given the right to participate in the community's decision-making.

In the Roman Catholic community, at a time when papal encyclicals were rare, Pope Leo XIII issued the 1891 encyclical *Rerum Novarum* on human rights. Though not intending to address the women's ordination issue, the pope laid out principles of social justice that came back to haunt the Catholic hierarchy during the twentieth-century critiques of their stance toward women. Shortly thereafter, Elizabeth Cady Stanton wrote and published the first feminist critique of religion in *The Woman's Bible*.

The Missing

Stories of the most conspicuous and generally successful leaders of the women's movement are the ones preserved in the pages of history, and yet the power of those who have lived and worked "under the radar" coalesced with that of their more public sisters. Both types of work are needed to effect change. So the blank spots on these pages, the white space in the margins, and the indentations of the paragraphs are filled with those less visible, quieter contributors to the progress that has been unfolding for generations.

The missing from this book also include many of the very well-known of modern times, who do not appear in these pages because they are scholars, rather than activists. They already have the public's awareness.

From the early seventeenth century through all of the nineteenth, there might seem to have been lulls in times between actions or between individuals' accomplishments on behalf of women in church and society, but those were not fallow years, nor resting time: they were part of the natural ebb and flow of energy, until a *kairos* arose for each next step.

EARLY TO MID-TWENTIETH CENTURY

While preceding pages in this chapter have illuminated some individual women's accomplishments, in the early to mid-twentieth century national and international events very rapidly forced a drastically different dynamic. The drama of exceptional individuals did not end, of course, but national attention necessarily shifted in the face of several societal developments that demanded *esprit de corps* more than focus on the individual. The battle for British women's suffrage came to a heated, public, and sometimes violent head in 1911. Ever-improving methods of communication and travel increased the possibility of learning about major issues in faraway women's lives. Two world wars necessarily drew women into public spheres and leadership in unprecedented numbers, and in a collaborative, secular atmosphere not restricted to coreligionists. And finally, increased access to secondary and higher education exposed more young women's minds to new ways of thinking.

There is irony in the fact that the Catholic bishops, aggressive in their support for Catholic education for all (in order to develop them as "good Catholics"), were unknowingly sowing the seeds of many a woman's critical thinking about the church and its leaders in subsequent decades. In particular, by mid-twentieth century the first critical mass of Catholic women college graduates emerged and became the well-educated leaders of both progressive and traditional causes in church and society.

Roots of the Catholic Women's Movement

In the Catholic Church of the United States, the earliest organization explicitly addressing the ordination of Catholic women was the St. Joan's International Alliance, with its roots in England. Yet that organization of British women was born of energy that flowed from even earlier times in France. It has been credibly argued that intentional Catholic feminism in France flowed from the revolution in 1789. France's description as "the eldest daughter of the Church" began to lose its accuracy in the face of the citizens' calls for *liberté, egalité, fraternité*. Though not called feminism at that time, women's desire for *egalité* was strong, as later illustrated by Delacroix in his 1830 post-Revolution painting called *Liberty Guiding the People* with its central image of *La Marianne*, the preeminent visual portrayal of the country, striding forward forcefully, French flag in hand. And because most French women were at least nominal Catholics (that having been the national religion), France became a seedbed of Catholic feminism.

Just a few decades after the French Revolution, in the 1800s there were many varieties of feminism in France, and most of its numerous organized groups (whether of secular or religious purposes) claimed Joan of Arc as their inspiration or patron. An example of this can be found in Elisabeth Arrighi Leseur's *Ligue des Femmes Françaises*, a forward-looking local social action and prayer group which she led and shaped. The members and the organization were dedicated to Joan of Arc and committed to Catholic action by doing personal apostolic and charitable work in order to "extend the work of the clergy."

> The members held regular conferences and spread this cult of Joan of Arc among women. . . . It was a question of raising up profoundly believing women in each parish, cultured, good managers of their households, devoted to others and apostles among the families they visited so systematically. This adult pedagogy helped close the gap so harmful to marital harmony because of the differences between male and female education. In this period of rising feminism and on the eve of the Great War, during which women assumed heavy responsibilities, a new type of Catholic [woman] appeared. . . . Her feminism was an outgrowth of their social concerns and her desire to be an apostle.[5]

Leseur died in 1914, thus overlapping in timing, ideals, and action with the earliest years of the St. Joan's Alliance, which for several decades has devoted its energy to both church reform and civil reform activities.

Emergence of the St. Joan's Alliance

Three years before the death of Elisabeth Leseur in France, Gabrielle Jeffery and May Kendall in England cofounded the Catholic Women's Suffrage Society in 1911. It was the only organized group of Roman Catholics in England established to actively and publicly participate in the nationwide pursuit of women's right to vote. Though Jeffery and Kendall mobilized the women originally to gain the vote—a "secular" goal—and were successful, Jeffery wrote shortly thereafter that "the final goal will be the ordination of women."[6] After women's (limited) right to vote was passed in 1918 in England, the group pondered its obvious power to effect change and decided to broaden its mission in order to promote the equality of rights between women and men in political, social, and church life.

Five years later, in 1923, the organization changed its name to the St. Joan's Political and Social Alliance, yet another women's group to invoke the patronage of Joan of Arc, a woman known to have been extraordinarily principled, courageous, determined—and successful in reaching her goal. As Barbara Barclay Carter noted in 1933, "Her [Joan's] answer to her judges anticipates by five centuries the modern woman's plea for the right to follow the calling to which her gifts and capacities summon her."[7]

In the next fifty years, geographical sections (chapters) of St. Joan's arose in twenty-four countries on five continents, including the United States.[8] During that same time span, the organization changed its name to the St. Joan's International Alliance (SJIA) to reflect its spreading geographical scope; and its primary objectives evolved into the promotion of Christian feminism, the advising of civil and religious authorities concerning issues relating to women, and service on various committees of the United Nations Educational, Scientific, and Cultural Organization (UNESCO). The alliance had an international structure, very well-educated members, and credible representatives, and therefore it became one of the earliest Catholic non-governmental organizations at the UN.

St. Joan's Alliance Takes Root in the United States

Finding the link between the European and the United States sections of the SJIA is difficult, for the complete archives of the latter are not centralized, are often informal and privately held, and the name of the group has changed several times since its formal establishment in 1911. During the subsequent fifty-four years, several well-educated, professional North American women learned of the organization and independently of one another joined the British section of St. Joan's. Among many others were three who became particularly well known in the movement: Georgiana Putnam McEntee became the first U.S. member in 1931, Dorothy Shipley Granger in 1943, and Frances Lee McGillicuddy in 1952. McEntee and McGillicuddy were especially active in the alliance, attending its periodic meetings held in Europe, corresponding with other members abroad, writing articles for *The Catholic Citizen* (the alliance's international newsletter), and even being elected to offices of responsibility.

Eventually a critical mass of members of the British group had developed in the United States: McEntee and McGillicuddy, aided by Dr. Elizabeth Jane Farians, Virginia Finn, Bernice McNeela, and Verna Mikesh started the U.S. branch of the SJIA in 1965.[9] Though not extensively involved in the organizational details of founding the North American section, Georgiana Putnam McEntee was a longtime influential leader in the organization. She turned up in the early 1970s at a meeting of the Philadelphia Task Force on Women in Religion in the company of Frances Lee McGillicuddy, then president of the U.S. section and SJIA consultant to the UN, and was described by Mary Lynch,[10] who met her there, as "the doyenne of the U.S. section [of St. Joan's]" thereby acknowledging the leadership McEntee exercised as the first U.S. member of the alliance.

Georgiana Putnam McEntee

As a candidate for a bachelor's degree in history at the College of Mount St. Vincent in Riverdale, New York, in 1917 the young Georgiana Putnam McEntee earned second prize for her historical essay submitted to *The Catholic Historical Review*. These two facts provide clues to her ability to stand out from the crowd, for it was only a very small minority of young Catholic women who attended college in 1917, and an even smaller minority of those students would have been capable of winning a national academic competition, as she did.[11] She set herself on a path in the scholarly life and taught history at Mount St. Vincent and at St. Joseph College for Women (Brooklyn); she earned both her master's and her doctoral degrees from Columbia University (in 1919 and 1929, respectively). In the 1930s, she was associate professor of history at Hunter College and within a decade became the dean there.[12] She joined the British section of Saint Joan's Alliance in 1931 and became its international vice president in 1939, serving in that capacity for several decades.

McEntee's 1927 book, *The Social Catholic Movement in Great Britain*, was circulated widely and cited often as the seminal study of that topic. In it she devoted several pages to the nature and impact of the St. Joan's Alliance and explained the reason for its inclusion in her book with the following words:

> More specialized in aim than the Catholic Women's League is the Saint Joan's Social and Political Alliance, formerly known as the Catholic Women's Suffrage Society. Brief mention will be made of its history and work because any group of women organized as these are, for the purpose of bringing about an improvement in the status of women, cannot fail to have an important influence on society as a whole. (238)

By integrating the issues of women's rights into her well-respected pioneering research, McEntee established a pattern for later members of the alliance. Very many of them were and are conspicuously well-educated and highly competent members of their professions or civic communities. In their research, writings, lectures, UN committee work, and teaching, they have used their formidable gifts in the service of women in church and society, becoming a type of global think tank on social and ecclesial issues related to women.

Dorothy Shipley Granger

Simultaneously, another early form of the St. Joan's Alliance existed in the United States, established by Dorothy Shipley Granger in the Baltimore-Washington area in 1943.[13] Granger's purpose was to mobilize Catholic women on sociopolitical issues for the advancement of women in labor unions and other public arenas, though not in the Catholic Church.

Born of a Catholic Maryland family of means and an impressive, far-reaching British family tree, Granger was educated at a private Catholic high school, at Cornell University, the University of Miami, and the New York School of Interior Decoration. At various times in her life she was identified as a "suffragist, women's rights activist, radio producer, Baltimore civic leader, and civic and social reformer." Granger played an active role in the Maryland chapter of the National Women's Party (NWP), fought successfully for the right of women to serve on juries, and later became known as a public advocate of the Equal Rights Amendment (ERA). She energetically engaged Catholic clergy and hierarchy (the willing and the unwilling) on the issues and rallied Catholic women to these nonecclesial causes. Granger's active membership in the NWP and in the International Federation of Catholic Alumnae (IFCA) gave her access to the membership lists of each organization, and by surveying those individuals she developed a pool of Catholic members interested in advancing the rights of women. In 1941 Dorothy Shipley Granger began correspondence with the St. Joan's headquarters in Europe,[14] and after submitting the necessary documents she received approval and established the first U.S. section of the SJIA in 1943. It was not long-lived.

Affiliating her work for women with an organization with a Catholic name did nothing to mitigate angry outbursts from several Roman Catholic clergy, as detected in this declaration by the IFCA's director, Monsignor Edward B. Jordan:

> A group going under the name of the "St. Joan Society" and purporting to represent the Catholic women of the United States, played into the hands of the National Woman's Party, which has been advocating for the Equal Rights Amendment for years. . . . So far as we have been able to determine, the society has never received ecclesiastical approval. To be sure, it prints on its official stationery . . . an excerpt from a prayer, which is attributed to a distinguished member of the Hierarchy [Bishop Edmond J. Fitzmaurice of Wilmington, Delaware], but we doubt whether this prelate ever gave the "St. Joan Society" permission to use his name in this connection.[15]

Though her assertive public support for the ERA was enough to set U.S. Catholic officialdom against her, Granger remained a committed and active member of Baltimore's Corpus Christi Parish, is remembered by some of the current staff there, and left a generous financial bequest to the parish upon her death in 1998.

In focusing the Mid-Atlantic chapter of St. Joan's on secular issues, Dorothy Shipley Granger followed the founding spirit and strategy of May Kendall and Gabrielle Jeffery in 1911, when they conceived of the organization as a way to mobilize Catholic women in England to win the right to vote. Only after success in that area did they refocus their mission to address church-related issues, which raises the unanswered question of why Granger did not do the same after her many successes in civic matters.

Frances Lee McGillicuddy

Regarding the work of the St. Joan's Alliance in the United States, McEntee the scholar and Granger the social reformer were followed by McGillicuddy the strategist and public face of Catholic women seeking fullness of life in the church and society. Born in Portland, Maine, her educational path took her to St. Elizabeth College in New Jersey for her bachelor's degree, Columbia University for a master's degree in French, and Middlebury College and the Sorbonne for postgraduate study. The breadth of her worldview, combined with her very assertive, extroverted, electric personality predicted that Maine was going to be too small an arena for Frances, and she chose to settle in New York City for the rest of her adult life.

McGillicuddy's earliest profession was the teaching of French in the New York public schools; and after the UN's founding in 1945, she became the official "observer" for the American Association of University Women and for the Federation of University Women, of which she was likely a member. Not content to merely "observe," in 1949 she wrote "A Guide to the United Nations' Special Agencies" and participated actively on various topics related to the health and welfare of women and children.

Then in 1951 the SJIA gained Category II consultative status at the UN's Economic and Social Council (ECOSOC). During those years McGillicuddy was introduced to the St. Joan's Alliance (British section) by Dr. Janet Robb, a friend of hers in the International Federation of University Women (IFUW) "who repeatedly urged me to join the Alliance."[16] She did so in 1952 and immediately became active and well known in the British section, attending its international meetings, visiting in the homes of members there, and writing for its international journal. In view of her already existing roles for two other UN nongovernmental organizations, she also agreed to serve as the SJIA representative to ECOSOC's Commission on the Condition of Women, monitoring issues relevant to her organization's purpose, presenting interventions,[17] lobbying with governmental committee members, and reporting back to St. Joan's members at their international meetings and in their newsletter, *The Catholic Citizen.*

Later Frances wrote that Florence Barry, a British member, had been trying to wear down both Joan of Arc (the saint) and Frances herself to establish a U.S. section of the organization, so she took up the challenge. "It should be noted," she wrote, "that the founding group of the U.S. Section—who happened to live in the New York area and had already heard of St. Joan's International Alliance—resolved to set up an American Section during lunch in the United Nations delegates' dining room and we spent an additional hour or two 'in the corridors' working out the details."[18] Frances reinforced this pivotal moment in a 1971 letter to Mary Lynch, saying: "The founding mothers [of the United States St. Joan's] were from the NY-Connecticut area."[19] Like Dorothy Granger before her with two different organizations, Frances's membership in St. Joan's gave her access to the list of North American women all across the country who, like herself, had joined the British section; and in 1965, most of them became the first members of the new U.S. branch.

In addition to her presidential responsibilities, McGillicuddy attended the 1971 International Synod of Bishops in Rome, with credentials as "Assistant Editor of the *Ecumenical Journal*" (founded by Arlene Anderson Swidler) and as an international vice president of the St. Joan's Alliance. It is probable that she and Mary Lynch (see chapter 2) met there and that McGillicuddy told her of Leonard Swidler's Philadelphia Task Force on Women in Religion. The following year, Frances brought Georgiana McEntee to a task force meeting in Philadelphia, at which Lynch and both the Swidlers were also present. To be in the same room with the formidable energy and focused commitment of McEntee, McGillicuddy, the Swidlers, and Lynch was to witness the unstructured but effective leadership community in the Roman Catholic women's ordination movement in the United States.

The unwavering mission of St. Joan's, as described in the 1970s by Frances Lee McGillicuddy, has been "We are feminists because we are Catholics. Though orthodox vis-à-vis the church, St. Joan's International Alliance is an organization of Catholics, rather than a Catholic organization . . . We do keep the Vatican and others informed—perhaps more than they would wish." She interpreted its self-description as "an organization of Catholics" to have been a deliberate strategy to maintain its freedom from control by bishops and the Vatican. Yet the depth of rootedness in the Roman Catholic Church was once captured in her explanation that "the encyclical *Pacem in Terris* inspired us to extend our egalitarian efforts to the Church itself."[20]

As her UN activity and her international work for St. Joan's increased, after several years in the classroom McGillicuddy retired from teaching and was able to work full-time at her passion for the improvement of women's lives worldwide. Frances served as the U.S. president from then until 1974, when longtime Saint Joan's Alliance (SJA) member Bernice McNeela succeeded her, and Rosalie Muschal-Reinhardt accepted the international vice presidency formerly held by Frances. Three significant developments affected McGillicuddy deeply: she had retired from SJIA leadership, membership in St. Joan's was not growing, and the brand-new Women's Ordination Conference (WOC) was aborning (see chapter 4). The impact of those elements was painful for her, as she may have wondered if there would be anything left of her life's passion and work. McGillicuddy sometimes expressed feelings of incomprehension and resentment that St. Joan's was not invited to collaborate with WOC after sixty years of pioneering, high-quality, effective, persistent work on their mutual cause. [21] It must be acknowledged now, if it has not been before, that it was precisely the initiative and labor of the St. Joan's Alliance members that set the stage for the next step in the movement. Their prolific scholarly work and astute strategizing with bishops, theologians, and clergy laid the foundation upon which WOC was able to build.

Reading her own writings and what others wrote about her gives evidence that Frances Lee McGillicuddy was intelligent, passionate about justice (both civil and ecclesial) for women, strong in her Catholicism, cynically witty, unrelenting in activism, creative in strategizing, and blunt in her speaking and writing. She died in 1992 and is buried in Calvary Cemetery in South Portland, Maine.

Subsequent Leaders of the United States Section of St. Joan's Alliance

In the McGillicuddy years, the United States section of St. Joan's worked almost exclusively on justice for women in the Roman Catholic Church, specifically their ordination; and during the period after her leadership, SJA members in the United States have broadened their activities to address many and varied arenas where women are at physical and intellectual risk. As time has passed, however, the social and ecclesial environments have moved toward activism to such a degree that few new members have been attracted to join the original group, a large part of whose purpose was explicitly to research, write, and work from within the Roman Catholic Church. In tracing the organization's history, Anne Marie Pelzer of Belgium wrote, "It was necessary, first of all, through a series of well-written papers, to deflate, one by one, the masculine myths that were then rigorously put forward in [Catholic] religious literature." She added, "The Alliance scorns the abuses and scandalous actions which guarantee immediate publicity. . . . It bases its actions on sound Christian premises, rigorous documentation and unassailable logic." [22] This is precisely what scholar-members of St. Joan's had seen as their unique gift to the church.

The scholarly work done by members of the alliance has earned lasting international renown and appears in any serious bibliography on the issue of women's ordination in the Roman Catholic Church. It began in 1961, when

Pope John XXIII convened the ecumenical council known as Vatican II. In his preliminary announcements he "invited the laity to express their opinions before the approaching Council," and the St. Joan's Alliance immediately went to work. They assembled from among their members an international task force comprised of one lawyer (Gertrud Heinzelmann, a Swiss) and five theologians (including Mary Daly and Leonard Swidler from the United States) who developed a paper[23] advocating the admission of women to the ordained priesthood. The paper was widely distributed in Europe to laity, clergy, and hierarchy, and became known in the United States when Rosemary Lauer wrote an analysis of it which appeared in *Commonweal Magazine* on December 20, 1963. Lauer's was the first article openly critical of the Vatican's stance toward women to appear in the U.S. Catholic press.

In subsequent years the group of alliance theologians produced papers of similar weight on the subjects of women's ordination to the diaconate and to the presbyterate, and the treatment of women in canon law in general. They proposed to the pope and cardinals that women serve as auditors at the council, and they condemned the Vatican's edict against installation of women as readers and acolytes in liturgical settings. The lobbying, debate, and discussion surrounding the appearance of such materials in print and in professional settings raised the visibility of the topic and the level of discourse. St. Joan's members in small groups or as individuals often met with their respective bishops to explain the organization's most recent research and keep them updated on other activities. If in-person conversation was not possible or not welcome, they kept up a steady stream of communication on paper. Many individual bishops were influenced positively by these actions, notably the Canadians, who issued a declaration of approval of women's ordination in 1971. Such supportive statements by bishops and cardinals— whether individuals or groups—were always reported in the St. Joan's international and regional newsletters and met with gracious thank-you letters from St. Joan's members and sections. St. Joan's members did, after all, believe that their special mission was to work within the church and to win support by using tactful intelligence rather than public demonstrations.

In addition to scholarly work, creative, clever, and often seemingly light-hearted projects were developed as well and were very often well received by bishops and cardinals. Around the country innumerable newspaper interviews, feature stories, catch-phrases, and lapel buttons all made the same point: ordain women.

Though more and more women were earning advanced degrees in theology and related disciplines, functioning as part of a "Catholic think tank" appealed to fewer of them in the milieu of social and ecclesial activism of the 1960s and 1970s. Dr. Elizabeth Jane Farians of Cincinnati (b. 1923), for example, left St. Joan's precisely because she felt that it was not activist enough.[24] During her years of membership, however, she gave of herself

unstintingly to developing strategies, projects, and *ad hoc* structures like the
1969 Joint Committee of Organizations Concerned with the Status of Wom-
en in the Church, assisted by SJA members Patricia Bruner and Bernice
McNeela. The Committee was composed of representatives from seven organizations with similarly overlapping purposes: the Deaconess Movement,
National Association of the Laity, National Coalition of American Nuns,
National Organization for Women, St. Joan's International Alliance, Sisters
Uniting, and Women Theologians United. One of their first projects was to
create and send a background paper and proposal to the American bishops to
"make a proclamation" concerning justice for women, to set up a national
office to deal with women's concerns, and to create and implement an anti-
discrimination policy against women. As a result of Farians's strategy, the
National Conference of Catholic Bishops did establish their long-lasting
Committee for Women in Society and the Church. Farians then expanded her
own horizons in founding the Ecumenical Women's Task Force, which
shortly after became part of the National Organization of Women.

The Joint Committee's exclusive focus in 1970 was on those United
States bishops who had shown themselves sympathetic to the cause of wom-
en in the church: William Baum, Joseph Breitenbeck, Charles Buswell, Leo
Byrne, James V. Casey, Carroll Dozier, George Evans, Raymond Gallagher,
Thomas Gumbleton, James Malone, Cletus O'Donnell, and Lawrence She-
han. Elizabeth, Bernice, and Patricia met with them twice while serving as
liaison from the Joint Committee to the committee of the U.S. Catholic
bishops on the permanent diaconate. The following year, at the 1971 International Synod of Bishops in Rome, the St. Joan's members who were there as
observers added to Farians's original list the names of thirty additional supportive bishops and cardinals from all over the world, based on their public
statements and private conversations. One European member of St. Joan's
calculated that in Germany, eleven of the twenty-two bishops were in favor
of ordination of women to the diaconate. Once back home from the synod in
Rome, the Canadian bishops as a body approved the concept of the ordination of women.

As a young woman, Elizabeth Jane Farians dreamed of being a teacher,
and after earning her bachelor's and master's degrees from the University of
Cincinnati she taught physical education for some years in the Cincinnati
public schools. But with the publicity surrounding the decision of St. Mary's
College (Indiana) to offer the first doctoral theology program for women,
Farians's heart recognized its true home, and she quickly matriculated in the
new St. Mary's program. Though her years of study were energizing and
enlivening, her employment path afterward was rocky and insecure, as one
after another college or university terminated her services because of her
outspokenness on issues related to women's oppression. Farians has picketed
for racial integration and gender integration; publicly and privately protested

unfair hirings and firings; lobbied bishops and politicians; organized, lectured, published, and strategized for change; demonstrated; and negotiated.
She marched in Selma with Dr. Martin Luther King, integrated swimming
pools and the Catholic Theological Society. Yet the event of which there is
most frequent mention by her and by others is that of June 1973 when
Farians became the first woman to deliver the baccalaureate address at
Brown University's commencement exercises.

As the bedrock for it all, Farians has written that she "was influenced by
the social teachings of the church and by the Catholic Worker movement"
and that, though her "roots were in Christianity," she is "no longer interested
in institutional religion or the traditional concepts of transcendent deity."
Because of the richness of her service to the cause of women's advancement,
Farians is listed in the *Directory of American Scholars* and in *Who's Who of
American Women*. Is it any wonder that this dynamo of mental and physical
energy was attracted to the St. Joan's Alliance? And in view of that organization's less aggressively confrontative style and methodology, is it any wonder that the attraction did not hold her for many years?

At its heyday in 1977 the U.S. branch of St. Joan's had a membership of
150. But as in Elizabeth Farians's life, ambivalent feelings about the Roman
Catholic Church have deterred or diverted many from investing their energies in church reform. Still others have walked away from the women's
ordination issue—and the church itself—as church authorities have revealed
their unwillingness to dialogue on the issue. Lastly, the normal passage of
time has led to family needs, personal health issues, and deaths that have
sapped the communal energy and public activity of the alliance. Though few
in number, in the early twenty-first century, members of the St. Joan's International Alliance are still working to eradicate gender-based inequities, more
often in the secular sphere than in the ecclesial. They participate in online
discussions, write articles, attend the biennial conference in Europe, and in
all arenas they keep the issues alive.

On the other hand, one cohesive group, the Minnesota Saint Joan Community, enjoys an energizing range of activity, and even some relatively new
members. Mary Kennedy Lamb, Verna Mikesh, and Dorothy Irvin were
leaders of the national U.S. section of SJA during its early years, and the
serendipity of their all living in Minnesota has created energy and focus for
their activities ever since. "Mary Kennedy Lamb took the first [local] organizational steps and served as the first president. Soon we in Minnesota separated from the national section in New York. At present some of our members
belong only to the Minnesota Saint Joan's, while others belong to the international as well."[25]

Cosponsoring relevant public lectures, offering feminist prayer and Eucharist opportunities, discussing current theology, holding meetings to plan
activities, regularly producing a newsletter, and supporting Dorothy Irvin's

archaeological calendar project (see chapter 6) are among their communal commitments. In addition, to honor SJA member Mary Lamb (1932–1996), the Archdiocese of St. Paul and Minneapolis annually recognized people who[26] promoted women's participation in the church, which was a creative strategy. The Mary Lamb Award ensured local awareness of the ideals of the St. Joan's organization.

A "Cousin Organization"

Roughly simultaneous to the early years of the St. Joan's Alliance in England, another organization was born in the United States which, at first, did not show a strong resemblance to its sibling. In March 1920, the National Council of Catholic Women (NCCW) was established by the U.S. bishops for the express purpose of developing for lay Catholic women a common voice, their united action, their active membership on national church committees, and their prodding of Catholic organizations in general to the service of the needy. However, their unexpressed purpose may have been to counter the more vocal and aggressive activities of the secular feminist movement.[27] In the same way Christianity has "baptized" non-Christian feasts and deities and social trends for its own purposes, the bishops may have unconsciously, or consciously, known that the burgeoning roles of women in society needed a religious counterpart if the church was to retain credibility with its female members.

Though the NCCW has been considered by many feminists to have been too cozy with the church hierarchy, and too reliant on the clergy, the fact is that their explicit goals have always been the empowerment of its members in order to empower other women, to maintain an active international outreach, and to advance the ongoing education of women, especially those in poverty.

One year after its founding, the NCCW was granted membership in the International Union of Catholic Women's Organizations at their meeting in Krakow, Poland. And fifty years after the NCCW was accepted into the International Union, they committed themselves to the larger group's four-year program

> to encourage all women to fully develop their potentials in world and church; to develop their own talents so as to become instruments of their own progress; to facilitate women's development of their own communities, their country, the world—on an equal footing with men; to contribute to the formation of Christian personalities, capable of working for new structures and forms of civilization, while safeguarding and trying to find values needed for pluralism and solidarity.[28]

The monthly journal of the U.S. branch of the NCCW was titled *The Word* and was very similar to, but more sophisticated than, the British St. Joan's Alliance *Bulletin*. Their content was remarkably alike: articles on serious contemporary theology, suggestions of practical applications of theology, news regarding women's advancement in various fields, articles on issues related to the church's teachings on social justice, and a group study guide for use by the members among themselves or with nonmembers. For a lively period of time in the 1970s Arlene Anderson Swidler was editor of the journal, which seems to have been a good fit—unexpectedly so, given her blunt and outspoken feminist critique of the Roman Catholic Church in other venues. As editor, she implicitly promoted simultaneously the aims of both the NCCW and the St. Joan's Alliance, of which she was an international leader. In fact, in its April 1971 issue, *The Word* published an article by St. Joan's member Mary Lamb titled "Human Rights" in which the author examined five common arguments against the ordination of women and then refuted each.[29] Publishing such an article may have been far from the intent of the bishops of the U.S. Catholic Church who established the NCCW; but in the 1970s, many Catholic bishops throughout the world were speaking publicly in favor of ordaining women (see chapter 5).

St. Joan's Alliance and Vatican II (1962–1965)

Throughout its history the St. Joan's Alliance and its synchronous organization, the National Council of Catholic Women, were knowingly and unknowingly preparing their members and constituencies for the Second Vatican Council. Theological education of their members occurred at their conferences, in their newsletters, in lectures at their meetings, and in the writings of members both in Europe and in the United States. As illustration of this ongoing work, Frances McGillicuddy once wrote:

> In addition to relaying our communal views to the United Nations, as early as 1959 the Council of the St. Joan's Alliance discussed the participation of women in the service of the Church. In 1961 we asked [the bishops] that if a diaconate was to be instituted as an independent ministry it be open to women as well as men. We [also] asked that lay men and lay women be invited as experts at Vatican II.[30]

From the founding days of the organization, both in Europe and in the United States, the active members of St. Joan's have been and are conspicuously well educated, strong-minded, excellent organizers, and recognized as professionals in their fields, very many of them having a commitment to serious, scholarly writing and intelligent, sophisticated leadership. They have been, one might say, an "elite" among the Catholic women of their time—though the egalitarianism flowing from both Vatican II and the American culture prevents one from using such a term. Thus the organization is very different in style from the post-1975, U.S.-founded Women's Ordination Conference (see chapter 3), with its members' wide range of experiences, more pragmatic methods, and activist methods.

The hallmarks of St. Joan's members are evident in three particular theologians who have long been members of the organization and of the Catholic avant-garde in general: Dr. Leonard Swidler and Arlene Anderson Swidler, longtime Philadelphia residents, and Dr. Dorothy Irvin. The Swidlers were theologians before they met the St. Joan's Alliance through members who were friends of Arlene. She, in her turn, sparked Leonard's interest in the theology underlying the goals of the organization.[31] Dorothy Irvin had studied under Leonard's mentoring at Duquesne and moved to Tübingen for continuation of her studies with him in pursuit of a doctoral degree. Each of the three returned to the United States with an energetic commitment to actualizing the goals of the St. Joan's Alliance—a branch of which already existed in the United States—through their research, lecturing, teaching, and writing (both scholarly and popular).

Resettling in the United States, Leonard resumed teaching at Duquesne University in Pittsburgh and in 1962 founded the *Journal for Ecumenical Studies*, a first of its kind in that theologians from all Christian faiths were invited to contribute to it. Arlene became managing editor of this groundbreaking publication. Dorothy remained in Germany and continued her studies at the University of Tübingen, earning a doctorate in theology, with subspecialties in Scripture and archaeology.

Within a few years, Arlene and Leonard moved to Philadelphia and became active and effective leaders in the church reform circles that were growing in the years immediately surrounding Vatican II. Leonard founded and coordinated Genesis III: A Task Force on Women in Religion, the method of which was to present educational panels and discussions of relevant topics on many of the college campuses in the geographical area. He began a long career of teaching at Temple University in the Religious Studies Department, and at the same time Arlene began her own teaching career at Rosemont, St. Joseph's, and Villanova Universities. In addition, they were raising two daughters, Carmel and Eva.

Shortly after Vatican II, the Swidlers arranged for their friend and mentor, Bernard Häring, CSsR, a forward-looking German theologian, to come to Temple University in 1968 to offer a course on the spirit and outcomes of the worldwide Second Vatican Council. As Häring's friends and colleagues, Arlene and Leonard shared the instruction and mentoring of the many students who enrolled for his courses.

Leonard Swidler was among the earliest lay Catholics in the United States to earn a doctoral degree in theology and to publish serious writings supporting the ordination of women. The scholarly work that propelled him into lasting international fame was his 1971 article "Jesus Was a Feminist." Always continuing their work in the St. Joan's Alliance, Arlene and Leonard attended its 1972 international conference as representatives of the United States section, after which Arlene wrote *Woman in a Man's Church.* The topics and timing of their work, their leadership in the St. Joan's International Alliance, and the fact that they were parents made them unusual in the early post–Vatican II church, and deserving of historical note. When work on women's ordination began to emerge from more theologians and practitioners, Leonard's academic focus shifted. Following Arlene's advice and pleased that others had taken up the cause with responsible theological scholarship, he focused his intellectual, teaching, and organizational energies on broader matters of church reform, such as ecclesiology, ecumenism, and interfaith works. Thus, in 1980 he cofounded (with Dr. Robert Schutzius) the national organization the Association for the Rights of Catholics and served as its president for over twenty years. After some time, Arlene Anderson Swidler developed a physically and mentally debilitating illness that took her life on May 24, 2008.

Meanwhile, their friend Dr. Dorothy Irvin had earned her doctorate in Tübingen, settled in Minnesota, and begun many years of teaching at the colleges of St. Teresa and of St. Catherine. Integrating her teaching and her passion for precise research, she continued to travel regularly to sites of early Christian communities in Italy, Turkey, and Jordan. In doing so, she began to notice that many frescoes, inscriptions, and texts pointed toward the ordination of women to the diaconate, presbyterate, and episcopate. In addition to leading tour groups to the sites themselves, Dorothy began in 2003 an intensive and creative dissemination of her research by designing and publishing annual calendars, cards, and bookmarks that contain the relevant texts, translations, and photographs. While selling them to individuals and groups, Irvin embarked upon a fundraising project to enable her to send one calendar to each cardinal around the world. These practical products of the print medium have put her research into the hands of many more persons than a scholarly article alone could do and are characteristic of the integrated work of members of the St. Joan's International Alliance. In *The Archaeology of Women's Traditional Ministries in the Church*, Dorothy Irvin has wed her chosen academic field to the service of women.

St. Joan's had developed theological, scriptural, and other materials for its members in seven different countries to use when personally preparing their respective bishops for the international synod, and the strategy had worked. Most of "their men" had been directly affected by the work of St. Joan's members in their dioceses, as shown in their interventions on the floor, their writings, and their interviews with the press—both at the moment of the synod and in subsequent years.

Bernice A. McNeela was the kind of leader every revolution needs. She was, by all accounts, calm, gracious, intelligent, ready to help whenever needed, and thoroughly committed to work toward full justice for women in the Catholic Church. According to E. J. Farians, "When she first came to one of the St. Joan's meetings in New York, she was very shy but very committed."[32] Mary Henold has described her as "a writer . . . a thinker . . . articulate . . . not an activist."[33] Many of the women who had emerged as leaders of St. Joan's before McNeela had vastly different personalities and temperaments from hers and yet relied upon her to be the steady, quiet hand in the organization. In fact, so much was she respected that she served as the St. Joan's delegate to Elizabeth Farians's joint committee and, upon Farians's request, took up the task of chairing the group. Later, in 1979, Bernice was elected president of the U.S. section and secretary of the international body. She "more or less took Frances McGillicuddy's place in St. Joan's,"[34] continuing to attend the biennial international gatherings until the early 2000s. Her death notice in Loyola University in Chicago's annual listing (Winter 2008) notes only that she earned her master's degree in social work there in 1952 and died October 7, 2007. She resided in Wheeling, Illinois, for much of her adult life, another woman of the generation whose educational and professional achievements were considered "ahead of their times."

Verna Mikesh was one of the original animators of St. Joan's on this side of the Atlantic, working with Frances McGillicuddy to establish the organization here in the 1970s. Another atypical Catholic woman who was highly educated for her time, Mikesh graduated from the University of Minnesota in 1940 and worked in the state extension system in the field of school nutrition from 1941 until 1971.[35] She published extensively in her field, and was publicly recognized as a valued member of the St. Paul, Minnesota, civic community. Evidence of the latter is the 1972 recognition of her as St. Paul Business Woman of the Year.[36] "I thought I'd get a job after I retired, to build up my Social Security," she said, "but I've been too busy with my projects to look for a job"—and one of those "projects" is the long-term leadership of the Minnesota St. Joan's community with its many activities (see above) designed to raise consciousness of ecclesial injustices to women.

C. Virginia Finn, of Milwaukee, was one of the earliest members of the U.S. branch of the alliance, worked with Frances McGillicuddy to establish it, and now enjoys the distinction of having served many years as president of the international body. In that capacity, Finn leads the biennial meetings of SJIA and has been its representative to UN nongovernmental work, especially in areas of acute need related to women and girls around the globe. She earned a law degree from Marquette University in 1989 and thus continued, herself, the unofficial and unarticulated tradition of St. Joan's members' commitment to their ongoing intellectual development.

SUMMARY

The design of women's advancement in social and ecclesial arenas has been that of an upward funnel, rising and widening through the centuries. They have achieved this through working toward the recognition of their fundamental equality with men. For those impatient with life processes, it can be helpful to develop a deep understanding of the past with which to season their vision of the future.

For several decades, when the subject of women's ordination has arisen in conversation, most Catholics have presumed that the movement is primarily of and for vowed women religious (Sisters). But contrary to that very prevalent opinion, this movement was initiated and supported by energetic, creative, and faithful lay women, beginning with the St. Joan's International Alliance and its roots in post-Revolution, secularized France. And while today those most active in the U.S. movement are of the middle class, the women of the U.S. St. Joan's and the NCCW seem to have been atypically highly educated for their day, and many of them financially secure. This era illuminated, as well, the debt owed to the academic world they inhabited for taking the women's ordination issue seriously: researching, writing, and lecturing until it became a topic of general conversation, and not only of scholarly circles.

NOTES

1. Among the several detailed, rich, and necessarily overlapping resources on this subject are Kennelly, Kenneally, Lindley, Ruether/Kelly, and the National Commission on the Observance of International Women's Year, www.womhist.alexanderstreet.com/dp59/doc26.htm.

2. Susan Hill Lindley, *You Have Stept Out of Your Place* (Louisville, KY: Westminster John Knox Press, 1996), 5.

3. Dead by hanging: thirteen women and five men; Giles Corey was pressed to death. Bridget Bishop, Sarah Good, Elizabeth Howe, Susannah Martin, Sarah Wildes, George Burroughs, Martha Carrier, and George Jacobs were among the victims.

4. *Chronology Highlighting Women's History in the United States* (Document 26), National Commission on the Observance of International Women's Year (Washington, DC: U.S. Government Printing Office, 1978), 207–16.

5. Janet K. Ruffing, ed. and trans., *Elisabeth Leseur: Selected Writings* (Mahwah, NJ: Paulist Press, 2005), 27, note 65.

6. "The Diamond Jubilee of St. Joan's Alliance," *The Catholic Citizen: Journal of St. Joan's Alliance* (May–June 1971), University of Notre Dame Archives, Mary B. Lynch Papers (hereafter UNDA CMBL) Carton 3, Folder 12.

7. Barbara Barclay Carter, "St. Joan's Quincentenary," *Commonweal Magazine* 14, no. 2 (Oct. 21, 1931): 597–99.

8. "Feminist Organizations Fighting 'Oppression' in the Catholic Church." *New York Times* (Dec. 1, 1975): 28.

9. James Kenneally, "Women Divided," *Catholic Historical Review* 75, no. 2 (April 1989): 262–63.

10. *The Bulletin of the U.S. Branch of the St. Joan's Alliance* (March–April, 1972): 1, UNDA CMBL Carton 1, Folder 16. (The term "doyenne" signifies the senior or eldest female member of a group.)

11. "Historical Records and Studies," *Journal of the U.S. Catholic Historical Society* (Nov. 1917): 114.

12. James Kenneally, "A Question of Equality," in *American Catholic Women: A Historical Exploration (Bicentennial History of the Catholic Church in America)*, ed. Karen Kennelly (New York: Macmillan, 1989), 263.

13. Ibid., 143.

14. "The Dorothy Shipley Granger Papers 1914–1998," Series IV, Subseries D, Harvard University Library, Schlesinger Library of the Radcliffe Institute.

15. *Quarterly Bulletin, International Federation of Catholic Alumni* 27, no. 3 (Sept. 1944): 7.

16. Frances Lee McGillicuddy, "President's Report," *Bulletin of the U.S. Branch of the St. Joan's Alliance*, ed. C. V. Finn (Milwaukee, WI: self-published, July 1974): 2, UNDA CMBL Carton 1, Folder unnumbered.

17. A. A. Swidler, "Frances McGillicuddy at UN," *The Word* 8, no. 8 (Oct. 1971).

18. Frances Lee McGillicuddy, "President's Report," *Bulletin of the U.S. Branch of the St. Joan's Alliance* (July 1974): 2, UNDA CMBL Carton 1.

19. Ibid.

20. Frances Lee McGillicuddy, *The Bulletin* (Nov. 1972): 2, UNDA CMBL Carton 3, Folder 11.

21. Author's 2008 conversations with Dolly Pomerleau regarding phone calls from McGillicuddy to the latter in the 1970s.

22. Anne-Marie Pelzer, *History of St. Joan's Alliance*, 10, www.womenpriests.org.

23. Gertrud Heinzelmann, *We Shall Keep Quiet No Longer! Women Speak to the Second Vatican Council* (Zurich: Interfeminas Press, 1961).

24. Mary J. Henold, *Catholic and Feminist* (Chapel Hill: University of North Carolina Press, 2008), 71–74.

25. Verna Mikesh, "From Our President," *Voices and Visions, Newsletter of the Minnesota Saint Joan Community*, ed. Mary Meeker (Summer 2007): 1.

26. "Parish Newsletter" (New Brighton, MN: St. John the Baptist Parish, July 4, 2006).

27. James Kenneally, "A Question of Equality," in *American Catholic Women: A Historical Exploration*, ed. Karen Kennelly (New York: Macmillan, 1989), 141.

28. *The Word* 8, no. 5 (May 1971): 11–12.

29. Mary Lamb, "Human Rites," *The Word* 4 (April 1971): 9–10.

30. Frances Lee McGillicuddy, "St. Joan's Alliance Crusades for Equality," *Brooklyn Tablet* (Dec. 12, 1972): 2, UNDA CMBL Carton 3, Folder 11.

31. Interview of Leonard Swidler by author (Feb. 2, 2007).

32. Letter from E. J. Farians to author (March 14, 2007).

33. Henold, *op. cit.*, 79.

34. *The Catholic Citizen* 2000, no. 2, inside cover, UNDA CMBL Carton 3.

35. *University of Minnesota Newsletter* (Winter 2009), www.extension.umn.edu/source/winter09-04.html.

36. *Park Bugle* 5, no. 2 (Aug. 1978): 9.

Chapter Two

Braid

Immediately Post–Vatican II

In August of 1972, a forty-seven-year-old Roman Catholic woman named Mary Bernadette Lynch wrote, "Looking over my 25 years of participation and preparation for the work of the Lord, I now realize that it has been a hunger for ordination."[1]

EARLY YEARS

The name of the woman who wrote those words is often invoked as that of the one individual who started the contemporary movement toward women's ordination in the U.S. Catholic Church. Though this is not quite accurate (as Lynch herself was consistently careful to make clear) her prodigious, generally single-handed work most certainly advanced the issue rapidly and publicly. She had a short lifespan of only fifty-four years, of which the last nine were intensely focused on the situation of women in the Catholic Church and the prohibition of their ordination to the diaconate and to the priesthood. It is those nine years—not whether or not she was the first to publicly organize others around the issue—that earn Mary Lynch a place of prominence in history.

Alongside the popular image of her as an assertive reformer, Lynch's life reflects the fact that she was also very much a traditional pre–Vatican II Catholic in her spirituality and theology. A "cradle Catholic" born to John C. and Ethel Jule Lynch on February 28, 1925, Mary acquired her formal education from first grade through graduate school in Catholic institutions (from which she saved every report card and transcript, until her death) during the

era before the Second Vatican Council's updating of Catholic theology and
practices. Graduating from Ohio Dominican College in 1948 (at that time
called St. Mary of the Springs College), she left her family and hometown of
Columbus, Ohio, for Washington, DC. There, at the Catholic University of
America, she earned a master's degree in social work in 1951, specializing in
child and adolescent care, and she deepened her conviction that social work
was, for her, a ministry. She continued to nurture that religious interpretation
of her work through many years of spiritual direction and retreats, reading
her well-worn *Prayer Book for Social Workers* and an Act of Consecration
for those ministering in that field. [2]

Following her studies at Catholic University, Lynch returned to Columbus in 1951 and served Catholic Charities as administrator of the De Paul
Center for Boys. Her skills in administration of such facilities were widely
recognized, and after the De Paul Center work she was invited to serve one-
year stints in other locations (Oklahoma City, Dayton, Wilmington, and Des
Moines) whose Catholic child-care services needed reorganization. She attributed this widespread need to two facts: the social work field as a whole
was reexamining the appropriateness of its way of delivering care to children
and adolescents, and a spirit of change was afoot. In addition, many of the
religious communities formerly running such institutions were withdrawing
from them. Often the withdrawals were due to the communities' inability to
educate enough members as quickly as necessary to staff and implement new
approaches in the field and consequent professional regulations. Stepping in
to ease the departure of such religious communities and to pave the way for
the future reinforced Mary's expressed view of her work as a valuable ministry to the church.

Examining her retreat notes and reviewing the materials she used for her
spiritual reading leads one to surmise that taking on "Sisters' work" was an
early manifestation of Lynch's lifelong attraction to the communal vowed
religious life and her struggle to discern if that was her vocation. Even in
1967, when forty-two years of age, she reminds a friend, "I wrote to you last
February concerning . . . the establishment of a religious community." [3] And
in 1968, her friend, supporter, and probable spiritual director, Rev. Louis A.
Ryan, OP, was helping Mary to clarify her desire to pursue "lay affiliation"
with a religious community. Ever the organizer, she even created and wrote
samples of "constitutions" for such a relationship. [4] During that same year,
she wrote to one Ann Ryan:

> I suppose you would call us one of the "pre-communities" you mentioned in
> the NCR [*National Catholic Reporter*] letter. We have been in spiritual direc-
> tion for eight years and are gradually forming plans for an association of
> professional apostles dedicated to the Apostolate of Childhood. The aim of this

apostolate would be the development of the total personality of the child as embodied in Montessori principles.[5]

To another she wrote, "We also feel that there must be many AMI [*Association Montessori Internationale*] teachers who may be interested in this spiritual union we would like to formulate, to meet the spirit of the times."[6] Mary Lynch even named the hoped-for community the Order of the Servants of the Children of Light, and developed "A 20th Century Apostolate Designed for Child-Care Workers," also called "The Apostolate of Childhood."[7] Accompanying Lynch on this spiritual journey, and the only other member of the "pre-community" referred to above, was Aileen Murphy, a nurse described variously by Mary as her friend, coworker, support, partner, and companion. They had met in 1960, the day before Lynch was to leave Columbus for a year of social work administration in Oklahoma with the Catholic Extension Society. Simultaneously, Murphy was about to return to her home in Toronto after visiting a friend in Columbus who insisted that she meet Mary Lynch before departing. So persuasive and convincing was Lynch, perhaps having inherited her father's skill as an "auto salesman" (so noted on her birth certificate), that Aileen Murphy agreed to uproot herself from Toronto and meet Mary Lynch in Oklahoma City, there to temporarily relocate their lives of service and search.[8]

SPIRITUAL GROWTH

Beginning with that year in Oklahoma City, Aileen and Mary lived a peripatetic and purposeful life similar to the Dominican tradition that was so familiar and attractive to Mary. On the surface she was responding to professional requests for her organizational and administrative skills in Catholic child care, but beneath it all there was, perhaps, the desire to serve as the Dominicans did in their early years, moving from place to place wherever needed. Not only had she become familiar with that tradition through the Dominican Sisters at St. Mary of the Springs College, but her advisor Louis Ryan was a Dominican priest, and his influence cannot be minimized. Lynch saved for decades a published article written by Ryan on the spirit of St. Dominic. In addition, some of her written comments in retreat notes explicitly acknowledge her attraction to the Dominican spirituality. As late as 1975, she wrote to a friend, "I have made a decision to pursue the entrance procedures of the Adrian Dominicans, so I'm therefore withdrawing as a resource person [to an unnamed organization]. I have been pursuing the idea of [starting] a new community for some time but feel now that it is a premature idea. . . . At this time I feel that the Adrians would be best for me and my background."[9] On the other hand, as she noted during one retreat, another very significant influence on her spirituality was that of Ignatius of Loyola. In her own

written notes she expressed a preference for his method of interior development because it moved one toward "flexibility, mobility, plurality of services, and identification with Christ."[10]

FINDING HER SECOND VOCATION

Since a successful spiritual search requires open eyes and ears, it ought not
be surprising that the next turning point in Mary Lynch's journey occurred
when she saw the *National Catholic Reporter* issue in February of 1970, in
which she read Jeanne Barnes's letter arguing for the ordination of women to
the diaconate. In 1964, in Article 29 of its dogmatic constitution on the
Church, *Lumen Gentium*, the Second Vatican Council had moved Paul VI to
restore the permanent diaconate. He did so for men in 1972, writing, "The
deacon is at the disposal of the bishop in order that he may serve the whole
people of God and take care of the sick and the poor. . . . Furthermore, he is
entrusted with the mission of taking the holy Eucharist to the sick confined to
their homes, of conferring baptism and of attending to preaching the word of
God in accordance with the express will of the bishop."[11]

Reading Barnes's letter opened Mary's mind to the diaconate as a route
for her in the church to live a life of spiritually motivated service—and
community, if possible. She may have even felt reassured upon realizing that
ordination of women to the diaconate had been an ancient practice, clearly
based on the Christian Scriptures, and not a deviation from church tradition.
Not one to let an insight go unacknowledged, she quickly wrote to Barnes
and expressed her gratitude and her new-found hope for a future in service to
the church "after 20 years of searching for effective means of reaching the
spiritual lives of others."[12]

From that time on, Mary Lynch had a new focus to her life. Through
social work, she had met Maria Montessori's pedagogy and spirituality;
through Montessori, she had developed her unrealized dream of founding a
religious community; through that desire to wed spirituality and service, she
came to understand the diaconate as her logical path. Acting upon that realization, she tapped a deep passion and energy for making ordination a reality
for Catholic women so that, after many very successful years in social work
administration, she wrote, "My life needs paring down so my work is truly
the work of the Lord."[13]

Beginning in 1970, Mary's pace quickened, and her activity displayed
single-minded focus on the many aspects of living out her new realization:
her newly understood call to ordination to the diaconate. She intensified her
correspondence with Jeanne Barnes, noting in 1971, "More than anything,
tho, I am struck by the quiet, calm, insistent, rational, *woman-like* manner
that comes across so beautifully in your bulletins."[14] Eventually Jeanne and

Mary became co-ministers to the many women and men who responded to Barnes's letter in the *National Catholic Reporter*. Their goals were to encourage them, to alert them to educational opportunities, to describe strategies for local and national consciousness-raising, to review current readings, and to suggest sympathetic contact persons. Their response to each woman and man who wrote was more than impressive in its reverence, kindness, compassion, challenge, and practicality. Within a few months, Barnes augmented the individual correspondence with an alternate monthly newsletter called *The Journey*, proclaiming its significance in the banner of each issue: "A journey of one thousand miles begins with a single step." [15]

Swirling about at that time were manifestations of rapidly growing interest on many fronts, giving evidence that Catholics were ripe for dialogue on the subject of women's ordination. The social and ecclesial environments were leading to thought and action around the issue because of the publication of Pope Paul VI's statement *Ad Pascendum*. In addition, the Catholic Theological Association appointed six of its theologians to study the permanent diaconate for the U.S. Bishops Committee on the Permanent Diaconate. One key question was whether women should be allowed ordination to the diaconate, and the theologians' conclusion was in the affirmative.

The *National Catholic Reporter* published many letters received in response to Barnes's original one, and in September 1970 ran one titled "Dear Sheila, You Can't Be a Priest Because." In the same month Mary M. Schaefer of Toronto edited, printed, and mailed the first issue of *Diakonos*, a periodical addressing the issue of women's ordination to the diaconate. [16] The Philadelphia Task Force on Women in Religion was in full swing under the leadership of Arlene Anderson Swidler and Leonard Swidler. The *National Catholic Reporter* reported in November that "Dr. Elizabeth Farians is calling upon bishops of America to lead the world in re-educating the Church and ridding it of its anti-feminism. . . . Miss Farians pointed out that some groups of Catholic women are willing to 'sell women short' of their full God-given right." [17] Farians being a member of the St. Joan's Alliance, her entrance into the public debate demonstrated the long commitment of that organization to women's issues. But theory and theology were not enough for Lynch's social worker outlook: problem-solving was her strong suit, and she was eminently practical in her approach to setting things right.

FOCUSING THE CALL

In November of 1970, Mary Lynch moved to Wilmington, Delaware, upon the invitation of that diocese to work with and reorganize their child-care system. This temporary move proved fortuitous in the light of Mary's developing clarity about her ministerial calling for it placed her in close geographical proximity to retreats, seminars, workshops, and strategizing groups in Philadelphia and New York. Personal notes indicate that she took advantage of the bounty. She attended a significant conference at Graymoor Ecumenical Institute (New York) on the subject of women's liberation where the speakers included Sidney Callahan, Dorothy Day, Betty Friedan, Jaroslav Pelikan, Joyce Richardson, and Mary Luke Tobin, SL. In March of that year, she wrote to Jeanne Barnes: "I have become active in the Philadelphia Task Force on Women in Religion. In fact, Frances McGillicuddy [then president of the U.S. St. Joan's Alliance] was at our last meeting." The Task Force's main activities in 1970 were monthly ecumenical panels which they implemented at local colleges on the subject of women in religion. Active members included the Swidlers, Sue Toton, Mimi Carroll, Gloria Hernandez, Judy Heffernan, Gaile Pohlhaus, and Virginia Ratigan, several of whom were also members of St. Joan's. So important to her was this group that Lynch maintained, until her death, some of the relationships formed there.

It was during the year in Wilmington that Mary Lynch decided to apply, in March 1971, to the Catholic Seminary of Indianapolis (CSI) for the master of divinity degree. In her application to the seminary, Mary Lynch describes her own process of spiritual search:

> Through my years of experience in dealing with the emotional and social lives of others [as a social worker], I saw this as an indirect means of affecting the spiritual lives of others. It was also, one of the only means available to women. Now I'm convinced that with further studies in the ministry available, I can be of more direct service to the spiritual needs of others. Upon completion of the course I feel that I will then be prepared to fill an official position in the Church where my experience and training will prove to be an effective means of serving, directly, the needs of the Church in our times. [18]

Her acceptance letter from Theresa A. Mount, SP, the academic dean, noted, "You are the first woman to ask to follow the program leading to the Master of Divinity," though it is not clear from the letter if Theresa meant the first Roman Catholic woman anywhere, or the first at CSI. Shortly thereafter, in December 1971 Judy Heffernan of the Philadelphia Task Force wrote Lynch with the news that she, too, had been accepted into that seminary for the following fall and was deeply indebted to Mary as a role model. It is safe to conclude that there was support for women at CSI from those two examples and from the fact that Theresa Mount served at that time on the Task Force for Women in Theological Education for the American Association of Theological Schools. [19]

During that same period, just before Lynch began her seminary studies for the master of divinity degree, Lynch's views of women's potential service in the church widened from solely the diaconate to the presbyterate, what she called the "full priesthood." In a discernment process around that time she acknowledged this, saying, "When I went to CSI I *brought* a growing interest in full ministry."[20] There can be little doubt that this change of outlook had come from her exposure to the theological ambiance of the Philadelphia Task Force on Women in Religion, as well as from reading with Jeanne Barnes the letters sent by many women whose hunger was to serve as a priest, not as a permanent deacon.

Still, her dream of finding a community life with a spiritual base endured and was often expressed:

- When accepted for seminary studies in Indianapolis in 1971, she wrote to Jeanne Barnes, "It might just be possible for us to set up a house for interested women to come and explore together some of the avenues [for the future of women in Catholic ministries]."[21]
- In the magazine *Concern*, she underlined a description of a way of life that "presupposes a core group whose members feel the call to a deeper life of prayer at this time in their lives."[22]
- During the same time period, she was searching for "guidelines" to incorporate into her dream of finding or founding a house of prayer with an apostolic orientation. She also noted, by underlining in her reading, that "this is the contemplative life—listening to the Word, making our home in the Word, dwelling in the Word and being a disciple of the Lord."[23]
- In August of 1971 Lynch wrote to Sandy Bousquin in Boston that she was going to try to start a group residence for women seminarians at CSI. The inference was that she hoped Sandy would join the endeavor of theological study and communal residence.
- A few years later she wrote, "My entire life [I have tried to discern between] the cloistered life such as Cenacle Sisters or a teaching order."[24]
- Among the papers Lynch saved till her death was an article titled "The Unique Life of the Sisters for Christian Community."[25]
- Another was titled "Plans for an Experimental Group Desiring Affiliation with the Daughters of Charity."[26]
- As late as 1975 she participated in the conference of Christian Life Communities held at the University of Massachusetts, where she delivered a scheduled presentation and attended a session on spirituality by William Callahan, SJ, as well as one concerning Christian Life Communities members' training program. She was always seeking to learn from successful models of community life.

During her seminary studies in Indianapolis, none of those dreams came true in the way she hoped, but Lynch and Murphy found a home there and lived their form of community life during Mary's seminary years.

A DIFFERENT COMMUNITY

In fact, a very different sort of community was forming around Mary Lynch, though she did not realize it and did not call it by that name. When Lynch moved to Indianapolis for seminary studies in the summer of 1971, Jeanne Barnes had just moved to Highland Park, Illinois, and they met a few times that year, each continuing in co-ministry to the many correspondents, as well as publishing the *Journey* quarterly. Mary began to take on more of the work, explaining to inquirers in October 1971 that Jeanne Barnes "is swamped with correspondence and she asked me to share it with her as her time is limited at present."[27] In February 1972, Jeanne expressed concern about her ability to continue handling the increasing volume of correspondence, mentoring, and support needed. Simultaneously, Mary Lynch was finding herself with flexible time available to her as a seminary student, a pleasant contrast to her many years of social work administration. The two of them agreed, therefore, that Mary would pack up the correspondence in her car and drive it back to Indianapolis and that she would also edit and produce the newsletter. At that point she became the successor to Jeanne Barnes as leader of the Deaconess Movement.[28]

The metaphorical community that Lynch began to lead was large—seventy women desiring ordination and many more who actively and passionately supported the concept—and it was exhilaratingly worldwide in its scope. At the same time that she was receiving letters from inquirers about the movement, Mary Lynch received notices, articles, clippings, and newsletters about the rising interest worldwide in women's ordination. Members of the St. Joan's International Alliance were already studying and engaging bishops on the issue, Frances McGillicuddy told her, and the chronological and ideological overlap between Saint Joan's and the Deaconess Movement became clear. Lynch began then to attend some national and international meetings of the alliance.

Lynch learned from her European contacts that Sr. Elena Rojas had delivered a presentation on women's ordination to the pre-synod gathering of priests and bishops of Spain in early 1971. After the actual synod, Bernice McNeela, also of the St. Joan's Alliance, notified her in November 1971 that Archbishop Leo C. Byrne of St. Paul "has received negative mail in response to his speech regarding women which he made at the synod [in Rome]." She asked Lynch to urge those on her mailing list to send Byrne letters of support and thanks for his presentation. Frances Lee McGillicuddy sent to Lynch the text of Cardinal George B. Flahiff, CSB, of Winnipeg's paper presented at the same synod of bishops, regarding discrimination against women in the church. She did not indicate how the other bishops had responded to Flahiff's paper.

That same year, a sampling of related yet varied types of developments received publicity. The second national workshop on the newly restored permanent diaconate for men was held in Detroit. Cardinal John J. Krol of Philadelphia dismissed four pastor-appointed altar girls at St. Matthias Parish. Mary Lynch wrote a long letter to each U.S. bishop, to Cardinals Krol and Deardon, and to Pope Paul VI reminding them of the ancient tradition and the contemporary theology about ordaining women to the diaconate. As is evident in the history of this issue in all religions (see Lindley 1996), the more overtly active women and girls have become about it, the more resistant many clergy and hierarchy have been.

Mary Lynch found her name on the mailing list of innumerable newsletters and bulletins from around the world, each describing projects and activities related to the ordination of Catholic women—some to the diaconate and some to the presbyterate. In many activities, such as Rojas's presentation to the bishops' synod in Spain in 1971, the U.S. women lagged behind their sisters and brothers in other countries.

There were at this time many groups and individuals rallying around the diaconate issue and feeding information about their activities to Lynch, including announcements of retreats, conferences, workshops, training programs, and academic courses—even one about the ecumenical international deaconesses conference to be held in New York City in June of 1972. It seemed that the entire Christian community was exploring the issue of women's ordination, and at the same time even the National Conference of Catholic Bishops called for an exhaustive study of whether women should be ordained. This was perceived as "progress" by many Roman Catholics and was greeted by many with an enthusiasm that might have been more understandable at an actual decision to ordain women.

"As you'll note, we are more of a movement than an organization," Lynch wrote in the *Journey* in August 1972.[29] She was the "attractor" for the energy in the movement, both nationally and internationally, and the high energy level indicates her feeling of accomplishment at seeing many clergy, several bishops, and some cardinals publicly support her work. Just as it had been important to her to learn that the bishops approved ordaining women in the early church, she made constant overtures to bishops and clergy to "officially" restore the female diaconate. The North American cardinals and bishops were slower than their European and Asian brothers to speak and write publicly in support of the issue, but some of them eventually became known for their support of the cause in published articles and in talks with groups (see chapter 5).

PREPARATION COMPLETED

Upon Lynch's completion of her master of divinity degree in spring of 1974, Bishop Maurice J. Dingman, whom she had met in Detroit in 1971, invited her to come to Des Moines and develop a house of prayer for his diocese. It was then that she wrote to Bernice McNeela in October 1973, "Getting settled in our house here in Des Moines. Two Sisters and three of us lay people live here. I have a great opportunity to look over the needs of the Diocese and see where to get involved."[30] This was the closest thing to her dream, yet she left no comment about the experience of living in a mixed community of men and women, laity and religious.

In the process of discerning whether or not her future should be in the vowed religious life, Lynch left the first evidence of her awareness of the power of the lay life in the church. An article titled "The Vows and Christian Life" regarding the responsibility of all the baptized seems to have made a significant impression on her.[31] She underlined the following passage, perhaps as the theological foundation for her impending prophetic role, and she kept a copy of the article until her death:

> The laity are—by reason of the knowledge, competence or outstanding ability which they may enjoy—permitted, and sometimes even obliged, to express their opinion on those things which concern the good of the Church.[32]
>
> The meaning of the Christian life in general involves, in the broadest outline, love of God, realized through love of Christ in and *through a community* established for and by this love in the life of the Spirit.[33]

Once again, as when she learned that the early Christian churches ordained women deacons, it was reassuring to Lynch that these teachings of Vatican II actually encouraged Catholics to speak their minds. Not a dissenter, she wanted to be sure that her beliefs and behavior be integrated with the church's teachings.

RESOLUTION OF CONFLICT

Her underlining of these passages illustrates Mary Lynch's lifelong and often-expressed dilemma: whether to operate as an individual Catholic lay person, or to found or find a community that would help her to be a "more perfect" Christian. As a union of the two dichotomies, Lynch felt the inner spiritual need to make vows of some sort as an individual, yet in the way that members of religious communities do. There were, after all, few models for her other than those of the vowed, communal religious life. So on August 12, 1974, she pronounced private vows of faithful service to the Gospel in the presence of Bishop Dingman in Des Moines (see appendix B). Though there were to be two other women making the same vows, one changed her mind just before the ceremony, and Aileen Murphy was the only other person to join with Mary Lynch in this step. By then Mary's ministerial focus had shifted from her earlier dream of founding a Montessori-based child-care community to the care of women called to ordained ministries, but she and Aileen Murphy were at last the tiny nucleus of the community Lynch had always sought.

Retreat notes of later years in Mary Lynch's life reveal the enduring and deep-rooted traditionalism of her religious outlook, originally forged during her many years of Catholic education. And it was precisely this very traditional theology of priesthood that brought her to the ordination debate. Her often painful spiritual quest was simply for God: "I desire to be one with God." Her spiritual passion was explicit in her theology: "I come alive when I think of complete identification with God and [I] see priesthood as ultimate access to God—through Christ the High Priest."[34] She wanted to be ordained because she believed that ordination would ensure her union with God—a belief that she never explicitly repudiated in writing, even while newer theologies of priesthood flourished in the Catholic Church after Vatican II. A short time after she wrote that statement, she began to reflect on the fact that not only could *she* not come as close to God as she desired, but *all* Catholic women were being denied that possibility. This she considered to be a painful wrong that the church was imposing on more than half its membership.

THE ANIMATOR

Beginning in 1972, with her willingness to take on leadership of the Deaconess Movement initiated by Jeanne Barnes, Mary Lynch gradually became the animating and organizing leader that her years in social work administration had prepared her to be. She realized that official change in a hierarchical church had to come through bishops, so she contacted them as individuals and as a group, garnering their respect and, in some cases, their friendship. She felt that bishops would listen to women's religious communities on this subject because of their numbers, their influence in dioceses, their level of education, and their known commitment to the service of women. So she cultivated relationships with individual Sisters as well as with communities' leaders and with the Leadership Conference of Women Religious. She believed that the women called to ordination needed not only emotional support, but educational preparation and empowerment in order to be agents of change themselves. So she was a conduit for those issues. She became connected to many varied organizations that had similar aims: spiritual, ministerial, theological, and formational. And to all, she explained that because the church is a society and societies change slowly, the work to be done would take a long time and require what she called "delicacy."

Bishops

With respect to her relationships with bishops, "the personal was the political" in the strong friendship she enjoyed with Bishop Maurice J. Dingman (Des Moines). He saw in her a deep reservoir of spirituality, evidenced by his entrusting to her the development of a house of prayer and spirituality for the people of the diocese following her degree completion. He saw, too, her relentless sense of responsibility that led him to gift her with work-time to advance the women's ordination movement. Their initial conversations about her work to be done in Des Moines prompted her to tell a friend in June of 1973, "I'll be able to put full-time into the movement now."[35] It seems clear that she and Dingman had discussed the fact that her time and talents would not be fully utilized in developing the house of prayer and that she could expand her service to the church by simultaneously leading the ordination movement. Later, a note from a Bill Brown to Mary Lynch says, "I had lunch with Bishop Dingman during the NCCB meeting, and we were chatting about you. He is high in his praise of you!"

Another note reveals a different sort of connection with bishops, less personal than Lynch's friendship with Dingman but revealing of her varied approaches to the hierarchy. In December of 1973 Archbishop Enrico Bartoletti (Lucca, Italy) wrote to thank her for a paper she had sent him, along with a lapel button of some sort: "which brought a lighter touch to a recent meeting, as well as making your point very clearly!"[36]

Religious Communities

Similarly, she built upon her lifelong personal attraction to religious communities and developed it into productive strategies. One such strategy was to gain a speaking engagement at the August 1973 Leadership Conference of Women Religious (LCWR) meeting and to obtain assurance from Ellen L. Burns, ASCJ, who was chair of the LCWR pastoral ministry committee, that the committee would work toward formulation of a statement on women's ordination which would then be presented to the body for discussion and acceptance or rejection. Furthermore, she motivated Avis Clendenen (at that time a Sister of Mercy in Chicago) to propose to her community's province chapter of April 1974 a statement of support for women's ordination. Following ratification of the document at the province level, the Chicago delegates took it to the June 1974 national chapter of the Sisters of Mercy, where it was "overwhelmingly approved."[37] As was the custom then, the decisions of the chapter were sent to all the bishops of dioceses in which any Sisters of

Mercy were serving, thus broadening the circle of consciousness-raising and giving bishops some idea of the breadth of support for the issue among women religious. Thereupon, the community sent it to the national Bishops Committee on the Permanent Diaconate.

That same year Ellen Roach, CSJ, agreed to take a similar statement to her community's province chapter, and it is likely that there were other Sisters who did the same in their respective communities.

Other Organizations

During this time period, Lynch increased her participation in the events of other organizations presumed to be sympathetic to her goals. The more persons she could educate on the subject, the more successful she felt the movement could be. This conviction took her to Milwaukee for Alverno College's Conference of Women Theologians in January of 1974;[38] to Denver the same winter for the national meeting of Diaconate Directors of the United States;[39] to a "consultation for Sisters at the Chicago Theological Union" in March; and to Rome in October "to cover the proceedings of the synod of Bishops." (Though there is no record of how her synod invitation came to pass, one might suppose that this task was undertaken for the Diocese of Des Moines upon recommendation by Bishop Dingman, for whom she was working at the time.)

Upon the conclusion of the two-week synod in Rome, Mary Lynch stopped in Paris to meet the leaders of an organization called *L'Amicale des Femmes Aspirant [sic] au Ministère Presbyteral* (AFAMP), whose newsletters and members had convinced her to start a U.S. branch of the association. She and their leaders hoped "to work out plans [for the AFAMP] internationally. She was also a speaker at their *Session d'Effort Diaconal*, where she reminded the participants, "We must become so credible that they recognize [us] as a competent body."[40] After returning to the United States, Lynch began to use the name Association of Women Aspiring to the Priestly Ministry (U.S. Section) to describe what had been called until then the Deaconess Movement. This name change reflects the shift in Lynch's own aspirations from the diaconate to the priesthood, as well as the desire of many of the women to whom she was ministering on this issue. On the home front, during the same month as the bishops' synod in Rome (October 1974) twelve members of the National Leadership Board of the U.S. Sister Formation Conference made a public statement asking for "the restoration of the diaconate [for women], ordination to priestly ministry, [and] inclusion of more women in all decision and policy-making bodies of the church."[41]

In subsequent decades, Lynch's international efforts developed into the Women's Ordination Conference's leadership in the first formal unification of similar organizations at the First European Women's Synod in Gmunden,

Austria (1996). There Andrea Johnson gathered a caucus of the representatives of similar Catholic organizations from other countries and proposed the formation of a federation-type relationship which subsequently became known as Women's Ordination Worldwide—with its felicitous acronym (see chapter 6).

BIRTHING TIME

After returning from the synod in Rome and from the planning meeting with the women in Paris, Mary Lynch relayed to Nancy Lafferty, FSPA, "The influential people I have met in Rome and Paris are convinced that working toward women's ordination is timely and necessary." Consequently, shortly after her experience there, Lynch wrote a letter to seventy Catholic women and men, most of whom represented relevant national organizations, religious orders, and seminaries. Her energy had been heightened in Rome, and she evidently realized that the moment was ripe for the next phase to begin. She had been personally cultivating relationships with several groups and decided to begin with them. (Because of its timing, this December letter is today often described wryly as "Mary Lynch's Christmas card.") Of the seventy persons invited, thirty-one attended the first meeting on December 14, 1974, in Chicago where they agreed to plan a national conference for the fall of 1975 "for those who want to be ordained and for those who support them." Over time, the invitation has taken on the symbolism of a "Christmas card," and surely its message seems to have been a proclamation of good news and tidings of great joy to all those holding this vision for themselves or for their church.[42]

The purpose of the proposed conference was established as "education and strategic input," and thirteen members of this December group agreed to implement the plans, with Mary Lynch appointed as overall coordinator. Her first step upon returning home was to write a letter to each U.S. bishop to inform him, to indirectly reassure him, and to ask for his financial support. Sending this letter was yet another manifestation of Lynch's desire to be in harmony with the church and to not be perceived by the bishops as anything other than a coworker with them in the vexing problem of a growing priest shortage. Only after the letter went out to each Roman Catholic bishop on January 1, 1975, did she run an ad in the weekly *National Catholic Reporter* announcing the event to the public and inviting participation.[43]

Perhaps some of the bishops were emboldened by receiving the forthright letter from Lynch, and no doubt energy around this issue was bubbling in many places. So, shortly after receiving the announcement of the coming national conference on women's ordination, several bishops, including Carroll Dozier (Memphis), published pastoral letters on women and church.

Dozier referred to women as "the church's readiest participants." Joseph L. Bernardin (then of Cincinnati) urged equality for women in his article in *Commonweal Magazine* "Women, Ordination and Tradition," and William D. Borders (Baltimore) published his pastoral letter "Women and the Church."

Correspondence continued to pour in to Lynch: the report of a Baltimore parish council (Our Lady of Perpetual Help) asking Borders for "an end to the altar girl ban," for they had been successfully serving there after appointment by their pastor, Rev. James Dowdy, since 1973;[44] an apology from a pastor in Clarksburg, West Virginia, for not being more active in the organization, but saying, "I have been sowing positive seeds of encouragement and acceptance of women in ministry in the local area. We now have women lectors and women distributors of Communion in the parish."[45] Support arrived from Rev. John T. Finnegan, president of the Canon Law Society of America, who wrote Lynch in January 1975 to say, "My very best wishes to you, Mary. I feel that God is blessing your work and your approach and will perhaps do significant things through your ministry."[46] In the next month her mail contained this poignant note from Michael Rose, SJ, a priest in Guyana: "I am a Jesuit priest who desperately wants women to be admitted to every ministry in the church including the priesthood, as I believe this to be God's Will. But I receive very little support, even moral, in my own country. . . . So I am trying to keep up with events in other countries." In the same month Elizabeth Carroll, RSM, delivered her landmark address at the National Conference of Catholic Bishops Bicentennial Hearings in which she called for complete participation of women in the ministry and life of the church: "The question is no longer why should women be admitted to orders, but why should women not be admitted to orders?"[47]

In mid-February of 1975 Mary Lynch convened the second planning meeting for the November conference. The planners gathered at Rosary College in Illinois and moved the monumental task closer to its actualization. A short time later, theologian Rev. Richard McBrien wrote a very positive nationally syndicated column about his experience with the conference planners. It was laudatory of the leadership skills he witnessed, the theological sophistication of the participants, and "the pastoral maturity" he observed, pointing out that those qualities are prerequisites for priestly ministry.

Lynch fit in a quick trip to Philadelphia in April of that year, reconnecting with her friends in the Task Force on Women in Religion,[48] and the next issue of the *Journey* announced that she would be attending a meeting of the U.S. section of the St. Joan's International Alliance, to be held at Barat College (Chicago), and assured the readers that she would report back to them on the proceedings. Those who were active at the Chicago meeting were Marie Bailey, Frances Brophy, Cynthia Jo Dentiger, Virginia Finn, Frances Lee McGillicuddy, Bernice McNeela, Rosalie Muschal-Reinhart,

Mary Roach, and "the Philadelphia group." The commitment and activities of the like-minded organizations were coalescing and were parallel to Mary Lynch's involvement with all of them: St. Joan's, the Deaconess Movement, AFAMP, the Association of Women Aspiring to Priestly Ministry (AWAPM), and the Philadelphia Task Force.

AVALANCHE

Mary Lynch was trying to juggle a number of leadership tasks during 1975: responding to letters that continued to pour in from women seeking ordination and from men and women who supported the movement, writing and editing the *Journey*, serving as the U.S. representative to St. Joan's, organizing and inspiring the AWAPM, and now coordinating the entire upcoming November women's ordination conference. All these responsibilities coexisted with her personal mentoring and counseling of many women, her speaking engagements at national and international conferences, and the nurturing of personal contacts with hierarchy and other clergy.

So it is no wonder that on June 2, 1975, she wrote, "I've moved away from the [conference] coordinator's job as it would be too time-consuming and I want to concentrate on the Program Committee and AWAPM."[49] Four weeks later, she sent an official letter of resignation from that post to Nadine Foley, OP, assistant coordinator of planning for the national conference, who then succeeded Lynch in the overall leadership role. The new understanding was that Mary would serve as chair of the program committee and, by virtue of that position, function as a member of the overall executive committee. In July a dark cloud hung over Mary Lynch as she wrote in her retreat notes, "Finances pressing—Feeling depressed—when [I've] always been optimistic. . . . Desire for community seems less possible—things looming over me. Peace getting disturbed—events seem to be thrust on me. What to do with them."

The power of this bout of depression and upheaval is significant, for it coincides with her withdrawal from leadership of the fall 1975 conference. Her feelings expressed during that retreat were reasonable, given the amount of activity she was trying to maintain, but they were also probably the first indications of what would develop into the long illness that led to her death in 1979.

To the executive committee she wrote in October 1975, "This is to inform you of my resignation from [even] the Executive Committee. I feel that I cannot do justice to this committee as I have been doctoring and not been in good health. I want you to know that I have given a great deal of thought to this and do it for the sake of keeping the Committee very strong."[50] Nadine Foley's letter of response was caring, warm, and supportive, including the understanding comment that at the last meeting of the executive committee several members noted that she (Lynch) "didn't seem herself." Foley explicitly assured Mary Lynch of their gratitude and support.

PREPARING FOR A NEW LIFE

Because of Lynch's original insight and energy, the first national conference concerning the ordination of Roman Catholic women saw the light of day in Detroit from November 28 to 30, 1975, and was titled "Women in Future Priesthood Now: A Call for Action." Though Lynch had stepped away from the overall leadership of the event, Nadine Foley introduced her from the stage at the opening event. Foley expressed her gratitude for "the power of one woman asking one question," and the audience exploded in sustained applause.

As a result of the very well-planned, implemented, and publicized gathering, over 2,250 names were added to the mailing list for the new organization that would be called WOC (Women's Ordination Conference). The energy of extraordinarily gifted and spiritually motivated women exploded into projects and ministries that would change the face and feelings of the Roman Catholic Church in the United States. No one expected, of course, that the goal of ordination would be achieved during the course of that November weekend; yet no one really anticipated the power of the long-submerged passion of Roman Catholic women who felt called to the ordained ministry and wanted the opportunity to test their call in the same way that boys and men have done for centuries. Jeanne Barnes's Deaconess Movement and its forty members of merely five years earlier had grown to over 2,500, changed its name, and expanded its goal from diaconate ordination to priestly ordination.

Mary Lynch was much diminished in her energy at the Detroit conference, and the earliest stages of her final illness seemed tragically timed to synchronize with the birth of the outward manifestation of what she had prayed, hoped, and worked for: the empowerment of Roman Catholic women to express themselves and to transform the church. The interplay of dying and giving birth to new life was powerfully clear. Was it coincidence or had her passion consumed her? Was it "tragic" timing or was it fortuitous in that she became ill only after she saw a community of shared passion to whom she could hand over the work?

The relative disorganization of the final issue of the *Journey* (Winter 1975–1976) demonstrated in another way that Mary's illness was progressing, and in that issue she hinted at indications of the movement's probable evolution into a new organization. Shortly after the issue of the *Journey* came out, in January 1976 the original planning committee for the Detroit conference met for one last time, and Lynch was able to be present. The members (Dolores Brooks, OP; Joan Campbell, CSM; Mary Lynch; Rosalie Muschal-Reinhardt; Donna Quinn, OP; and Margaret Urban, OP) voted to create a national organization, as had been mandated by the participants in the Detroit conference, and to set in motion the steps necessary to bring that about.[51] Lynch noted in subsequent communication, "Our Task Force [Committee] disbanded after the follow-up meeting. Those who want can continue on a new committee which will get organized on March 6 [1976]. They will try to implement the suggestions that the Conference [made]."[52]

Despite the progress of Lynch's illness and her gradual stepping off the national stage, her mailbox was as full as ever and called for her attention. In June it contained an "official" proclamation of gratitude, signed by each member of the Core Commission of the new organization: "Mary Lynch is a member *emeritus pro vitae* [*sic*] of the Core Commission. We proclaim this in recognition of her prophetic role and complete dedication in generating and carrying forth the issue of women's acceptance into the priestly ministry and calling forth at the same time a renewal of the presbyteral ministry in the Roman Catholic Church. In Sisterly love, [the nineteen signatures follow]."[53]

On another day, she received notification of her nomination by overwhelming majority to the newly forming Core Commission of the nascent organization. Her response indicated that she was not able to serve. In July a simple yet poignant request came from Ada Maria Isasi-Diaz (chair of the nominating committee for the organization-to-be) that Lynch share with the new organization the AWAPM mailing list in order to consolidate it with the emerging WOC membership list. Serving as coordinator of the U.S. AWAPM had been a symbol of Mary's identity in the movement, and her willingness to give the mailing list was tantamount to giving away a part of herself. Yet in September, she informed Beatrice Dagras, SB, her AWAPM counterpart in Paris, "I am offering it [the list] to the larger group known as the Women's Ordination Conference."[54] In a sense the U.S. branch of AWAPM, too, was dying and would be reborn within WOC.

One day, the mailbox contained the published proceedings of the Detroit conference, edited by Anne Marie Gardiner, SND. To her Lynch wrote, "I suspect that it is part of God's design that many of the most involved among us are fatigued and are glad to let others carry on."[55]

Sprinkled among the types of mail with which Lynch was familiar from her long work in the movement, a new type began to appear: get-well notes of a most caring and admiring nature. She (or the executor of her estate) saved several cards and notes from bishop-friends of hers and from clergy, but not very many from the women she had worked with, for many of them had by then transferred their focus to WOC from the AWAPM. Themes of these notes were concern for Mary's health, desire to show her the impact she had on their lives, and desire to show her how her work would affect the

Catholic community. For example: in July Regina Griffin, RSCJ, wrote, "I heard from Sr. Kathy Power several weeks ago that you have not been feeling well. I am keeping you in my prayers."[56] Rev. Carroll Stuhlmueller, CP, a friend and advisor, wrote, "Praying that you make a good decision regarding the future of your newsletter [*The Journey*]. It has done so much good already that I'd hate to see it discontinued. I pray too for your health, so that you can return to full activity."[57] Lynch was on the verge of divesting herself not only of the AWAPM mailing list but also of the newsletter which had been her primary link with the members themselves. But more than a year into her illness, March of 1977 found Lynch still serving the church with her focused passion on the Priestly Life and Ministry Committee of Corpus Christi Church, her local parish in Columbus, Ohio.[58]

In October of the next year, former coworker (presumably from her social work years) Sue Pattan Zitzinger wrote to tell Mary "what a far-reaching influence your fleeting presence made upon my life as it undoubtedly has on many others. Your smiling leadership and example of persistence, responsibility and discipline on the job seemed to result in success and fun simultaneously."[59]

The second national WOC conference came and went (November 10–12, 1978), and there is no mention of Mary's involvement in its preparation or outcomes. She spent Christmas that year in St. Vincent's Center, a residential nursing facility in Columbus, Ohio. Bishop Ernest L. Unterkoefler of Charleston, South Carolina, wrote in April, "You are a noble Christian woman bearing up with magnificent nobility and patience."[60] Her dear friend Bishop Maurice J. Dingman wrote, "You have done so much for the cause of women in the Church. I have always admired your patience and how you balanced that with great zeal. God will reward you generously. I am proud of your years in the diocese."[61] Later, he admired her "single-handed leadership." An illegibly signed message from a woman reads, "I have always felt that the women in the priesthood movement owe its origin and push to you. When priesthood for us finally comes, every woman priest will owe a debt to you."[62]

During the last months of Lynch's life, the WOC Core Commission wrote her to say, "Your sisters are with you as we fully recognize you as the first prophetic priest who is a woman in America."[63] Catherine Stewart Roche of New Mexico wrote, "Thank you for your life and your vision. Thank you for dreaming the impossible dream and sharing it so that others could dream and dream out loud."[64] By the month of June, the severity of her illness became even clearer: "I hope you've had more comfortable days . . . and are responding well to chemotherapy."[65] Many, like Rev. Tom Allen, learned of Mary's very serious medical condition from WOC's newsletter *New Women, New Church*. He wrote her, "I learned via WOC that you are ill and so I quickly write to lend you my support and prayers in Jesus. I always remember you in the courage of your conviction."[66]

Amid all the supportive correspondence found among her papers, the last two pieces were both dated July 19, 1979, and epitomize a grateful love for her presence on this earth. In the first, Judy Heffernan's words ring as clear reminders of all the letters we ourselves have never managed to write to someone who has been important to us: "I think of you so often with love and gratitude and joy and am so sorry I so rarely write to tell you . . . (Knowing always that the Spirit came to me through you!)."[67] If that first letter mirrors Mary Lynch's yearning for community and human love, then the author of the second can stand symbolically as a loving link with the church, in the person of Rev. Carroll Stuhlmueller, CP. He wrote, "I thank God that you have been able to return [home to Columbus] and be with those who love you very much. At the same time, I weep with many of your other friends, to know of your serious sickness."[68]

A month later, on August 24, 1979, Mary Bernadette Lynch left this earthly life. The memorial card distributed at her funeral liturgy four days later at St. Vincent's Children Center is carefully nuanced. "Go forth with the Sign of Faith, in the Peace of Christ," from the Roman Ritual, is printed on the front of the card, making it clear that she lived in faith and within "the Faith." Her work to change the Catholic Church had been done from within, and with great "delicacy"—a requirement she herself had expressed as the most likely to produce results. Though there are other written descriptions of Mary Lynch among her papers, the back of the memorial card lists eighteen attributes which may be presumed to be the opinions of those who knew her best: "joyful, faithful, compassionate, hope, strength, awesome love, comforter, healer, nurturer, teacher, poor in spirit, thirsting for justice, longing for truth, pure in heart, praying always, peacemaker, cross-bearer, woman for others."

The several lay ministries allowed in 1979 within the Catholic funeral liturgy were all performed by members of the Lynch family, and the Eucharistic presiders were five male priests.

SUMMARY

Mary Bernadette Lynch's life bridged two clearly delineated periods in Catholic Church history: the pre– and the post–Vatican II periods. This is seen in both the external fact of her life's dates and also in the inner development of her intellectual and spiritual life. She was typical of thousands of devout Catholic women of her time: born into a traditional and specifically North American Catholicism, educated in Catholic schools for nineteen years, and nourished by an individualistic piety which led her to hunger for intimacy with God. Lynch differed from the others, however, in the path she took to reach that end.

The Catholic culture of the time formed Lynch to be compliant with the teachings of her church, not rebellious. She applied her professional insights about social change to the Roman Catholic Church, acknowledging the very long time and the very particular gifts—"delicacy," among others—that were necessary to change that culture. Mary Lynch's spirituality drew her toward the familiar form of the vowed religious life of her day and found in the social work profession an orientation to service similar to that of Catholic Sisters. During her social work career she learned the spiritual aspects of the Montessori educational theory, and that awareness stimulated her to seriously consider creating a lay community for others in service to the church. Her hopes and passions were deeply rooted in her fundamentally traditional Catholicism and not in heresy, schism, or rebelliousness.

Circumstances allowed Lynch to collect the stories of individual women's calls to ordination, including her own, in unconscious preparation for the day when they might be invited to pursue sacramental ordination within the church and should have their documentation at the ready. Credibility, competency, and contacts were important to her as an individual and as "pastor" of the movement. This meant engaging in theological studies as well as in pastoral work on parish committees or as a Communion minister. She saved the lists of participants from courses, lectures, workshops, retreats, and meetings in order to build a community of support for the movement. Lynch's degree in social work and her two decades of professional experience in administration, organization, and social systems were at the service of a new community: that of women seeking ordination and those supporting the concept.

When considering Lynch's place in the history of the women's ordination movement, it is worth noting that much of her work presaged that of those who came after her. Her personal connections with Catholic women and men in France, England, the Philippines, Belize, Canada, Belgium, Spain, El Salvador, Mexico, Italy, and elsewhere clearly foreshadowed the later groundbreaking research and writing of Frances Bernard O'Connor, CSC, regarding the hopes of Catholic women in the developing nations. Lynch's unification of the Deaconess Movement with AFAMP and her involvement with the St. Joan's Alliance foreshadowed the 1996 federating of women's ordination groups around the world into the organization known as WOW. The *Journey* newsletter of Jeanne Barnes and Mary Lynch was reincarnated as *New Women, New Church* after the birth of WOC, serving the same purposes for the movement, the members, and the church at large.

This chapter may seem to have highlighted the roles, influence, and activity of male clergy and hierarchy more than the reader might have expected. But the fact that Mary Lynch herself saved so many materials related to them reflects her confidence that the task was to befriend, teach, and "convert" the people in power "with great delicacy" because in their hands rested the ability to change the church structures whose design impeded women from full ministry. During this period of the movement, the individual strands of her life, of the other women's, of the bishops', and of the supportive organizations ceased to be parallel, individual strands and wove together as a thick, rich braid.

NOTES

Special acknowledgment is here given to the archives of the University of Notre Dame (UNDA) where the Mary Lynch Collection (CMBL) is housed. She saved many of her papers untitled or undated, but every effort has been made to arrive at such information by way of internal evidence in the papers themselves.

1. Report by Mary Bernadette Lynch (hereafter MBL; 1972), University of Notre Dame Archives, Mary B. Lynch Papers (hereafter UNDA CMBL) Carton 6, Folder 5.
2. Books found among collected papers, UNDA CMBL Carton 6, Folder 19.
3. Letter from MBL to unnamed friend (Oct. 24, 1967), UNDA CMBL Carton 1, Folder 16.
4. Correspondence between MBL and Louis Ryan (1968), UNDA CMBL Carton 3, Folder 38 and Carton 6, Folder 15.
5. Letter from MBL to Ann Ryan (June 19, 1968), UNDA CMBL Carton 1, Folder 2.
6. Letter from MBL to unnamed friend (Feb. 28, 1967), UNDA CMBL Carton 1, Folder 16.
7. Letter from MBL to Ann Ryan (June 18, 1968), UNDA CMBL Carton 5, Folder 37 and Carton 6, Folder 15.
8. Clipping from the *Indianapolis Star* (April 12, 1972), UNDA CMBL Carton 5, Folders 5 and 6.
9. MBL letter to unnamed friend (Aug. 5, 1975), UNDA CMBL Carton 3, Folder 38 and Carton 1, Folder 11.
10. MBL Spiritual Retreat Notes (July 1972), UNDA CMBL Carton 5, Folder 30.
11. Paul VI, *Ad Pascendum* (1972), document on *The Restoration of the Permanent Diaconate*.
12. Note from MBL to Jeanne Barnes (March 1970), UNDA CMBL Carton 2, Folder 31.
13. MBL spiritual retreat notes (July 1972 or 1975), UNDA CMBL Carton 5, Folder 3.
14. Letter from MBL to Jeanne Barnes (Jan. 10, 1971), UNDA CMBL Carton 1, Folder 3.
15. *The Journey* I, no. 1, UNDA CMBL Carton 6, Folder 13.
16. *Diakonos* newsletter, ed. Mary M. Schaefer (Toronto, Sept. 1970), UNDA CMBL Carton 4, Folder 6.
17. *The Catholic Citizen* (1970–1971), UNDA CMBL Carton 3, Folder 12.
18. General correspondence, UNDA CMBL Carton 1, Folder 16.
19. Discernment reflections by MBL, "Why Abandon Social Work?" UNDA CMBL Carton 4, Folder 46.
20. Letter from Theresa A. Mount to MBL (1971), UNDA CMBL Carton 1, Folders 1 and 2; emphasis mine.
21. Letter from MBL to Jeanne Barnes, UNDA CMBL Carton 1, Folder 3.
22. *Concern* (Spring 1971), UNDA CMBL Carton 4, Folder 28.
23. Andrea Wild, *The Work of the Spirit Is Alive in Our Times* (Denver, CO: Queen of Peace Oratory, Spring 1971), UNDA CMBL Carton 4, Folder 28.
24. MBL, "Why Abandon Social Work?" UNDA CMBL Carton 4, Folder 4.

25. Marilyn L. Sieg, "The Unique Life of the Sisters for Christian Community" (Aug. 21, 1973), UNDA CMBL Carton 4, Folder 10.

26. Unknown (undated), UNDA CMBL Carton 4, Folder 48.

27. Letter from MBL to inquirers concerning the Deaconess Movement (Oct. 21, 1971), UNDA CMBL Carton 2, Folder 2.

28. MBL personal notes (Feb. 1972), UNDA CMBL Carton 4, Folder 46.

29. MBL, *The Journey* (Aug. 1972), UNDA CMBL Carton 1.

30. Letter from MBL to Bernice McNeela (Oct. 1973), UNDA CMBL Carton 3, Folder 26.

31. Gary F. Greif, "The Vows and Christian Life," *Review for Religious* 26 (Oct. 1967): 805–33, UNDA CMBL Carton 3, Folder 30.

32. *The Documents of Vatican II: Lumen Gentium*, ed. Walter M. Abbott, SJ (New York: Guild Press, 1966), par. 37.

33. Greif, *op cit.*, 817; emphasis mine.

34. MBL spiritual retreat notes (1973), UNDA CMBL Carton 5, Folder 3.

35. Note from MBL to an unnamed friend (June 1973), UNDA CMBL Carton 2, Folder 1.

36. Letter from Enrico Bartoletti to MBL (Dec. 1973), UNDA CMBL Carton 3, Folder 2.

37. Avis Clendenen, "Proposal to Chicago Province Chapter" (Apr. 1974), UNDA CMBL Carton 2, Folder 1.

38. MBL personal notes (Jan. 1974), UNDA CMBL Carton 3, Folder 36.

39. MBL personal notes from National Meeting of U.S. Diaconate Directors (undated), UNDA CMBL Carton 6, Folder 15.

40. MBL lecture notes from L'Amicale des Femmes Aspirant au Ministère Presbyteral Conference (Paris, Sept. 28–29), UNDA CMBL Carton 3, Folder 20.

41. Statement of National Sister Formation Conference concerning ordination for women (Oct. 25, 1974), UNDA CMBL Carton 2, Folder 2.

42. Letter from MBL to prospective participants in first planning meeting of a national conference (Dec. 14, 1974), UNDA CMBL Carton 2, Folder 45.

43. Ibid.

44. Proposal from James Dowdy to William D. Borders (Jan. 1975), UNDA CMBL Carton 5, Folder 3.

45. Letter from Alan Eddington to MBL (Jan. 13, 1975), UNDA CMBL Carton 1, Folder 11.

46. Letter from John T. Finnegan to MBL (Jan. 20, 1975), UNDA CMBL Carton 1, Folder 11.

47. Address by Elizabeth Carroll (Feb. 4, 1975), UNDA CMBL Carton 4, Folder 4.

48. MBL personal papers (Apr. 23, 1975, and June 23, 1975), UNDA CMBL Carton 1, Folder 11.

49. Ibid. (June 2, 1975).

50. Letter from MBL to executive committee of Detroit conference (Oct. 25, 1975), UNDA CMBL Carton 1, Folder 14.

51. Minutes of Detroit conference planners (Jan. 17, 1976), UNDA CMBL Carton 2, Folder 48.

52. MBL report on planners' meeting (Jan. 17, 1976), UNDA CMBL Carton 1, Folder 15.

53. Proclamation from WOC Core Committee to MBL (undated), UNDA CMBL Carton 7, Folder 1.

54. Letter from MBL to Bernice McNeela (Sept. 8, 1976), UNDA CMBL Carton 1, Folder 15.

55. Letter from MBL to Anne Marie Gardiner (1976), UNDA CMBL Carton 2, Folder 42.

56. Letter from Regina Griffin to MBL (July 13, 1976), UNDA CMBL Carton 1, Folder 15.

57. Letter from Carroll Stuhlmueller to MBL (Sept. 14, 1976), UNDA CMBL Carton 1, Folder 15.

58. *Parish Bulletin* (Corpus Christi Church, Columbus, Ohio, March 10, 1977), UNDA CMBL Carton 4, Folder 25.

59. Letter from Sue Pattan Zitzinger to MBL (Oct. 27, 1978), UNDA CMBL Carton 4, Folder 15.

60. Letter from Ernest Unterkoefler to MBL (Apr. 23, 1979), UNDA CMBL Carton 4, Folder 15.

61. Letter from Maurice J. Dingman to MBL (Apr. 24, 1979), UNDA CMBL Carton 1, Folder 16.

62. Illegibly signed letter to MBL (May 15, 1979), UNDA CMBL Carton 1, Folder 15.

63. Letter from national WOC office (Rochester, New York, May 23, 1979), UNDA CMBL Carton 2, Folder 21.

64. Letter from Catherine S. Roche (May 28, 1979), UNDA CMBL Carton 1, Folder 15.

65. Illegibly signed letter to MBL (June 6, 1979), UNDA CMBL Carton 1, Folder 15.

66. Letter from Tom Allen to MBL (June 13, 1979), UNDA CMBL Carton 2, Folder 21.

67. Letter from Judy Heffernan to MBL (July 19, 1979), UNDA CMBL Carton 1, Folder 15.

68. Letter from Carroll Stuhlmueller to MBL (July 19, 1979), UNDA CMBL Carton 2, Folder 21.

Chapter Three

Mosaic

Role of Women Religious in the Movement

PERCEPTION AND REALITY

For more than a half century the women's ordination movement in the Roman Catholic Church was initiated, led by, and composed of lay women, from May Kendall and Gabrielle Jeffery who founded the St. Joan's Alliance in London in 1911, through Georgiana Putnam McEntee and Frances McGillicuddy who activated it in the United States, and Jeanne Barnes and Mary Lynch who founded and led the Deaconess Movement in the early 1970s. As further indication of its lay leadership, until recent years only one Sister[1] had been listed on the membership rolls of the U.S. St. Joan's Alliance: Anna Dengel, MM, founder of the Medical Missionary Sisters, who was awarded honorary membership for the work of her community on behalf of women in Africa. Illustrating the lay nature of St. Joan's are the photos and lengthy interviews of some of its members, published in the *New York Times* in 1975.[2] Furthermore, the earliest writers in the United States on the subject of women's ordination were lay persons: theologian Rosemary Lauer's article in *Commonweal* maintains pride of place as the first specifically Catholic feminist writing published in the United States.[3] Nor were Mary Daly, Rosemary Radford Ruether, Arlene Anderson Swidler, or Leonard Swidler (see chapter 1) members of vowed religious communities. Still, the persistent error about the composition of the movement has been that vowed women religious[4] have been responsible for its founding and its continued existence.

Examination of the registration roster[5] for the 1975 Detroit conference, too, reveals the falsity of the common lore. Of the total 1,254 persons registered, there were 653 Sister-participants, identified by title, community initials, residential addresses, or this author's personal acquaintance. Among the 651 remaining registrants, some probably were Sisters but did not use any identifiers other than their given and family names. This was a growing practice among Sisters of the time in order to emphasize their unity with all women, rather than setting themselves apart as different by using a religious title. The deliberate omission was also motivated, at times, by their need to avoid potentially incendiary attention from the clergy or hierarchy. In any case, even allowing for a few unidentified Sisters to increase the number 653, there was an almost even representation of lay women and Sisters at the first nationwide U.S. gathering related to women's ordination. From these statistics, and more to follow, it is clear that Sisters have not "owned" the movement. Despite this, the roster of speakers did display a preponderance of women religious, and because of this the troublesome false perception did develop and rooted itself tenaciously.

Furthermore, the first issue of *New Women, New Church*, WOC's periodical newspaper, was the only issue in which Sisters were extraordinarily numerous contributors.[6] In the very first issue there were twenty-two articles written by Sisters and only fourteen by other women. The ratio shifted in the second issue, which ran only two stories by Sisters and five by other women; and by June 1994 the proportions had shifted even more, with two articles by Sisters and seventeen by other women. In the arena of formal national leadership, shortly after the 1975 WOC founding, only one member of the three-person executive team was a Sister: Joan Sobala, SSJ. Since then, there has been only one other woman religious in that leadership role, and she filled an "interim" term as the national administrator: M. Fidelis McDonough, RSM (1982–1983). Yet the popular misconception has been a long time dying and still raises its head occasionally: that the movement was started, and has been mostly populated and controlled, by Sisters.

It was extraordinarily difficult to free the ordination movement from the power of that error for deep-rooted reasons. Throughout the twentieth century and even earlier, the teachings of the Catholic Church on the states of life and paths to holiness presented them in the order of their "superiority": priesthood, vowed religious life, marriage, and the single life. Internalizing that hierarchical reasoning led many Catholics (including some Sisters themselves, of course) to infer, when the subject arose, that Sisters were logically the best women qualified for ordination because they were "holier" than other women. The double message, which was harmful to both groups, was that lay women are less than holy, and Sisters are less than womanly.

The roots of this stratification of lifestyles lie in the widespread and long-lasting seventeenth-century Jansenist belief that sexual desire and sexual activity (and many other human traits) are base and make one less than holy; therefore those who abjured their physicality were considered the nobler, the purer, the worthier in the Roman Catholic Church. Whether consciously or unconsciously held, this did contribute to the public's impression of Sisters as holy women, for they traditionally live a vow of lifelong chaste celibacy. Adding to the force of that teaching-by-stratification was the confusing nature of the North American communal religious life itself: simultaneously active (teaching, nursing, working in administration, working in social services) *and* cloistered (prayerful, tightly restricted as to movement outside the convents, contemplative). Sisters were believed to be not only effective professionals but also the church's full-time holy women. Similarly, we have noted that the root of Mary Lynch's desire for ordination was based on the fact that she wanted to be "closer to God," and she believed that priests, with their ordination promise of celibacy and their function as ritual leaders, were the closest people to God. Considering this background makes it more obvious just how extraordinarily atypical have been leaders like the St. Joan's Alliance members and others who, themselves at the bottom of the church's holiness scale, transcended those theological, psychological, and cultural castes in their work for all women's acceptance as candidates for the ordained priesthood.

LATE TO THE MOVEMENT

Several elements of U.S. convent life delayed the entry of Sisters to the women's movement in general and the women's ordination movement in particular. Community rules and superiors prevented them from moving freely into any activities not directly related to their work or their personal spiritual lives. In many communities the life was rooted in a rural European farming schedule and customs that they had brought with them from the countries of their founding across the Atlantic. The community schedule included inflexible times for rising and retiring, strenuous work both day and night at community-assigned tasks (e.g., teaching, farming, nursing, doing housework, carrying out maintenance), and obligatory participation in religious exercises and community activities several times daily. Reading material was supervised. Every moment was filled by the schedule, and accountability to the Sister Superior for not following it was required. In addition, individual Sisters had no money in pocket, purse, or piggy bank. Most did not have access to even small amounts of money to pay for a bus, cab, or train; nor did they have the use of cars to get to lectures and meetings. In short, they were deprived of the experiences that might have sparked their participation in the movement.

The life of non-cloistered Sisters resembled a high-speed treadmill, and eventually four specific developments increased the speed.

Papal Exhortations

Pope Pius XI in his 1929 encyclical "The Christian Education of Youth" set the stage for change[7] when he emphasized explicitly that those engaged in educating the young should be well prepared and impeccably credentialed. Then again, when advising superiors of communities in 1950, Pope Pius XII urged, "See to it therefore, that they [the Sisters] are well-trained and that their education corresponds in quality and academic degrees to that demanded by the state. . . . Give them also the opportunity and the means to keep their professional knowledge up to date."[8]

Government Requirements

In the 1920s, U.S. state regulatory agencies[9] began to require certification and continuing education for the majority of works in which religious communities found themselves. These requirements applied to the private sector, as well as to the public.

Human Limitations

U.S. bishops were loathe to allow the women's communities to reduce their workforce in the schools for the sake of their own education so, in order to meet the papal and government requirements, many Sisters were assigned by superiors to attend college classes every weekend and all summer in pursuit of undergraduate degrees (often in fields not of their own choice or ability). This practice of part-time, year-round education seemed interminable and often required eight to ten years to earn a bachelor's degree. (The process was so long that many of the Sister-students met as their own college classmates some of their former pupils.) The process was dispiriting and exhausting, and therefore often a Sister's effectiveness in her assigned, full-time work suffered.

Unforeseen Factors

In the early 1940s (during and after World War II), an overlooked breed of candidate approached the religious life. Either their mothers or they themselves had worked outside the home during the war, so their eyes and minds were opened to women's abilities and expanded and equal roles in the workplace. These women were predisposed to the active aspects of the religious life more than the contemplative (except, of course, for those who chose the entirely contemplative life in such communities as the Carmelites, the Poor Clare nuns, and others).

Fulfilling the mandates from church, state, and superiors sent some of these women into a variety of educational environments as students: some were coeducational and some non-Catholic if they were the most convenient or the least expensive or the site of excellent programs in certain fields. To greater and lesser degrees, Sisters returned home to the convents as women with new experiences and new ideas, often eager to talk about their interactions on campus and the ideas in their courses. Eventually the communities themselves were changed by new knowledge and new attitudes.

The cohort of postwar active types was strengthened in the early 1950s to mid-1960s by an annual influx of novices whose age, education, and societal environment had led them to seek in the religious life more than the traditional women's roles they had seen all around them. For example, the 1956 entering class in the Baltimore Province of the Sisters of Mercy was composed of twenty young women. Seven of them had already begun or completed their undergraduate degrees, two more had earned master's degrees, and the remaining eleven had come directly from college-preparatory high schools. Most of the twenty had been strong high school and college student leaders, elected to head student governments and other organizations, or appointed to roles like editor of school papers and yearbooks, and chair of other activities and projects.

Very many communities were attracting the same type of applicants, and the entering cohorts of the mid-1950s were the first to be assigned to full-time undergraduate studies in their early community life so as to be fully professionally prepared before going into their ministries. After earning a bachelor's degree, some of them were sent very soon to pursue graduate degrees (full-time or part-time) in order to meet the ever-rising state registry and certification standards. Some few were assigned to begin doctoral studies.

This double infusion of two "generations" of intelligent, active, leader-type members was typical of many non-cloistered religious communities of women at that time. Some communities chose to focus and hone the inchoate skills that might otherwise have swamped them, and others were unwilling or unable to do so. It is no surprise, then, that these were precisely the years of the founding of two nationwide organizations that gave the most spiritual and professional support to the Sisters in leadership positions in their communities: the Sister Formation Conference (1954–1964) and the Conference of Major Superiors of Women (later named the Leadership Conference of Women Religious; 1965–present).[10]

MOMENTUM FOR CHANGE

Though neither academic degrees nor youthful energy propelled them out of their active-cloistered lives, religious communities took very seriously Pope John XXIII's announcement of plans for a worldwide Catholic bishops' gathering (to be called "Vatican Council II"). Suddenly their rather random convent conversations about change were not only approved but mandated by the pope's call to all Catholics to prepare for the coming council through study and prayer. Taking this exhortation to heart, many communities created multifaceted processes for members' education in contemporary theology and spirituality. Central to this theological enterprise was Belgian Cardinal Léon Joseph Suenens's book *The Nun in the World* and its insights into the purpose, nature, and mission of the vowed religious life.[11] It appeared in 1962 and quickly became the single-most influential book of the twentieth century regarding women's vowed religious life.

Soon after the council ended, its documents became widely available,[12] including "The Decree on the Adaptation and Renewal of Religious Life," called *Perfectae Caritatis*, and very many women's communities around the world embraced its theology and its implications. Flowing from study of this material, four developments occurred among women's communities:

- deepening personal and communal study of and reliance on Scripture,
- implementing the implications of the new ecclesiology,
- reexamining founders' purposes and their contemporary relevance and viability, and
- adapting to the council's implied shift of the vowed communal life as a form of the lay state of life, rather than the "semi-clerical" as had been the case.

In the light of all this input and the resultant changes in thinking and behavior, the leaders of the religious communities wanted to better understand their members and their readiness to become Gospel-motivated agents of change. So the Conference of Major Superiors of Women commissioned sociologist Marie Augusta Neal, SND (Emmanuel College), to design a survey[13] to be completed by each Sister in the United States (135,106) and to analyze and publish its results. Deep among the hundreds of questions on this First Sisters' Survey in 1967 was question number 232, asking, "Have you ever seriously considered the ordained ministry for women?" The mere inclusion of that particular question opened the issue for the first time in individual Sisters' thinking. For some it validated what they had already believed, and for others the question was the instrument that set them to thinking on the topic.

The responses to question number 232 hardly predicted that Sisters would ever become a strong part of the women's ordination movement: 85 percent replied "No" to the question; 11 percent said, "Yes, but not for myself"; and a mere 3 percent said, "Yes, and for myself."[14] But by the third administration of the survey (1989) the results had changed dramatically for this question: the number of those who had not seriously considered it fell to 52 percent; 40 percent had seriously considered it, but not for themselves; and those who considered it for themselves had risen to 7 percent. The power of Neal's survey overall is unquestioned in its effectiveness as a description of U.S. Sisters at three successive moments in time. But what is generally overlooked is its (perhaps) unintended, inherently Socratic pedagogy: teaching by questioning. Merely raising the question of women's ordination in a responsible, professional research project legitimated to some degree its debatability and its importance, and invited the responder to take the question seriously. Neal may have done more for the ordination movement among Sisters than anyone by asking her simple question and surfacing the latent desire of many who answered it.

The third of Neal's surveys also revealed in question number 219 that by then, 85 percent of the Sisters had earned undergraduate degrees and 64 percent had also earned advanced degrees beyond a bachelor's. This commitment to education had an empowering effect on community members, as many came to know themselves to be ministerially competent, well prepared, and able to navigate well in the world outside the convent walls. The image of the naive, innocent nun was vanishing, to the great discomfort of many adults inside and outside the Catholic Church, both lay persons and clergy. The fact that very many communities had begun to require some undergraduate theology courses of their members meant that a few of them developed a taste for that academic field and were later assigned to or chose to pursue graduate studies in it. The astonishingly prescient M. Madeleva Wolff, CSC, poet and president of St. Mary's College (Indiana), was the first Catholic educator in the United States to open (1947) master's and doctoral degree theology programs to women. By this initiative, she indirectly prepared women to engage the Roman Catholic clergy and hierarchy in theological discourse on an equal, often superior, footing. Though neither woman was directing her work toward the issue of women's ordination, both Wolff and Neal used their respective areas of expertise—academic administration and sociological research, respectively—to lay the foundation for much that would develop among women religious in the days and years to come.

All of these ingredients and influences—and many more—resulted in Catholic Sisters becoming arguably the largest subset of highly educated women on the planet. To that fact one must add the social movements of the day, successful steps in renewal of their own communities, newfound modest financial stability, and outlook of the two postwar cohorts of Sisters. The reservoir of resulting energy could not but burst forth. Some Sisters channeled their efforts into so-called secular arenas of reform and justice, and some devoted themselves to church reform in general. Among these latter women were several who chose to apply their education, talent, and energy to the women's ordination movement.

TYPES OF INVOLVEMENT

Individuals

During the brief period of the Deaconess Movement (1970–1974), very many Sisters did write to Jeanne Barnes and Mary Lynch to express interest in advancing that issue and in being ordained themselves to the diaconate.[15] For some, the desire may have been due to the combination of the then-prevailing understanding of the diaconate as a subservient ministry in the church with the residual self-understanding of many Sisters as servants, rather than leaders. Still others who enthusiastically supported the Deaconess Movement looked upon ordination to the diaconate as a strategy, a "foot in the door" that would eventually lead to ordination to the priesthood.

Organizers and Administrators

Yet, as mentioned in earlier pages, the program of the pre-WOC gathering in Detroit in 1975 ("Women in the Priesthood Now: A Call to Action") created a different impression about Sisters' level of interest. A Sister, Nadine Foley, OP, chaired the planning committee upon Mary Lynch's request, after Lynch herself had to drop out of the role. In addition, of the twenty-four "slots" in the schedule, eleven were filled by Sisters, six by other lay women, four by Roman Catholic priests, one by a Roman Catholic lay man, and one by a female Episcopalian priest. Most likely this preponderance of Sisters on the program was due to the fact that Lynch had invited thirty-five women of religious communities to serve on the planning committee. Undoubtedly, cost was an issue in inviting speakers of high quality, and so the members of the planning committee suggested one another and other members of religious communities, knowing that they would expect little or no financial remuneration. The leadership roles included facilitating sessions, leading small group discussions, delivering addresses, and presiding at prayer. Thus, even though the actual number of the over 1,200 attendees was rather evenly distributed between women religious and other lay women, the faces most often in front of the audience were Sisters'.

Three years later, the planning committee for the second national conference ("New Women, New Church, New Priestly Ministry," Baltimore, 1978) included only one Sister, Gratia L'Esperance, RSM, and was chaired by Dolly Pomerleau, cofounder of the Quixote Center. Planners scheduled forty-eight events, of which other lay women led twenty-one sessions and Sisters led twenty-seven.[16] In addition to the simple percentage shift in the two groups since only three years earlier, the conference design itself reduced the impression of Sisters' "monopoly" on the movement: After a brief welcome to the event by Mary Luke Tobin, SL, the three principal addresses immediately following were delivered by theologians Sheila Collins, Mary Hunt, and Elizabeth Schüssler Fiorenza.

Just as the identity of the contributors to the second issue of *New Women, New Church* had shifted with Pomerleau's leadership of the 1978 event and Rosalie Muschal-Reinhardt's of the infant organization, Sisters were ready to step back from some of their former highly visible roles. In this they followed a prevalent principle in contemporary communities: one's service is to be discerned according to the need of the specific time and place and then relinquished. Sisters' direct and indirect contributions to the women's ordination movement did not end with the 1978 conference but became distributed more evenly with other lay women's. This parity lasted until a steady, drastic decline in the number of women choosing a vowed religious life across the country greatly lessened the number of them to be found in most movements for ecclesial or social change. In addition, after Pope John Paul's 1994 ban (*Ordinatio Sacerdotalis*) on merely discussing the topic of women's ordination, many Sisters who remained committed to the issue altered their style of activism out of reluctance to expose their communities to punitive action from the Vatican or their local bishop.

As WOC evolved into the largest and the most visible national organization promoting the ordination of women in the church (St. Joan's Alliance being its older, less rambunctious sister), it gradually assumed a familiar, functional structure. Thus in 1979 an *ad hoc* committee proposed the establishment of a Core Committee and an advisory board composed of eight lay women, one lay man, and six Sisters: Teresita Basso, PBVM; Elizabeth Carroll, RSM; Kathleen Keating, SSJ; Jacqueline Merz, SSND; Jamie Phelps, OP; and Marge Tuite, OP.[17] In succeeding years fewer and fewer women religious have served WOC as members of either of these governance or advisory groups, for the reasons noted above, but among them have been Helen Marie Burns, RSM; Elizabeth Carroll, RSM; Gretchen Elliott, RSM; Maureen Fiedler, SL; Celine Goessl, SCSC; Theresa Harpin, CSJ; Theresa Kane, RSM; Martha Ann Kirk, CCVI; Donna Quinn, OP; Mary Luke Tobin, SL; Charlene Walsh, RSM; Jacqui Wetherholt, SSJ; Barbara Wheeley, RSM; and one other Sister of Mercy who chooses to remain anonymous.[18]

At the same time that WOC was shaping its identity, Ethne Kennedy, SH, founded the National Assembly of Women Religious (NAWR), whose purpose was complementary to the Conference of Major Superiors of Women/ Leadership Conference of Women Religious. Whereas the latter was an organization of Sisters in formal leadership roles in their respective communities (i.e., superiors), Kennedy created NAWR for the rank-and-file Sisters in the early 1970s and later broadened its membership to other lay women as well. Kennedy also edited the organization's newsletter and published a book called *Women in Ministry: A Sister's View* and edited another, *Gospel Dimensions of Ministry*.

Renaissance Women

As noted in chapter 1, the early members of St. Joan's Alliance very often put their professional training or academic background to the service of the ordination issue, and similar resourcefulness can be found among U.S. Sisters. Women were not admitted into Catholic graduate theology programs before 1947, and women religious, as explained above, were not applying for graduate education in general in significant numbers until the mid-1950s. Thus it was only in the 1960s that numbers of Sisters began to emerge as widely recognized theologians and authors, including the earliest, Mary Lawrence McKenna, MM (1967), with her book *Women of the Church: Role and Renewal*. Two years later Agnes Cunningham, SSCM, published her book *Ministry of Women in the Church*, and Albertus Magnus McGrath, OP, wrote *What a Modern Catholic Believes about Women* in 1972. Later, McGrath explicitly charged the church with gender discrimination when she stated, "Vatican II did not recognize women as belonging in all things equally with men to the people of God."[19]

Her roles as college president, community president, and president of the Leadership Conference of Women Religious (LCWR) earned Elizabeth Carroll, RSM, a speaker's slot at the bishops' bicentennial hearings in 1975, where her topic was "On Women." Her paper there included the key statement "She must be guaranteed by the Church that freedom to be and to become all that, under the Spirit, she is capable of. Within the Church this will mean the revival of ordination to the diaconate, for which we have clear evidence in the early Church. It will also mean the institution of the orders of priesthood for women."[20] Carroll's address at the 1975 pre-WOC gathering in Detroit ("The Proper Place for Women in the Church") expanded the theme, and her article "Women and Ministry" appeared in *Theological Studies* the following December. These three events propelled Carroll to the forefront of the reform movements in women's religious life and in the church at large.

Sharing center stage with Carroll at the 1975 Detroit gathering were Anne E. Carr, BVM; Mary Collins, OSB; Dorothy Donnelly, CSJ; Margaret Farley, RSM; Nadine Foley, OP; Nancy Lafferty, FSPA; Marie Augusta Neal, SND; and Mary Daniel Turner, SND, most of whom held doctoral degrees in Scripture, theology, philosophy, or related fields. Three years later the WOC conference in Baltimore heard social analyst and educator Marge Tuite, OP; psychologist, Fran Ferder, FSPA; and Maureen Fiedler, SL, who presented her groundbreaking research concerning the degrees of readiness of Catholics to accept the ordination of women.

Almost twenty years later, after completing her term of office as president of the Sisters of the Holy Cross, Francis B. O'Connor, CSC, set about an iconoclastic task. She had worked for many years in Bangladesh, and after she had returned to Indiana, her service as community president required regular visits to the areas around the world where the Sisters worked. Upon leaving office, she returned to three of those sites (Bangladesh, Brazil, and Uganda) for her creative research project. There she initiated discussions and held interviews with many Catholic women in order to learn their experience and outlook concerning their status in the Catholic Church. In all the selected locales, O'Connor heard the women voice sentiments similar to those of women in the "developed" nations. "How is it," she asked at the conclusion of her work, "that women in such disparate cultures, races and language groups, thousands of miles apart, on four different continents could have identical questions about their church, and envision similar solutions?"[21] In publishing this pioneering research she disproved the oft-invoked dismissal of the Catholic women's movement as a concern of only the elite, educated, financially secure women of the northern hemisphere. As the women of St. Joan's Alliance had done, and as Fran Ferder, Maureen Fiedler, and Marie Augusta Neal had done, Francis O'Connor used an academic background and experience that seemed unrelated to the ordination issue in order to contribute significantly to it.

Educators

Beginning in 1727 with the Ursuline Sisters' arrival in New Orleans, the primary ministerial purpose of most U.S. Catholic religious communities was to answer Catholics' needs for education, both secular and religious. Their task did not end with the school dismissal bells, for they engaged in tutoring, in music and art lessons, in religious education for Catholics in public schools, and in evening adult education programs. From the 1970s onward, their service has also been requested on parish councils, professional organizations, and civic and cultural associations. The human interactions that resulted from such involvements—from classrooms to boardrooms—led to conversations and questions that seemed far afield from the business at hand. As these associates, students, family members, and friends raised questions concerning issues of the day, Sisters had to educate themselves. Even if one were not formally educated on ethical questions in health care, for example, or equal pay for equal work, or women's ordination, the inquiries from students, patients, or colleagues pushed the Sisters to read and reflect on those areas.

Some Sisters have worked directly for the ordination of women through organizations, prayer, and activities, but equally significantly, others among them have taught the next generations of "people in the pews": the students

who would become theologians, scholars, speakers, organizers, teachers—
and priests.

Prophetic Voices

The word "prophet" is often used in a much more dramatic and skewed sense
than its etymology and theological usage justify. The word means simply
"one who speaks out," not "one who foretells the future." Prophecy is specific only in that it points out a link between particular behavior and probable
outcomes of that behavior. It challenges the hearer to change direction for her
or his own good ("If you continue excessive gambling, you will lose your
money, home, and family") or for the good of a group ("A nation that lives
by the sword will die by the sword"). Furthermore, a prophet's message can
be determined as valid or invalid, true or false, only after the fact—sometimes very long after the fact. In this spirit and with these understandings of
the term "prophet," consider now two iconic women who have spoken out
conspicuously concerning the Catholic Church's current stance regarding
women's ordination: Theresa Kane, RSM, and Joan Chittister, OSB.

The casual observer might say that both are self-confident, outspoken,
well-educated women religious of the twenty-first-century United States and
leave it at that. But there are complementary differences that serve to nuance
the similarity of the two women. The roots of Theresa Kane's Mercy community are in the nineteenth-century urban lodgings of Dublin's poor, whereas those of Joan Chittister's Benedictine community are in the eleventh-
century rural monasteries of Germany. The former community is indebted to
the spirituality of the itinerant religious of old who went out each day to find
where they might be needed, while the latter is profoundly influenced by a
tradition of contemplative stability and scholarship. The two women were
born one year apart (1935 and 1936), grew up in the pre–Vatican II Catholic
Church, and made permanent vows in their respective communities in the
early 1960s. As adults, each earned graduate degrees but in very different
fields: Chittister in communication and Kane in hospital administration; but
each built upon her early field of study in conspicuous ways, as communica-
tor and as administrator, respectively.

Theresa Kane, RSM (born in 1935), entered the Sisters of Mercy in 1955,
and in the 1960s served as president of St. Francis Hospital in Port Jervis,
New York. After completing the term of that assignment, she was appointed
in 1966 to serve as administrator for the community's New York province, at
that time based in Dobbs Ferry. In that role, she gave her attention and
energy to the development and leadership of over four hundred Sisters and,
with her council, bore a certain level of responsibility for the individual
women as well as for the general oversight of their community-sponsored
institutions and ministries. From that period onward, Theresa's work was of

ever-broader scope and ever-more-complex nature related to the vowed religious life. After serving as province administrator, she was quickly elected in
1977 to the presidency of the national Mercy community. This full-time
work entailed participation in the LCWR, of which she was elected the
president after only one year of membership.

The LCWR represents the vast majority of Catholic women's religious
communities in the United States and provides similar advantages to its
member organizations as any professional organization does: education in
relevant societal trends, updating of news in their specific field, moral support from peers, and stimulus to improve one's work and organization. Because its members all deeply value prayer, reflection, and theological input,
the LCWR also schedules such experiences on its conference agenda. As
president of this organization for a two-year term, Theresa Kane received a
"routine," *ex officio* invitation in the autumn of 1979 to welcome Pope John
Paul II on his visit to Washington, DC, in the name of the U.S. Catholic
Sisters.[22]

Until this time, Theresa Kane had not been usually identified with the
issue of women's ordination although she had attended, as one among many,
the Detroit gathering in 1975. Significant to this fact is that neither in Detroit
nor at the Baltimore 1978 conference was Kane on the speaking roster, for it
was not until after her controversial welcome to the pope in 1979 that she
became an internationally recognized public figure, associated primarily with
the women's ordination movement. Though in subsequent years Kane spent
much time and energy on other issues of "secular" social reform, especially
for women, it was the quite brief moment in the Basilica of the National
Shrine of the Immaculate Conception that identified her ever after—for good
or for ill. Even these many years after the event, it remains difficult to
understand which aspect of Kane's address her fierce opponents considered
to be inappropriate. Was it her confident manner, her subdued brown suit,[23]
her restrained message (which did not mentioned the word "ordination"), the
fact that the world witnessed her bold action via television, or her gender?
Was it partly the atmosphere created by women wearing blue armbands, led
by Dolly Pomerleau and Maureen Fiedler? The reaction during and after
Theresa's words begs the question of whether the whole event would have
developed differently if a man had spoken the same words to a pope (see
appendix C). The two sentences problematic to the Vatican were the following:

> Our contemplation leads us to state that the Church in its struggle to be faithful
> to its call for reverence and dignity for all persons must respond by providing
> the possibility of women as persons being included in all ministries of our
> Church. I urge you, Your Holiness, to be open to and respond to the voices

coming from the women of this country who are desirous of serving in and
through the Church as fully participating members.

The one brief phrase "all ministries of our Church" was the easiest for the
Vatican to reject, but it is likely that the other unacknowledged elements in
the event exacerbated the Vatican's reaction, either consciously or unconsciously. Never in the modern era had anyone publicly and formally addressed a pope to his face in opposition to his stance on a controversial issue,
and John Paul's displeasure was long-lasting. Equally strong was Kane's
confidence that she had acted appropriately for the good of the church:

> Although I did not mention ordination explicitly, in stating "all ministries of
> our Church," indeed I did include ordination [by using that phrase]. When I
> was asked to offer clarification of my greeting with the Vatican Office of
> Religious in November 1979, we had some stressful exchanges when the
> officials wanted me to state that I did not include ordination when I stated "all
> ministries." I responded, "Indeed I did include ordination and want it so stated
> that I did."[24]

In subsequent months, Theresa Kane requested a conciliatory conversation
with the pope, but John Paul refused her. Later he met privately with Mehmet
Ali Ağca, the man who shot and attempted to assassinate him in St. Peter's
Square in May 1981. The irony of this papal inconsistency has often been
noted by essayists, journalists, and lecturers. Though Pope John Paul II declined to receive her, Kane did secure an appointment in Rome with Cardinal
Eduardo F. Pironio, the Vatican's head of the Office for Institutes of Conse-
crated Life, and overheard him discussing with two North American bishops
her possible removal from office. As the months went on, a representative of
the Vatican phoned one of the community's province presidents to ask if she
would resign from that position and take over Theresa Kane's. The Sister
president refused, which Kane later called "a very courageous act on her
part." After Cardinal Cody and others of the hierarchy learned that Kane had
only two years left in her term of office and could not be reelected (according
to the Mercy community's constitutions), they seemed to drop the matter.

While recriminations were abundant, accolades, too, poured in to express
thanks to Kane for her action. One item among the latter category was of
particular historical interest: the April 1980 scroll prepared for her by the
U.S. Section of the St. Joan's International Alliance.[25] They named her
American Woman of the Year, calling her "A woman of hope and courage
who spoke firmly and respectfully to Pope John Paul II . . . urging him to
respond to the women of this country by providing them the possibility as
persons to be included in all ministries of the Church." It was a gracious and
heartfelt acknowledgement of solidarity of purpose and aims, and the award

overshadowed the previous gap and occasional irritation between the older and newer ways of advancing the issue of Catholic women's ordination.

There had been no immediate penalty imposed or price required of Theresa Kane by the Vatican; but from 1978 to 1984, they tangled once again in a prolonged conflict whose fires were fed, some opine, by John Paul's displeasure over her words in Washington. During the year before her welcome of the pope, Theresa Kane and her council established a study process[26] that they believed would be of great use to Catholic hospitals in the United States. The project's purpose was to study the question of whether or not direct sterilization is intrinsically evil and therefore unallowable in Catholic institutions or agencies. It was designed to tap both the experience of the Sisters of Mercy and colleagues in their extensive hospital network and the philosophical, medical, and theological expertise of others.

The multiyear process had barely begun, the dialogue not yet deeply engaged, when the Vatican was informed of it *sub rosa* and stepped in to stop it immediately. In addition, Pope John Paul II required Theresa Kane and her council to sign a formal declaration of their intention to support the teachings of the church not only in practice but interiorly and intellectually, as well. After several rounds of correspondence and several variations of a formulation, their signed statement was accepted and then rejected. The Mercy leaders labored to provide versions of the statement acceptable to the Vatican and true to themselves but were painfully influenced by the knowledge that any degree of noncompliance could have devastating effects on the ministries and members of the entire community. Possible punitive action by the Vatican was explicitly threatened, and Kane and her colleagues were aware of the recent experience of the Society of Jesus. After a period of similar tension with the Vatican, the Jesuits were informed in 1981 that the pope had appointed a "personal delegate of the Holy Father" to oversee the Jesuits instead of allowing a normal, internal election to be held for their next father general. In any case, for the sake of the community's well-being, in 1984 the Mercy leadership signed a statement that was acceptable to the Vatican, and the study was permanently put to rest.

Like others mentioned in these pages who have paid a painful price for their support of women's ordination in the Catholic Church (see especially chapter 6), Kane has not allowed herself to be hardened by the negative aspects of her experiences. In 2000 when Sharon Euart, RSM, was at the Vatican for a meeting of canon lawyers, John Paul II inquired of her twice concerning Theresa Kane and went out of his way to send his greetings to her through Euart. Kane has repeatedly interpreted this gesture as an indication that he had moved toward some degree of understanding of her actions and of her as a person. In the years after 1979, Kane applied her energy to teaching at Mercy College in Dobbs Ferry and maintaining an active roster of speaking commitments to reform-minded groups of Catholics across the country.

Similarly to Theresa Kane's history of Mercy community leadership, Joan Chittister, OSB, served her community as prioress of the Erie Benedictine Sisters for twelve years and as president of the Conference of American Prioresses for sixteen years. In these capacities, she too was a member of LCWR and served as president of the organization. Following that period of time, in contrast to Kane, Chittister chose scholarly and inspirational writing as her primary ministry, rather than classroom teaching. Through years of research, deadlines, and writing on spiritual topics she came to the attention of the Catholic public. She made a field that was often considered arcane or unnecessary both accessible and engaging for a broadly varied readership. Over time Joan's vistas broadened, and her weekly syndicated columns and published books probed spiritual foundations and ramifications in areas of contemporary struggles for justice such as war, immigration, poverty, and women's status in society and church.

A pivotal event in Chittister's life that highlighted the tensions between the Vatican and women religious vis-à-vis the ordination issue occurred in 2001, when the Women's Ordination Worldwide coalition planned its first international conference and invited her to be a keynote speaker at the event in Dublin. After some twenty-thousand copies of the program were in circulation around the globe, the Vatican began to react and informed the then-prioress Christine Vladimiroff, OSB, that she was to forbid Joan to attend or to speak at the conference.[27] Sanctions would be imposed if this mandate were not followed. In a surprising decision, Vladimiroff invoked the centuries-old Benedictine tradition of involving the entire community in discernment concerning matters of importance to the whole. This formal process is not merely a matter of walking into a meeting and casting a vote, but is a span of days or weeks requiring prayer, study, discussion, sometimes fasting, and often painful struggle to come to consensus. In the end, the outcome was that all of the 127 other active nuns of the monastery formally declared that "for the good of the church" Joan Chittister should go to Dublin for the speaking engagement. In addition, thirty-five of the youngest Sisters officially notified the Vatican that if Joan were penalized in any way, the same penalty should be imposed on them, too—even to dismissal from the community.

It is not surprising, then, that Joan went to Dublin feeling the profound support of her community. But there was one more obstacle to overcome: her own physical body interfered, and she appeared on the stage of the Dublin meeting bent over and frail-looking after very recent serious surgery. So on June 30, 2001, it was Joan's broader "community"—international, non-monastic, lay, or vowed women and men—who stood with her in prolonged and roaring embrace as she hobbled across the stage with the help of a cane. She had come for the good of the church, and her topic was to that point: "Discipleship for a Priestly People in a Priestless Period."[28] Describing the lived consequences of "an eminently male-oriented, male-defined and male-controlled world" such as the Catholic Church, Chittister reminded her hearers that "in the women's question the church is facing one of its most serious challenges to discipleship since the emergence of the slavery question when we argued then, too, that slavery was the will of God for some people—but not us."[29]

As Communities

The support of religious communities for the women's ordination movement usually and easily falls into the categories of financial and in-kind contributions, human and material resources, and publicity. But prior to the Benedictines' communal support for Joan Chittister, other communities were taking action. For example, at their 1977 province chapter,[30] the Sisters of Mercy passed a formal proposal for a process to be implemented by their elected leaders: Joan Specht, RSM, and her council (see chapter 2). Shortly thereafter, Specht (provincial administrator) met with Cardinal John P. Cody, at which time she presented to him Avis Clendenen and her credentials for ordination. He declined to ordain her. "Joan Specht also wrote to all the American bishops following our conversation with Cody, encouraging them to meet with women in their dioceses who were experiencing a call to ordained ministry."[31]

Many Catholic women's communities provided considerable support for the Detroit ordination conference of 1975 from the very outset. The initial brainstorming meeting convoked by Mary Lynch was held on the campus of the Dominican Sisters' Rosary College in Chicago. Of the thirty-six participants in the meeting, thirty-four were women religious. This reflects the predominance Lynch gave to Sisters when she extended the original invitations. The following November, of the forty-nine groups and individuals on the 1975 conference program that were credited with public relations and financial or in-kind support, twenty were women's communities or one of their sponsored institutions.[32] Among them were the Community of the Holy Spirit, the Dominican Sisters of Adrian, the Franciscan Sisters of Mary, the Franciscan Sisters of the Perpetual Adoration (Iowa), the Good Shepherd Sisters of New York, the Religious of Christian Education, the Religious Sisters of Mercy (New York and Omaha provinces), the School Sisters of St. Francis (Illinois and Omaha), the Sisters of Charity of Cincinnati, the Sisters of Charity of St. Vincent de Paul, the Sisters of Loretto of Kentucky, the Sisters of Notre Dame de Namur of Boston, the Sisters of St. Joseph of Cleveland and of Wisconsin, the Sisters of St. Joseph for Peace, the Third Order of St. Francis, and the Sisters of the Holy Child. In addition, the

LCWR and National Assembly of Women Religious, in which were included communities additional to those mentioned above, publicly endorsed the 1975 gathering. Individuals in some of these groups publicized the coming event in their respective community newsletters, on high school and college campuses, and in other Catholic organizations to which they belonged.

Those other organizations included, but were not limited to, emerging "special interest" groups of Sisters such as the National Black Sisters Conference (founded in 1968 by M. Martin de Porres Grey, RSM); the National Coalition of American Nuns (1969 by Margaret Ellen Traxler, SSND); the National Association of Women Religious (1970 by Marge Tuite, OP); *Las Hermanas* (1971 by Gloria Gallardo, HSS, and Gregoria Ortega, OLVM); and Network (1971 by forty-seven Sisters). While the ordination of women was not the primary goal of any of these smaller organizations, their commitment to solidarity with women seeking fuller lives in church and society led individual members to channel their energy toward the ordination matter as needed. As examples of this overlapping of commitments, Tuite and Traxler, as well as M. Shawn Copeland, OP, of the National Black Sisters Conference, and Maria Iglesias, SC, of *Las Hermanas* were prominent speakers at the 1978 national conference on women's ordination.

The massed intellectual and spiritual energy of thousands of women religious was like a river gathering strength as it spread the length and breadth of the country, from urban areas like Los Angeles to little towns like Sebago, Maine. As with any flood, the ordination movement stirred fear and tension in some, as well as energy and new life in others.

RESULTING TENSIONS

Among Sisters Themselves

Given the widely diverse backgrounds, ministries, theologies, spiritualities, and educations of Sisters, it is natural that there would be internal disagreements among community members on the issue of ordaining Roman Catholic women. Many a strained dinner conversation has ensued. One of the earliest and strongest statements concerning the responsibility of women religious to work actively toward this goal was a 1971 address in Ireland for the St. Joan's International Alliance by Rita Hannon, SUSC. The mere title of her talk, "The Treason of Women Religious," foreshadowed frank and confrontational content that was, indeed, the tone of the presentation. In the opening paragraphs of her talk, Hannon stated that, though there had been prelates, priests, and one pope [John XXIII] who have supported the aims of the alliance, "it is to the eternal shame of women religious that with very few and notable exceptions they have made no contribution to the advancement of women either within or outside the Church." She added that "their silence amounts almost to contempt," and concluded, "Much has been written and said about the things that cause women anger, frustration, disillusionment with the Church . . . There have been a few Catholics among such writers and speakers, but where were the nuns? If they had written, spoken, lectured on these matters as assiduously as they have guarded their chastity, the world today would be a much better place." [33]

Though presented in Ireland, Hannon's remarks are relevant to the U.S. ordination movement because she delivered them to a St. Joan's Alliance meeting, whose importance to the movement on this side of the Atlantic is detailed in chapters 1 and 2, and because the St. Joan's editor chose to publish it on the front page of its periodical. It is possible (though not necessarily to be presumed) that Hannon delivered it to an accepting audience, among whom were at least some supporters of her view. It is unlikely that she was expressing a purely idiosyncratic view of her own, and it is possible that the acceptability of raising this topic in St. Joan's circles may have had something to do with Frances McGillicuddy's long-standing negativity [34] about Sisters' roles in the U.S. movement. Frances was, after all, an officer of the St. Joan's International Alliance; she planned and attended its international conferences; and she subscribed to its periodical, *The Catholic Citizen.*

Whereas Hannon tried to shame Sisters into greater involvement in 1971, the argument toward less involvement is evident in some of the writing of Sandra Schneiders, IHM, published in 2000. She argued the inadvisability of ordaining women religious, based on the theological question of whether one can credibly stand between the theology of the sacraments and the polity flowing from contemporary ecclesiology. In Schneiders's view, the essence of the religious life is its prophetic nature, and in the stratified class structure of the Roman Catholic Church, it is impossible to be prophetic if ordained, and thus a member of the very structure needing critique. Her argument was grounded in the understanding that there is a "fundamental tension [contradiction] between an intrinsically hierarchical vocation and a prophetic one." This, she wrote, "could cause agonizing problems for congregations [of Sisters] because ordaining any of its members . . . would fundamentally change the character of the congregation." [35]

Hannon and Schneiders, two women religious, stand as chronological and ideological bookends for the era, and between them stand the varying beliefs and opinions of twenty-first-century women religious involved in the movement.

With Other Lay Women

In the three decades between Hannon and Schneiders, it must be noted that there was a significant antipathy within some other lay women toward Sisters working for the same cause. It was often unverbalized by the former and therefore unknown by the latter, but some written comments do remain for examination. In a 1973 letter to Carol Coston, OP, executive director of Network,[36] Frances McGillicuddy acquainted her with the work of the St. Joan's Alliance and then moved into a brief and pointed critique of the *modus operandi* of Sisters: "My past personal experience was that those I met in Rome and elsewhere were striving for acceptance by priests rather than by women. . . . For this reason I think that for the time being any "working together" of nuns with the overwhelming majority of women will have to be on an *ad hoc* basis."

Following the 1975 Detroit gathering, McGillicuddy's ill will toward Sisters and their influence in the movement was so strongly expressed in a letter to Rosalie Muschal-Reinhardt that the latter sent her a formal, written reply refuting each of Frances's assertions and surfacing the question of whether these positions reflected "an underlying principle of St. Joan's." Rosalie indicated that she would seek clarification from the alliance's executive committee and would then decide whether or not to remain a member of the organization.[37] She had been a very active leader in St. Joan's, both stateside and internationally, and she was hoping to remain in solidarity with them even as she helped to bring about the new entity (WOC) that was emerging. Rosalie's *de facto* role as a "bridge" between the St. Joan's Alliance and WOC emerges in the above-mentioned letter, as does her awareness that Frances is probably acting out of feelings of uselessness and loss of standing in the new organization: "I shall continue to pray daily for women like you, Frances, who were prophets to us. I also pray that in our attaining our goal, you understand that others now join you in the prophecy."

It is tempting to dismiss McGillicuddy's views as the angry stance of one person facing her loss of influence, but other women[38] have expressed sentiments similar to hers:

> I am wondering how many other women besides myself, are really "ticked off" about the attitude of women who are nuns. . . . I am "up to here" with the way they are pushing us out, matronizing us, and I guess the last straw was when the women who are [liturgical] readers and extraordinary ministers [of Communion] were "bumped" out of their places for the Easter liturgies and replaced by women who are nuns.

These two women reflected feelings that went largely unspoken among others for several years: that Sisters wanted to run the movement, that they were controllers and not true co-laborers, and that their manner was just another example of oppressive clericalism. Closer to the fact is that women in general, *including Sisters*, were becoming stronger, more self-confident, more experienced, and more outspoken, just as Mary Lynch, Jeanne Barnes, Frances McGillicuddy herself, Arlene Swidler, and so many other women had become. The roots of the tension can be found in the image of Sisters up to that time: passive, abnormally humble, sweet, reserved, and accepting of whatever came their way. When those unhealthy attitudes within Sisters and the behaviors that flowed from them began to change, the contrast was jarring to many Catholics. Response to the human development of women religious may have been overreliance by some or resentment by others, but by neither attitude were Sisters allowed to simply be women.

Between Communities and the Hierarchy

Not only were some lay Catholics on edge about this profound change in Sisters' thinking and behavior, as described above, but many U.S. and Vatican authorities were as well. The first experiences of the tension revolved around the Sisters' pursuit of college and university degrees—which had been mandated by the state governments and two popes. As communities rotated a few Sisters each year out of classroom teaching and into classroom learning, the expense of running parish schools rose because the pastors had to hire lay persons to take their places. The result was that pastors were obliged to provide "real" salaries for the lay persons, by contrast with the meager stipends or compensations given to Sisters. At the next higher level, review of the diocesan budget projections each year brought the issue to the bishops' attention. This trend began in the late 1950s in diocesan institutions, such as parish schools and diocesan high schools, and since the 1970s has become a serious challenge to community-founded Catholic colleges and universities.

A very different issue and dynamic raised the hackles of Sisters' communities in the 1970s. With the Vatican II documents urging the renewal of religious communities by serious study of their founders' mission and their own contemporary ministries and lifestyle, both women's and men's communities assigned their own now-well-educated members to the task of recapturing history. In the process, many groups found that the official, public, church-sanctioned story about them was seriously flawed and often simply untrue. As Kenneth Briggs wrote, "This led to a distrust of the Roman Catholic hierarchy by women religious. Sometimes the disconnect between the community and the founder's legacy seemed clearly an attempt to hide truth that embarrassed or offended Church authorities."[39] For one example, the Sisters, Servants of the Immaculate Heart of Mary in Scranton, Pennsylvania, and Monroe, Michigan, uncovered the fact that their founder, Theresa Maxis Duchemin, was of Haitian-African descent and that her bishop's racial prejudice led him to exile her from the very community that she had founded.[40] In other cases, individual founders were deemed by the local bishop or leading clergyman to be excessively proud, mentally ill, disobedient, or power-hungry. Often the offended bishop expelled the woman from "his" diocese, and she had to find shelter elsewhere.

Situations such as these were not universally experienced nor broadly known but were widespread enough that they contributed to the growing awareness of community members that Sisters (and all other lay persons) have no place in the formal structure of the church and no decision-making role in its life. Ordination of women could change all that, some believed, and many decided to work toward that goal of radically changing the church. On the surface these episodes seem unrelated to the issue of women's ordination, but in fact they are the backdrop against which later, specifically ordination-related crises have arisen with individuals, with whole communities, with the LCWR, and most recently, with the entirety of women's active vowed religious life as lived in the United States in the early twenty-first century.

Between Individuals and Hierarchy

In addition to the highly visible electricity between the Vatican and such women as Theresa Kane and Joan Chittister, similar disruption has besieged the lives of many individual U.S. Sisters because of the actions of some local bishops, clergy, or institutional administrators.

Carmel McEnroy, RSM, was a tenured faculty member teaching theology at St. Meinrad Seminary in Indiana when the 1995 Bishops' Visitation Committee arrived. Her work was well regarded within the institution and in broader professional circles. The school had recently been assessed favorably by the Association of Theological Schools, and McEnroy had been a full participant in the preparation and the follow-up for that evaluation process. However, "when the bishops presented their oral report to the school administration, Bishop Elden F. Curtis demanded that Carmel McEnroy be fired because she had recently been one of hundreds who had signed an open letter to Pope John Paul II asking for continued discussion of women's ordination. Six weeks later, she was dismissed from her teaching position, and the school went into a tailspin from which it has never fully recovered."[41]

McEnroy brought legal suit against the parties involved in her termination from teaching, but it was not litigated because the judge felt that it was a private, church-related matter over which the courts had no jurisdiction. Her subsequent work included writing a book about the (few) female nonparticipant attendees at the Second Vatican Council.[42] Though the Vatican II women of her research would seem to have achieved acceptance by the hierarchy simply by being invited to the council, the theme of their exclusion ran through details of the event, similar to her own experience of exclusion from her work in a Catholic setting. Eventually Carmel found a teaching position at Lexington Theological Seminary (Disciples of Christ), and after some years she returned to her religious community in Galway after decades of service to the U.S. Catholic Church.

Barbara Fiand, SND, had served for seventeen years at the Athenaeum in Cleveland, Ohio, teaching seminary students and earning the esteem of her colleagues and of those in broader circles of academia. Thus the dean's termination of her yearly contract in 1998 was unexpected. He took the action because seminarians (whose names are not publicly known) reported to him—falsely, she has stated—that Fiand publicly discouraged vocations to the ordained ministry as it presently exists because women should be included. Fiand strongly denied the accusations, which conflicted with her consistently high evaluations that had earned her the seminary's Excellence in Teaching Award on two occasions. Because of the national publicity given to her contract termination, there was an outpouring of support for her from all parts of the globe. Her forced departure from classroom teaching left the Athenaeum with no full-time female faculty members. Since that time, Barbara Fiand has developed a full ministry of leading retreats and lecturing and has written several published books.

Celine Goessl, SCSC, worked for the Diocese of Saginaw as a parish minister for decades, grappling all the while with the call she had felt since high school to pursue the ordained priesthood. In 1971, well before the ordination issue had heated up, Celine wrote her local bishop, Francis F. Reh, requesting ordination. She attended the Detroit gathering in 1975, and as a Sister of the Holy Cross (Michigan), like Kane and Chittister she served a multiyear term as province administrator of her religious community. Unlike them, however, her community's circumstances made her reluctant to risk exposing them to probable adversarial engagement with the Vatican should she move toward ordination in the Roman Catholic Women Priests (RCWP; see chapter 6). However, as has been true for many Catholic women, after decades of carefully hewing to the letter of the church's ordination law, she "went public" and accepted election to the WOC board of directors. In 2005, she publicly presided at an alternative liturgy on the sidewalk outside the National Conference of Catholic Bishops meeting in Washington, DC; and in 2011, she was elected to the position of her community's presidency. She and her community have, thus far, been spared any Vatican action, and Goessl, like other women, develops her priestly ministry by word of mouth and referral by others.

Louise Lears, SC, served the Archdiocese of St. Louis for fourteen years as an urban parish employee, the archdiocesan religious education coordinator, a graduate student in the doctoral program in medical ethics at St. Louis University, and adjunct faculty member in their Department of Theological Studies. In 2007, two women candidates for ordination through the RCWP approached her to serve as coordinator of the event, which she declined to do. She did, however, help them to find a local Reform Jewish Congregation synagogue that was large enough for the ceremony and whose senior rabbi (Susan Talve) was supportive of the women and of their request. Lears also advised them on miscellaneous matters and attended the event as a member of the congregation with no ceremonial role. She did stand and join forty to fifty others in praying a blessing for the women ordained.[43] For these actions Archbishop Raymond Burke brought canonical charges against her, processed them formally, and issued on June 16, 2008, a final "Statement Regarding the Canonical Discipline of Sister Louise Lears, SC." He formally declared her to be *persona non grata* in the St. Louis Archdiocese, banned her from employment in any Catholic institution in the archdiocese, and imposed an interdict on her, meaning that he forbade her from receiving the sacraments of the church.

The following year the National Coalition of American Nuns (NCAN) granted its annual Margaret Ellen Traxler Award to Louise Lears in acknowledgement of the severity of her punishment and "for her support of the right of women to be ordained in the Roman Catholic Church." Following Burke's punitive measures, Lears returned to her home base of Baltimore and took a teaching position at a local state university. Burke, however, was within weeks moved to Rome and promoted to chair the *Apostolica Signatura*, the Vatican's department that oversees the nominations and appointments of men to be bishops.

Louise Akers, SC, primarily an educator, served the people of Cincinnati for over forty years, both at the secondary and university levels. Like Lears, she was not much associated with the women's ordination movement but rather with a broad range of justice and peace issues such as poverty, interfaith relations, immigration, war, and racism. Because of her knowledge and experience in designing and implementing programs on these topics both in Cincinnati and beyond, as well as her international service-learning leadership, WOC sought her out in 2008 to serve as coordinator of its antiracism task force.

This work for WOC resulted in her name and picture appearing on the WOC website, which fact was reported to Cincinnati's Archbishop Daniel E. Pilarczyk in 2009 by parties unpublicized. Consequently he summoned Akers to meet with him, not for dialogue, but to tell her of his decision. He demanded that she publicly recant her belief that the ban against women's ordination is a matter of injustice within the Catholic Church. In addition, he told her that she was to withdraw her picture and name from WOC's website. If these requirements were not met, Pilarczyk would bar her from teaching any credit or noncredit courses or programs in a Catholic setting. Akers reminded him that belief is a matter of conscience and so she would not issue a statement of recant, but she did promptly see to it that her name and picture were removed from the WOC site. The penalty was imposed nonetheless.

It is true that other lay women and men and male priests have been treated similarly to the women described above, but the focus of this chapter is on women religious. Likewise, other Sisters (e.g., Barbara Ferraro, SND; Jeannine Gramick, SL; Patricia Hussey, SND; Agnes Mary Mansour, RSM; and Margaret Mary McBride, RSM) have been treated in the same way over time, but their actions were not specifically related to ordination. The increasing number of punitive measures that have been meted out on this issue have been during the years following Pope John Paul's ban on discussion of it, Pope Benedict's reinforcement of the ban, and their practice of usually appointing like-minded men to serve as bishops who will affect the lives of Catholics far into future decades.

Between Communities and the Vatican

As if in response to the entire bundle of developments in the vowed religious life described in this chapter, the accumulated issues seem to have become overwhelmingly intolerable in the eyes of the Vatican by the early twenty-first century. One manifestation of that sentiment was a symposium, "Apostolic Religious Life since Vatican II: Reclaiming the Treasure," at Stonehill College (Massachusetts) in September 2008. It was sponsored and organized by representatives of the Sisters' communities that were not members of LCWR, and it featured as keynote speaker Cardinal Franc Rodé, who was at that time the prefect (chair) of the Vatican department that oversees religious communities around the world.[44] In his prepared remarks to the audience Rodé stated:

> Though the background to the problems is the same, and there are common problems and challenges faced by both men and women religious (the engineering of language, the slant toward relativism, the fading of a sense of the supernatural, in some cases doubt about the relevance and centrality of Christ), it is also true that each group faces its own peculiar challenges. Women religious especially need to engage critically a certain strain of feminism by now outmoded but which still nevertheless continues to exert much influence in certain circles.[45]

Shortly after the conference, without any forewarning, on February 2, 2009, Rodé sent a letter to the major superior of each of the communities of active Sisters with mother-houses in the United States, announcing a formal Apostolic Visitation.[46] The unprecedented investigation was designed to examine the "quality of religious life" but did not involve men's communities, cloistered contemplative communities, or communities centrally based in other countries. Phase 1 of the process began immediately and required individual interviews of most communities' leaders, who were not informed of the reason why they were selected. Those interviews concluded by July 31, and Phase 2 began very soon thereafter, requiring completion of lengthy questionnaires.

Among the topics to be reported were membership lists (names, address-es, ages, ministries), lists of community assets and finances, and extensive information about community-sponsored ministries and institutions. The pro-cess also required descriptions of how community members lived their vows, assessed their community's future, engaged in spiritual practices ("according to approved liturgical norms"), and were held accountable, especially in matters of dissent ("public or private") from church teachings. Some of the more intrusive and private topics were dropped by Rodé after many commu-nity leaders registered their objections and the reasons for them. The deadline for sending in the September questionnaires was November 20, 2009, and most communities responded by then, after investing innumerable hours of work that had taken them away from their day-to-day responsibilities to the very community life being investigated. The process coordinator, Mary Clare Millea, ASCJ, was appointed by Rodé, with the blessing of Pope Benedict XVI, and she organized teams of religious to help with the collation of the surveys. She also solicited volunteers from various communities to imple-ment the next phase, which was the spring 2010 onsite visiting of various communities. Each visitor whom she appointed was required to sign a formal oath of fidelity to the teachings of the Roman Catholic Church.

At the end of Phase 3, Rodé's successor, João Bráz de Aviz, received in 2012 the confidential report and recommendations prepared by Mary Clare Millea and her assistants. Neither of these documents was available to the respective community leaders, nor were the names of the volunteers who did the collating, summarizing, and reporting. Unknown, too, were the names of those who funded the project. It was generally presumed that the project was even more expensive than planned, when Millea sent a request to all the communities to fund portions of the process and a request to all the U.S. bishops for contributions from their respective dioceses.

Surprise, short notice, haste, and withholding information are strategies employed in conflicts with enemies. Use of these strategies suggests that Rodé and his superior(s) perceived the Sisters as enemies of the church. However, the thousands of individuals in the United States and abroad who wrote letters, signed petitions, published articles, and granted public inter-views gave witness to the contrary view. Even the U.S. House of Representa-tives went on record with a formal, public resolution initiated by Rep. Marcy Kaptur (D-OH) detailing and "honoring the historical contributions of Catho-lic Sisters in the United States."[47] Motivated by the possible implications of the Vatican investigation, people worldwide rose up to express gratitude and admiration for individual Sisters and for whole communities that built and maintained the Catholic Church with their personal influence and through service in education, health care, and social services.

Exacerbating the tensions already rampant in the communities, in June of 2009 Cardinal William J. Levada, head of the Vatican's Department of the

Doctrine of the Faith, notified the executive council of the LCWR that he was beginning an investigation of the organization itself. He believed its leaders to be negligent for failing to require their communities' members to promote the church's teachings on three specific issues: the male-only priesthood, homosexuality, and the primacy of the Roman Catholic Church as the means to salvation. This second investigation was especially startling in view of the fact that each year the LCWR executive council members had gone to Rome for their voluntary accountability meetings with the appropriate Vatican representatives, and no such short-comings had been mentioned to them at those times. Levada reported that they had been warned of their failures eight years earlier but that they had neglected to reform their ways.

Curiously, there was little public discussion of this investigation of LCWR by Levada and his delegate Bishop Leonard P. Blair until April 18, 2012. In the official communication to the U.S. bishops, who were informed before the LCWR leadership group was, investigators noted that they had found "serious doctrinal problems" with the organization, especially in its choice of collaborations, speakers, and topics at their annual conferences. As a result of their study, Bishops Levada, Blair, Peter Sartain, and Thomas J. Paprocki developed a five-year process by which they would oversee the reform of the organization.

SUMMARY

In the process of their own consciousness-raising, Sisters were always seen as women experiencing the same social and ecclesiastical changes as other Catholic lay women. They were "advantaged' and "disadvantaged" to the same degree as other lay women of the time but in different areas of life. In the earliest years of the movement they were advantaged in resources and institutions: meeting spaces, copy machines, libraries, and "captive audiences" to hear their message. They had functional structures, events, and contacts in their own communities (local, national, international), in diocesan Sisters' councils, and in national groupings such as LCWR, NCAN, NAWR, Brothers and Sisters in Christ, and *Las Hermanas*. But they were "freedom disadvantaged," particularly when compared to other single adult lay women: they were not allowed to drive or to attend meetings or events of their own choosing, and they were controlled by rigid schedules not of their own making. But with education and experience, women religious became stronger and more self-confident as individuals with varying personalities and abilities just as McGillicuddy, Barnes, Lynch, and Swidler had become.

Even so, the contrast with their past behavior was unsettling to many Catholics and led to frequent tensions with other Catholic women, clergy, and hierarchy, and even within and among themselves. In any case, the matter has become a moot point because a decline in the number of Sisters has meant that there are dramatically fewer of them to engage in social or church reform movements. The era of their strongly active leadership-service in those public arenas was approximately fifty years. The reasons for Sisters' progressively less-visible involvement in the movement include the acutely increasing median age of Sisters, John Paul II's 1995 ban on discussion of the topic, and individuals' decisions not to subject their vulnerable communities to disciplinary action by local bishops or by the Vatican.

Beginning in the 1970s, Sisters emerged among the leaders of the women's ordination movement because by then they had the necessary experience, education, institutional resources, newfound personal strengths, and successes in renewing their own communities. For others to have expected them to stifle those qualities ignores the applicable question attributed to an early American slave woman, Sojourner Truth, in similar circumstances: "Ain't I a woman?"[48]

Because the participation of women religious in the ordination movement has been so varied in style, visibility, energy, and content, the most accurate comparable design is that of a mosaic whose separate pieces are created of similar materials and whose beauty lies in the variety of their relationships, colors, shapes, sizes, and positioning.

NOTES

1. Anne Marie Pelzer, "St. Joan's International Alliance: A Short History, 1911–1977," *Journal of St. Joan's International Alliance 1992* (Brussels, 1977): 1–16, www.womenpriests.org.

2. Judy Klemesrud, "Feminist Organization Is Fighting 'Oppression' in the Catholic Church," *New York Times* (Dec. 1, 1973): 28.

3. Rosemary Lauer, "Women and the Church," *Commonweal Magazine* 79, no. 13 (Dec. 20, 1963): 365–68.

4. The terms "vowed woman religious," "Sister," and "nun" are used interchangeably among Catholics, though the term "nun" is most appropriately used for contemplative, cloistered women; nor is the term "lay woman" the best to use for their counterparts. Contemporary ecclesiology considers the church to be composed of clergy and laity, and Sisters are not clergy. In the Roman Catholic Church all women are "lay women."

5. Anne Marie Gardiner, *Women and Catholic Priesthood: Proceedings of the Detroit Ordination Conference* (New York: Paulist Press, 1976), 207–37.

6. Laurie Wright Garry, *The Women's Ordination Conference (1975–1994): An Introduction to a Movement*, unpublished doctoral dissertation (Milwaukee, WI: Marquette University, 2000), appendix B.

7. Marie Augusta Neal, *From Nuns to Sisters* (Mystic, CT: Twenty-Third Publications, 1990), 28–29.

8. *Proceedings from the First General Congress of the States of Perfection* (Rome, 1950), www.vatican.va.

9. Timothy Walsh, *Parish School* (New York: Crossroad Publishing, 1996), 136.

10. The members of the Conference of Major Superiors (founded in 1956 at the request of the Vatican) voted to change the organization's name to Leadership Conference of Women Religious in 1971 and still uses that name.

11. Léon Joseph Suenens, *The Nun in the World* (Westminster, MD: Newman Press, 1962), throughout.

12. *The Documents of Vatican II*, ed. Walter M. Abbott (New York: America Press, 1966), 466–82.

13. Marie Augusta Neal, *A Report on the National Profile of the Third Sisters' Survey* (Boston: Emmanuel College, 1991), 35, Archives of the Sisters of Mercy, Belmont, NC.

14. Ibid.

15. UNDA CMBL Carton 1, throughout.

16. *Proceedings of the Second Conference on Women's Ordination: New Women, New Church, New Priestly Ministry*, ed. Maureen Dwyer (Rochester, NY: Women's Ordination Conference, 1978), 7ff.

17. Ibid.

18. *New Women, New Church*, Women's Ordination Conference Newsletter 1 (2011).

19. Mary Daly, *The Church and the Second Sex* (Boston: Beacon Press, 1986), 136, note 1.

20. Press release (Washington, DC: Center for Concern, 1975), 1.

21. Francis B. O'Connor, *Like Bread Their Voices Rise* (Notre Dame, IN: Ave Maria Press, 1993), 160.

22. Theresa Kane, "Welcome to Pope John Paul II" (Silver Spring, MD: Sisters of Mercy, 1979), 1.

23. Sisters of Mercy Archives (Silver Spring, MD, October 7, 1979), videotape.

24. Electronic correspondence between Theresa Kane and Barbara Wheeley (April 15, 2005).

25. Letter from Bernice McNeela to Rosemary (April 8, 1980), Smith College Archives, Carton 2, Folder 13.

26. For a thorough presentation of this matter, see Richard A. McCormack, *A Critical Calling* (Washington, DC: Georgetown University Press, 2006), 271–84.

27. *Now Is the Time: Proceedings of the First International Conference of WOW*, ed. Eamonn McCarthy (Dublin: Brothers and Sisters in Christ, 2002), 87.

28. Ibid.

29. Ibid., 29.

30. "Chapter" is the term used to denote the highest decision-making gathering in a province, a monastery, or national Catholic religious community.

31. Electronic correspondence between the author and Avis Clendenen (March 14, 2007).

32. Anne Marie Gardiner, *op. cit.*, 238–42.

33. Rita Hannon, "La Trahaison des Religieuses," in *The Catholic Citizen: Journal of the St. Joan's Alliance* 54, no. 12 (London, March–April 1971): 1, UNDA CMBL Carton 3, Folder 12.

34. Frances L. McGillicuddy, "Fall-Out from the NCCB Meeting," private paper (1975), Smith College Archives (hereafter SCA), Carton 8, Folder unnumbered.

35. Sandra M. Schneiders, *Finding the Treasure* (Mahwah, NJ: Paulist Press, 2000), 215–69.

36. Letter from Frances L. McGillicuddy to Carol Coston (June 14, 1973), SCA Carton 8, Folder 9.

37. Letter from Rosalie Muschal-Reinhardt to Frances L. McGillicuddy (May 16, 1976), SCA Carton 8, Folder 4.

38. Twila Dubay, untitled newsletter resembling that of St. Joan's U.S. Branch (Sept. 1976): 20–21, SCA Carton 13, Folder unnumbered.

39. Kenneth Briggs, *Double Crossed* (New York: Doubleday Publishers, 2006), 141.

40. Conversations between author and Margaret Gannon, IHM (1990–1996).

41. Carmel McEnroy, *Guests in Their Own House: The Women of Vatican II* (New York: Crossroad Publishing, 1996), throughout.

42. "Community Supports Ousted St. Louis Nun," *National Catholic Reporter* (July 2, 2008), www.ncronline.org/print/1330.

43. Thomas C. Fox, "Mercy Sister Theresa Kane Criticizes the Church Hierarchy," *National Catholic Reporter* (Sept. 29, 2009), http://ncronline.org/news/mercy-sister-theresa-kane-criticizes-church-hierarchy.

44. Franc Rodé at Stonehill College, North Easton, Massachusetts (Sept. 27, 2008).

45. Author's personal files.

46. Laurie Goodstein, "U.S. Nuns Facing Vatican Scrutiny," *New York Times* (July 1, 2009), A1.

47. Congressional Record (House), Resolution 441 (Sept. 22, 2009), initiated by Rep. Marcy Kaptur (D-OH).

48. Extemporaneous intervention at the Women's Convention, Akron, Ohio, 1851, commonly (but erroneously, some scholars say) attributed to Sojourner Truth.

Chapter Four

Circles

The Movement Organizes

The 1970s are commonly remembered as a decade of social upheaval, of church renewal, of spiritual exploration, of educational curriculum reforms, and of ubiquitous agitation in all those arenas. Vatican Council II, the national Civil Rights Act of 1964, the Vietnam War, the UN's "International Year of Women" (1975), women's increasing education and professionalization, and myriad other, lesser ingredients made for a zesty and unfamiliar stew. Given the tenor of those times, one would not have predicted that this period would see solid stabilization in at least one volatile area: the women's ordination movement in the U.S. Roman Catholic Church. Yet this was precisely the case, and it is the next development to be examined in these pages.

DESIGNING AND REDESIGNING A HOME FOR THE ISSUE

At the conclusion of the 1975 Detroit gathering on women's ordination, the participants' mandate to the conference's planning task force was clear: establish an organization to keep this topic alive and moving forward.[1] Into the gap leaped Bill Callahan, Maureen Fiedler, SL, and Dolly Pomerleau, who immediately opened the doors of the Quixote Center (QC) as an organizational hub for this issue. Very soon the movement had, in addition to a goal, a name (Women's Ordination Conference), a recognizable national structure, membership fees, budgets, a publication, and an advisory committee. It was the first time that the U.S. movement had a centralized home; its predecessor, the St. Joan's International Alliance, had operated on the considerable generosity and flexibility of its officers and members who used a spare room in one home, a dining room table in another, and their own wallets to absorb many of the costs.

National Directors

With the members announcing in Detroit their desire to have a home, with the "architects" of it in place at QC, and with the project manager (Ruth McDonough Fitzpatrick) hired, the foundation of this new, metaphorical home was laid, and construction began.[2] Fitzpatrick, working out of QC in 1976, quickly became the very effective public face of the organization and thereby of almost the entire U.S. movement. Her personality and leadership skills are reminiscent of SJIA's Frances Lee McGillicuddy, her predecessor: both were well educated, extroverted, ubiquitous, bold, and creative. Fitzpatrick's uniqueness lay in her skills in political analysis and her ability to design activities flowing from them. All too soon it became clear that the QC physical space was not large enough to contain the growing number of its projects and staff members, as well as all the creative energy bubbling within its walls. The commuting and salary arrangements were also not desirable for Fitzpatrick; perhaps, too, the QC work-collective model was constraining. Thus she moved the WOC office to her own home in Virginia (unwittingly reconstructing the model of the St. Joan's Alliance members mentioned above) while serving as an employee of WOC, rather than simply as a member of the organization. During this time, she announced that eighteen months after the Detroit gathering WOC's membership had already reached "1,300 men and women, clergy, religious and lay."[3]

All too soon, the organization outgrew the Fitzpatrick home and the one-person model for staffing, and in 1977 two women who had been active in the organization since the Detroit conference agreed to form a leadership team, and they relocated the office to Rochester, New York, where they resided. Rosalie Muschal-Reinhardt had completed her master of divinity in Chicago, was an internationally recognized leader in St. Joan's, and had recently settled her family in Rochester. She was a natural bridge between the earlier movement embodied in SJIA and its emerging incarnation as WOC. Ada Maria Isasi-Diaz brought deep commitment and a passion for theology.[4] She subsequently earned a doctorate in theology from Union Theological Seminary in New York and taught at Drew University graduate school of theology. Her unflinching convictions about society's need to embrace diversity helped the young WOC to grapple with its limitations in this area (see chapter 7). Her work during those years focused on the development and organization of local WOC groups across country, many of which are still active today. Joan Sobala, SSJ, came onto the staff after the other two and brought with her broad pastoral skills, realistic practicality, experience in the local church of Rochester, and links to the St. Joan's organization. Each woman's strengths and personalities differed from the others', and still they all shared a "dog-with-a-bone" commitment to work for reform of the Roman Catholic Church from within. In 1982, after five years of leading the very high-profile, high-pressure organization, each of the staff members in Rochester decided to pursue other ways to serve the movement.

M. Fidelis McDonough, RSM, of Pittsburgh and Marsie Silvestro of Long Island then stepped up as interim staff members and relocated the WOC offices to Greenwich Village in New York City for the years 1982 and 1983. The office rent in New York was unexpectedly steep for WOC, as was the cost of running a small business there. The commute to the rented office was long, the job expectations unclear, and it was difficult for them to cover the nation as a team of only two. The "home" of the movement was buffeted by these factors, and it was in such financial distress that it could not pay the staff salaries.[5] After both resigned, Maureen Fiedler, Laura Hochstein, and Arlene Anderson Swidler, members of the Core Team (an advisory board), sent an emergency letter to constituents: "If we do not get aid/assistance (Help!) in this matter, we are not averse to suggesting that we close down the office and organization permanently."[6]

After this clear and cogent call, the Core Team moved WOC back to Washington, DC, in January 1983, and Duffi McDermott was retained as yet another interim national director. Though her time of leadership in the organization was brief, she and the Core Team developed a new and well-received event: the Annual Banquet and Awards to Prophetic Figures, first held in October 1984. She and the advisory group created a varied roster of honorees for the evening: Theresa Kane, RSM, as an "activist"; the Catholic Community of Appalachia as "an egalitarian community"; and Elizabeth Schüssler Fiorenza as an "intellectual."[7] Each represented an important aspect of the U.S. women's ordination movement, as conceived by its founders and leaders. Over the years that followed, the term "annual" was set aside, but the awards were given at least seven more times between 1984 and 2000.[8]

Following McDermott's brief stint, Ruth McDonough Fitzpatrick once again took up the reins of the organization, renting an office and equipment in Fairfax, Virginia (a shorter daily commute for her than QC had been). From 1984 to 1995 her leadership moved the organization into a period of stability and growth, despite and because of her extroverted, flamboyant style. She welcomed and stirred controversy, kept the organization in the public eye by her skills in public relations, and relentlessly kept the Catholic hierarchy's attention on the issue. Fitzpatrick expanded the membership, deepened and broadened friendships with clergy and bishops, and established relationships with other organizations promoting reform of the Roman Catholic Church.[9] On the other hand, and not unrelated to the prominence of the issue in the United States and around the globe, in May of 1994 Pope John Paul II published his "apostolic letter" to the world's Catholic bishops. It was called *Ordinatio Sacerdotalis,* and it reiterated the Roman Catholic Church's ban on the ordination of women. Many who supported women's ordination were profoundly disheartened by the pope's letter, but Fitzpatrick's assessment of the letter's appearance put a wry spin on it: "Well, at least they are paying attention to us!"[10]

After benefiting from Fitzpatrick's creative energy for ten years, WOC observed its twentieth anniversary in 1995 with the convening of its conference in Crystal City in Arlington, Virginia. The turnout was not as large as hoped for, so the rented meeting spaces were conspicuously underutilized. Many participants were disgruntled by the schedule or the speakers, or they brought their discontent with them about what was happening in the broader Catholic Church. In any case, and for whatever reasons, shortly after the conference, Ruth McDonough Fitzpatrick resigned from her position with WOC. Immediately thereafter, board member Andrea Magazzu Johnson offered to serve as interim director, with Maureen Fiedler as partner. The two of them led the organization for a year, after which Johnson was hired by the board of directors as the full-time national executive director of the organization.[11]

Though newer to the organization than some, Johnson worked beside WOC's cofounder Maureen Fiedler in a complementary team during the year 1996. They extinguished several "house fires," solidified the legal and operational structures, activated a new board of directors (elected by the WOC membership), cultivated significant donors, and slowed the organization's downward financial spiral. The following year Fiedler moved on, as had been the original plan. During Johnson's subsequent years of service, she completed the stabilization of WOC's finances and intensified WOC's presence on the international scene. At a caucus during the 1996 First European Women's Synod (Gmunden, Austria), it was she who formally proposed that a global organization be created and saw the proposal through to acceptance by the international leaders present. Women's Ordination Worldwide (WOW) was born, and Johnson served as its international chair for one term and then as the U.S. representative to the WOW planning council until 2009.

Johnson being an astute political analyst and strategist, another of her priorities was to strengthen existing WOC relationships with numerous other Catholic Church reform movements, particularly the Women's Alliance in Theology, Ethics and Ritual; Call to Action; Dignity; CORPUS; and Future-Church. She saw, too, that it was necessary for the future of the organization to search out and strengthen the next generation of members and leaders. After Johnson's very amicable resignation in 2000, the board hired Deborah Halter of Arkansas, who served for less than one year.

Upon Halter's resignation, WOC board member Genevieve Chavez expressed her willingness, and the board of directors hired her to take up the work of national leadership in late 2000. As the first southwesterner in that position and a very long-distance commuter between her home in New Mexico and the WOC office in Virginia, Chavez brought a richly different tone and style of energy to recognizing or reactivating the many local WOC groups scattered around the country. From her prior service on the board she knew all too well the several dangers to which the organization was prone and knew that intensifying the nationwide members' connectedness and support was crucial to WOC's viability and effectiveness. In that spirit Chavez approached the planning of the twenty-fifth anniversary year conference. For the first time it was held in conjunction with another group's gathering: the 2000 Call to Action conference in Milwaukee. There were economic benefits to this approach, as well as the value of visibly situating women's ordination in the broader context of church reform. The pre-conference day for WOC members was marked by a multicultural panel, an ecumenical panel, a large-scale prayer event, and small group discussions. The evening anniversary reception and a return of the popular awards ceremony rounded out the full day. Genevieve Chavez retired from her position in 2003.

During the period of Chavez's leadership Evelyn Hunt served as the board president (2002–2006) and as a resource person (occasionally full-time) during the periods of Chavez's agreed-upon times at her New Mexico base. Hunt's involvement in other national organizations as well drew her to Washington and to the WOC national office on a regular basis. It can be fairly said that since her election to the board in 1998, Hunt has continued to serve the organization as ballast in stormy times and an unostentatious hand in fair weather.

Today's Directors

The next WOC election saw the realization of many members' hopes and Andrea Johnson's efforts to develop a younger generation of leaders. As board president and elsewhere she raised the subject often, clearly, and publicly. She strongly supported WOC's Young Feminist Network (YFN), and mentored younger women in the organization, thereby tilling the soil for the election of one of them, Joy Barnes, in 2004. Barnes had been on the national office staff as program director after proving her skills as a leader in YFN, and WOC's membership began to increase from that time. She served as national executive director until 2005 when she and her family moved out of the country. Aisha Taylor, YFN coordinator, lobbyist, and consultant for diversity issues, succeeded her. Upon Taylor's decision to pursue full-time graduate study, Erin Saiz Hanna took up the national leadership in January 2010.[12] Though the noticeable difference between this WOC leadership generation and the membership as a body seems to be its youthfulness, it must be recalled that they are today the general age that the founders and members of WOC were in 1975.

The activities of YFN can be captured only sketchily here, but WOC's thrice-yearly newspaper (*New Women, New Church*) has consistently reported their creative energy. With the leadership of Kerry Danner-McDonald (founding coordinator, 1996–1999), Stephanie Barnes, Joy Barnes, Laura Singer, and Aisha Smith Taylor the members threw themselves into their work. Among many other projects, they were panelists at a Chicago "Youth Ministry Day"; they planned and implemented retreats and leadership training workshops for members new to the movement; and they visited college campuses as resource persons for religious studies classes, for campus ministers, and for career fairs. They organized and led a "Leadership Tour" to Cuernavaca for the express purpose of meeting young Catholic women leaders in Mexico. At least two members of YFN were elected by the national WOC membership to its board of directors: Carmen Lane and Anne Pezzillo. By 2005, global economic realities had tightened many purse strings, and WOC's next generation took to the Internet to strengthen their existing international relationships and maintain their broad perspective.

While it is true that their individual leadership stints have been rather brief, such brevity seems to be the price to be paid for leadership at their quite normal stages of life. "Working for a good cause" does not pay off one's student loans; nor does frequent weekend work and extensive travel to national and international meetings lend stability to one's new marriage or committed relationship—not to mention new parenthood. In addition, being the public face and voice for Roman Catholic Church reform produces its own sort of wear and tear on the psyche: fewer and fewer Catholic women—most especially the younger—are willing to commit themselves to reforming an organization that discriminates against them and bars them from having any official voice that could lead to changes.[13] The research of William V. D'Antonio (Catholic University of America) indicates that the percentage of those who involve themselves in church reform has dropped annually and is likely to continue that trajectory.

Yet one very dramatic crisis within the organization stands as symbol for the movement's future. During the night of February 15, 2008, a devastating fire completely destroyed the rented WOC office in Virginia: computers melted, walls collapsed, and over one thousand books burned. The twenty-year physical home of the movement was no more. In an earlier day, such a catastrophe would have brought the movement to a halt, or at least slowed it profoundly. (There were those who wondered if the fire had been deliberately set by opponents to women's ordination, but investigators found that it began in a neighboring business sharing the same building.) With remarkable foresight these technologically sophisticated younger leaders had much earlier stored the organization's crucial databases and documents on laptop computers and in other safe cyberspaces. In addition, only five months earlier they had sent their paper files and materials to Marquette University's

Archives, home of all WOC's historical materials. Though the staff was functioning in makeshift arrangements and with reduced material resources, their plans to visibly welcome Pope Benedict XVI on his April 14, 2008, visit to Washington, DC, went as planned before the fire. Within five months, they had moved into a new rented site within the city of Washington, DC.[14]

At play in this phoenix-like drama were the earlier WOC leaders' foresight in relocating the archives to Marquette and always keeping appropriate property insurance; a younger staff's skills in cyber-storing, their physical energy, and their public relations skills in immediately getting the news out to constituents; and finally, the financial generosity of the organization's members and friends. Cross-generational wisdom and knowledge kept the movement alive.

National Activities

After creating a literal and metaphorical home for itself in 1975, and despite its frequent change of address, WOC became a stable, visible national phenomenon. Whereas the St. Joan's Alliance's style has consistently projected an image of dignified, intelligent, and (usually) serious restraint, its younger sister has displayed extroversion, media-use, and (often) fun as its *modus operandi*. The pre-WOC Detroit gathering splashed into national and international headlines in both church and secular society, as has each successive large-scale conference. Smaller events and projects have garnered local media attention and keep the issue alive in many parts of the country.

Large Gatherings

The themes and dynamics of the respective WOC conferences reflect the interplay of two factors: the developmental stage at which the organization and its members find themselves,[15] and the social and ecclesial realities in which the movement is situated. The clearest example of this can be seen in the Detroit gathering: the pioneering feeling of being part of a "first-ever" type of event with its place in history understood by all, in combination with the social and ecclesial developments of the 1970s, when anything seemed possible. Close analysis of subsequent WOC conferences reveals the same double dynamic, though the temptation has been to explain the different tenor of each solely in terms of matters internal to the organization.

The three most numerously attended WOC conferences, following Detroit, were held in Baltimore, Maryland; St. Louis, Missouri; and Arlington/ Crystal City, Virginia.

Baltimore

The Baltimore WOC conference was titled "New Women, New Church, New Priestly Ministry," and its published proceedings were edited by Maureen Dwyer.[16] While Mary Luke Tobin, SL, was serving on the planning committee for the November 1978 event, she received a letter in June from the intrepid St. Joan's Alliance spokesperson, Frances McGillicuddy, who offered some advice. Frances noted that "the first ordination conference [Detroit] was remarkably successful as a raiser of consciousness and propagator of the idea of women's ordination. It was admirably organized and received fabulous news coverage. Best of all, it terrified the bishops."[17] There followed her advice to not weaken the issue by falling into the semantic trap of substituting the word "ministry" for "ordination." McGillicuddy felt that the overall energy generated in Detroit had been dissipated by adopting the "ministries" mentality, when speakers used that term instead of "ordination" or when they advocated ordination to specific ministries, rather than ordination to the full priesthood. She saw evidence of this trend in speakers and writers then in the forefront of the movement and urged against it. Her letter surfaced several related neuralgic issues in the movement (see chapter 7): Would ordination to specific ministries (e.g., evangelist, catechist, reconciler, ritual presider) better serve the faith community than ordination of one person to the whole "package" of varying ministries, as is the practice today? Is there scriptural and/or theological justification for either type of ordination? If special training and education are required for either type, then the issue of "classism" arises when some have the financial resources to pay for preparation for ordination and others have not.

While it cannot be proven that McGillicuddy's letter of advice influenced the planning committee, her insights were timely and to the point; the Baltimore conference's opening address by social analyst Sheila Collins was titled "Chains That Bind: Racism, Classism and Sexism." She noted that institutional religion functions as "supporter and legitimator of sexual, racial and class oppression"[18] and asked her hearers to consider how women in particular can reclaim Christianity and delegitimate those oppressions. Collins then explored the entwined roles of capitalism and patriarchy in oppression and warned that they could be expected to affect any change-agent's work.

Immediately prior to Collins's address, many of the two thousand participants had massed at Baltimore's Inner Harbor and processed along some blocks to the civic center conference site dragging or wearing oversized paper chains and singing hymns and songs.[19] It was one of those typically U.S.-style WOC actions mentioned above: public, slightly rambunctious, and energetically confrontative. Dolly Pomerleau, Core Commission member and coordinator of the conference, designed and led the event just as she and Bill Callahan had led and organized the nascent movement since 1975. As the conference got under way, the nation's Roman Catholic bishops were a mere thirty-five miles away attending their annual fall meeting, and this drew several WOC women to the designated hotel in Washington, DC, to engage some bishops in informal dialogue. Pomerleau coordinated that excursion and thereby became the liaison between WOC and the bishops for a time[20] until Ruth McDonough Fitzpatrick shared that role with her while national director.

A common argument of ordination opponents has been the dismissive rebuttal that it is a preoccupation of only the educated, angry "women's libbers" of the United States and therefore not representative of "the Church Universal." Thus the program included a plenary session "More than One Continent?" which was designed to open the eyes of the global church, as well as of the participants themselves. The panel included five women from Belgium, India, Mexico, Paraguay, and Uganda, each of whom presented a paper on the state of the question in her respective country. Each speaker covered similar issues: her culture's presuppositions about religion in general, how the churches have shaped those presuppositions, the function of Catholic priests, and an assessment of the clergy's success or failure in that culture. They discussed the types of women seeking ordination as well as those who were unable to pursue it. The women described their own experiences of baptizing, marrying, anointing, absolving, and presiding at liturgical rituals of all sorts.[21] They were, in a sense, living the goal of the ordination movement and did so, presumably, "without benefit of the sacrament." One of the panelists concluded her remarks by expressing solidarity with U.S. women "in *your* remarkable endeavor for a great cause [emphasis mine]." That single word may have revealed the speaker's acknowledgement of U.S. leadership of the movement; or it may have implied that Americans need to "get things legal" by changing church law, whereas women elsewhere were actually functioning as priests.

St. Louis

"Ordination Reconsidered" was advertised as being designed for women feeling themselves called to ordination. In hindsight, however, the very title of the 1985 conference may have contained a double entendre as an intentional tactic to sow doubts about the necessity of the church having an ordained priesthood at all. Or perhaps, of course, it meant to simply indicate that the women who attended would have the opportunity to reconsider (once again) their calls, this time in the focused company of other women who experienced the same questions. There was one keynote speaker (Mary Jo Weaver), several facilitated group discussion sessions, a drama about one of the first Episcopalian women ordained (Jeannette Picard), a liturgy (with

Theresa Kane, RSM, as homilist), and an exercise in each participant's personal next steps.

The multiplicity of topics and exercises unrelated to women's ordination proved frustrating for many of the approximately 250 participants (about only half of whom felt called to ordination, despite the pre-conference advertising), and there was no post-conference survey planned as to their next steps. Because of this, a fiercely determined group of about sixty participants chose "Ordination Now" as their next pursuit and made a commitment to gather in Rochester, New York, six months later to develop their own strategies to advance the issue. About forty of those sixty women were able to attend the Rochester meeting.[22] Thus was born a satellite project of WOC, which continues to current times and is known as Renewed and Priestly People: Ordination Reconsidered Today (RAPPORT; see chapter 5).

Arlington/Crystal City

"Discipleship of Equals: Breaking Bread, Doing Justice" was a gathering fraught with predictable tension over the theme. Even before this 1995 conference, theologian Elizabeth Schüssler Fiorenza's call to reform the church into a "discipleship of equals" had lodged in the consciousness and common parlance of many WOC members. For some, the phrase signified a church of attitudinal and functional equality, which they maintained could be achieved even in the existing church if women enjoyed full equality. For others the phrase meant a radically structure-free church without any potentially oppressive components such as priesthood, hierarchy, and papacy. Despite the differences of opinion about the conflicting theologies, the conference attracted almost one thousand registrants[23] to celebrate the twentieth anniversary of WOC's founding and functioning as the home of the issue of women's ordination. Two bishops, Charles Buswell and P. Francis Murphy, participated in portions of the weekend with no special recognition or function. Speakers Schüssler Fiorenza and theologian Diana Hayes made explicit their belief that ordination was not a desirable goal for the good of the church ("ordination is subordination"), and the small group discussions and open microphone times revealed a profound division among the participants on this subject.

The split was so evident that journalist Dorothy Vidulich sought out conference participants who expressed their outrage at the two speakers' "relentless destruction of ordination." Maureen Fiedler and Jeannine Gramick, WOC board members at the time, said that the board had explicitly charged the conference planners to incorporate both visions: "discipleship of equals" and "ordination to a renewed priestly ministry" throughout the program. Gramick was particularly upset that the style of prayer and worship throughout the conference was "non-denominational or New-Age spirituality" and not a "Catholic, Eucharistic style of worship." Ida Raming called it a "treachery" to women called to ordination.

YFN was coming to maturity at the same time as that incendiary conference, and thirty of its members shared their ideas, frustrations, and hopes about WOC and about the Roman Catholic Church. Some of their private exchanges took place in the halls and over meals, but the members went public by presenting a panel called "How the Roots Grew Wings," with Kerry Danner-McDonald as its chair. Later they held an open caucus that was billed as an intergenerational dialogue. Their initial presentation allowed them to vent their feelings of anger and of "tokenism," and they later agreed that their primary goal in the near future would be to increase strong visible leadership by young women and women of color.[24]

As the passage of time would show, the Arlington/Crystal City gathering was the last WOC conference of its type.

Milwaukee

The 2000 Milwaukee conference proved to offer a viable new model for the future work of the organization and of its members, situating both in a larger context than usual. The financial crisis following the 1995 gathering led those responsible for the organization to be fiscally prudent; and the anger and disappointment of many 1995 participants led the planners for 2000, chaired by Marian Ronan, to create a more irenic and celebratory atmosphere. To keep down the costs, it was a one-day event; and to increase the number of registrants, the gathering was "attached" to the Call to Action (CTA) national conference, which opened the next day. This strategy had a third benefit, which was an increase in the CTA registration because many WOC members stayed on; and yet a fourth benefit was the opportunity to attend the very rich CTA program—with no drain on the WOC coffers.

To say that the event was "irenic and celebratory" by no means implies that it avoided difficult issues or differing opinions. The three plenary speakers, for example, addressed profoundly hard realities related to the theme: the conflicts inherent in feminist theologies vis-à-vis the Roman Catholic Church (theologian Sheila Briggs), the race and class issues that will continue to plague the church (ethicist Barbara Hilkert Andolson), and the real-life challenges faced by an ordained Episcopalian priest (sociologist Paula D. Nesbitt). Smaller, special-interest groups considered topics of discrimination based on race, class, gender-orientation, ecclesial status (lay vs. ordained), and marital status. Other interest groups discussed the issue of ordination as it related to vowed religious communities, to small Catholic communities, to Catholic feminist groups, and to younger women.

The day began with Sophia-based prayer and ended with an active and broadly participative prayer ritual of bread and wine based on the Catholic

Eucharistic liturgy, thus making visible the organization's roots. The evening hours were filled with celebration of the twenty-fifth anniversary year: a large reception (including some women and men from the CTA conference) with refreshments and a ceremony of honoring the new recipients of the occasional WOC awards.

Viable though Milwaukee's 2000 model may have been, by the year 2005 developments in the culture, the movement, and the organization called for something still more different from the past. WOC's role in the founding and leadership of WOW suggested not merely lectures and activities on internationalism at a U.S. location, but actual cosponsorship with WOW of a conference in Ottawa, Canada. This thirtieth anniversary of WOC and the tenth of YFN included presentations by Elizabeth Schüssler Fiorenza and Rosemary Radford Ruether, which led to similarly divided responses in Ottawa as at the Arlington/Crystal City gathering in 1995.[25]

On the last evening of the Ottawa meetings, WOC held a reception at which it made its occasional awards, this time to concepts and organizations as well as to individuals. YFN's award was accepted by Stephanie Barnes in the name of the organization; the "ministers who walk with women called" award was accepted by Rene Smith Buchanan for RAPPORT; the "ministers of prophetic obedience" award went to Judith Heffernan; and the "ministers of irritation" award went to Chicago WOC for starting a billboard campaign that spread across the country and for its "Pink Smoke Over the Vatican" demonstration during the conclave prior to election of John Paul's successor. Though the Ottawa event was attended by only about four hundred women and men, both U.S. and Canadian, holding it in Ottawa did provide the opportunity to join the celebratory atmosphere surrounding the first Roman Catholic Women Priests (RCWP) ordinations in North America, which took place aboard a ship on the St. Lawrence River the day after the conference closed.

An altogether different model for a WOC gathering emerged in Boston in 2008. It was a weekend sponsored and planned by no sole entity, such as Call to Action or WOC, but rather by a coalition of reform groups: CORPUS, Federation of Christian Ministries, RCWP, and WOC. Whereas it had become increasingly difficult to convene 1,200 or so Catholic women on the subject of ordination, as in 1975 (Detroit), a more modest goal succeeded. About three hundred women and men assembled to consider "Inclusive Ministry and Renewal in a Complex Age."[26] The keynote speaker was a man, Matthew Fox, and twenty-six small group workshops considered a variety of subjects related to ministry, with both female and male presenters. After the close of the conference and separate from it, RCWP held an ordination liturgy of four women.

Chicago

In 2010, WOC held a small gathering one evening in Chicago where fewer than two hundred persons gathered to observe WOC's thirty-fifth anniversary and to celebrate the women and men who had spent energy and resources on "Making it Happen in Our Lifetime."[27] The evening featured the premier of a documentary film by Jules Hart called *Pink Smoke Over the Vatican*, which situates the movement in church history and examines the reaction of the Vatican to it.

The change in scale of the gatherings has been due to fiscal realities of the organization and of the global economy, as well as WOC's necessary return to a one-person staff for whom the planning of a large national event would be impossible. Other factors have led the organization to change its style[28] of public events: collaboration with other reform-minded groups at times has created productive synergy; participation in international events expands horizons and intellects; and contemporary technology makes it very possible to schedule live discussions, presentations, and films, and even to create a "virtual" support community of the like-minded. In addition, theologians, Scripture scholars, archaeologists, and historians have laid out all the necessary reasoning, and two popes have expressly reiterated the ban. On both sides of the question, everything that needs to be said has been said. Still, the morale and spiritual enrichment of Roman Catholic women seeking ordination remains in need of challenge and support, and meeting those needs has been an important purpose of WOC's conferences.

Special Projects

The oldest and most widely known project of WOC has been the regular publication of its newsletter, *New Women, New Church* (*NWNC*), which first appeared in December 1976 within twelve months of the organization's founding.[29] For more than thirty-five years, this small publication has served as an educational and motivational vehicle for the ordination issue, much as its predecessor, *The Journey*, had done under Jeanne Barnes's and Mary Lynch's editorship. The transition from one to the other was announced in *NWNC* in December 1976: *The Journey*, as published for so many years by Mary Lynch, was in danger of becoming defunct due to financial difficulties. In view of the fact that this publication had been a pioneer in providing wide communication among persons advocating the ordination of women, no one wanted to see this newsletter "die a pauper's death." Thus, WOC's Core Commission accepted Lynch's agreement to consolidate and to provide her mailing list to WOC. This gave the merged publication an even greater reach than either one had enjoyed while separate.

Today, the *NWNC* collection *in toto* serves as a history of the development and of the thinking and activities of proponents and opponents alike, though reflecting, of course, the organization's perspective, as do most professional journals. Consistent features of the newsletter have been reports on WOC-sponsored events such as public group witnesses, a calendar of coming relevant meetings around the nation, book reviews, theological articles, and brief biographies of women called to ordination. Action Alerts, such as writing to one's bishop on specific topics of praise or protest, appear regularly. Order forms are always included for educational and motivational merchandise, ranging from lapel buttons and bumper stickers to stationery and monographs. The choice of news coverage mirrors the same types of effective projects as those reported in the earlier St. Joan's Alliance newsletters. The educational function of *NWNC* is felt broadly in the U.S. Church, as the paper reaches each subscribed member, as well as certain specially targeted audiences. By 2010, Erin Saiz Hanna, national director, noted that the total quarterly distribution entered five thousand homes, offices, and libraries. [30]

Energy ran high during WOC's first year, and the second prong of its long-term commitments developed: the commissioning of professional-quality research projects, often in collaboration with QC staff members. The first to be published was Maureen Fiedler and Dolly Pomerleau's monograph based on their attitudinal survey: *Will the People Ever Be Ready?* (1976). [31] Shortly after that in 1978, psychologist Fran Ferder produced her landmark book *Called to Break Bread*, in which she studied one hundred Roman Catholic women who felt called to ordination to the priesthood. This research can be considered a companion piece to the earlier Fiedler-Pomerleau study: the first one studied the church members, and the second studied the members who desired to serve and were qualified. In 1977 WOC commissioned *Project Priesthood*, a survey of eighty-five Catholic women called to ordained ministry, which Kathleen Sharkey analyzed and published. Thirteen years later Maureen Fiedler and Karen Schwartz published their WOC-QC monograph *Benevolent Subversives: A National Study of Roman Catholic Women Called to Priesthood*. The next year, WOC published *Guidelines to Organizing a Witness [Event] in Your Diocese*, and one year later *A Directory of Catholic Women in Ecclesial Ministries*.

Based on her long study of the issue of women's ordination, Fiedler concluded that the church members and society at large were ready for women's ordination but that significant church teachings still stood in the way. Thus she and Linda Rabben published in 1998 a study of changes in specific Catholic Church teachings on many subjects over the centuries which could lead logically to the possibility of change in its teaching about women's ordination. [32] Because the mutability of church teachings relates to many Catholics' concerns about issues other than women's ordination, this study has received popular attention.

A strong thread of educational commitment is evident in the widely varying projects of WOC: the thirty-five-year-old newsletter; the national conferences; the research and publications; the lecture tours of Ludmila Javorova,
Ida Raming, and Iris Mueller; the Bishop Murphy Scholarship Fund, established by the board in 1999 with seed money from Bishop P. Francis Murphy's posthumous gift; the annual World Day of Prayer (since March 25,
1997); and the educational and motivational materials designed for individual and group usage, grounded in the Gospel and the documents of Vatican II.
Of course, the public witnessing events garner instantaneous awareness and
education of a different type and are usually held outside the building where
the nation's bishops are meeting (Washington, DC; South Bend, Indiana; and
Baltimore) or on the sidewalk near a church where ordinations or other major
church events are occurring. Often the participants and bystanders wear a
purple scarf or stole, which was adopted at the first WOW conference as the
international symbol of support for women's ordination, the symbolic peni-
tential color calling for the hierarchy's repentance over its discrimination
against women. WOC was visible and audible during ceremonies surrounding the Washington, DC, visit of Pope John Paul II, in conjunction with
synods and papal elections at the Vatican and at the Washington headquarters
of the National Conference of Catholic Bishops, including the occasional
"priestly pumpkin" prank there at Halloween.

BROADENING THE BASE OF OWNERSHIP

The early leaders of WOC chose an effective strategy for their purposes of
consciousness-raising and staying in touch with the real concerns of the
people in the pews: geographical dispersion. In one sense this was an easy
goal to accomplish, for the national gatherings drew women from all over the
United States, and when each returned to her local faith community (diocese,
parish, campus, hospital, religious community) WOC returned with her. Yet
some of the women were inexperienced in organizational development or
were limited by their full-time work in the home and/or outside it. They
wanted help.

While the geographical diversity of the earlier U.S. St. Joan's Alliance
was evident, dotting the continent from California to Florida, Minneapolis to
Alabama, and points in between, the alliance was hampered by not having a
full-time employee who could pursue the goal with deliberate intent and
accountability to a board. Conspicuous in that monumental task for WOC
was codirector Ada Maria Isasi-Diaz, whose specific role in the early administrative office was to strengthen already-existing regional groups and help
create new ones when requested. With her youthful physical energy, her
passion for the issue, and her almost full-time focus, in the late 1970s, she

traveled from Rochester, New York, through the length and breadth of the country listening, lecturing, assisting, and achieving significant results. In only six months, Isasi-Diaz visited local groups in Virginia, Louisiana, Alabama, Georgia, Florida, Maryland, Washington, DC, Pennsylvania, Oregon, Washington, Montana, and seven cities in California.[33] In most of those locations, the groups (or individuals) have remained active for over thirty years and by no means represent the full number of regional groups in existence today.

With similar deliberate intent, twenty years later WOC's national director Genevieve Chavez set herself the particular task of strengthening the movement in the southwestern states. It is usually easier to collect large audiences in the eastern and north central states where the distances between cities are shorter and the Catholic population is denser, but Chavez's prescient focus was developed amid the Hispanic culture where she herself lived. Soon YFN caught Chavez's spirit, and they planned some of their retreats and learning experiences in Mexico; and Theresa Trujillo was elected to the WOC board of directors, bringing her energy, fresh eyes, and experience from Cuernavaca, where she was working at the time.

Some local groups have come and gone, making significant contributions to the movement during their existence and then disappearing as an organization. Often the individual members have remained committed to the issue, raising the questions and working in their respective environments to advance the cause of church reform, including the ordination of women.

One such local group was the Baltimore Task Force on Women and Religion (BTFWR), which formed in 1973, well before the Detroit ordination conference or the formation of WOC. The animators of the group, Margaret Mohler and Thekla Rice, were practical, well-educated strategists, and enjoyed the support of Archbishop William D. Borders and Auxiliary Bishop P. Francis Murphy as well as that of nearby QC's staff members. Their first project, in 1973, was to establish and organize a nine-session course, "Women, Religion and the Church," required of all transitional diaconate candidates and held at St. Mary's Seminary and University. The course ran for several years, and received high acclaim from students and the seminary administrators.[34] The relatively open attitude of the Baltimore clergy and congregations can be attributed, in part, to the fact that the motherhouses of several Sisters were located in the archdiocese, and the motherhouses were powerhouses of post–Vatican II renewal. In addition, the presence of the Jesuit theologate, Woodstock College, had long stimulated Maryland parishes, religious communities, and Catholic educational institutions.

In May of 1975, Rice and Mohler initiated a local data-gathering project called "Visibility of Women in Parishes" similar to those conducted in several dioceses in the United States around the same time. Rice and former St. Joan's member Mohler coordinated teams of Catholic women who visited each parish in the Baltimore Archdiocese on the same weekend for a parish liturgy. The teams used the forms provided by the planners, noting gender-balanced language (or lack of it) in sermons, music, and prayers, as well as female participation in the liturgical ministries. They scrutinized parish bulletins for language and for committee leadership patterns. The visitors filled out the evaluation sheets that were then collated by the teams and sent to the pastors, the bishops, and the heads of archdiocesan committees with encouraging but honest cover letters. As a consistent group of volunteers gradually developed, they scheduled public witness activities, lectures, and discussion groups in parishes and on campuses; wrote articles and letters; published a handbook on discriminatory language in liturgy; and became the local media's "go to" source on issues related to women in the church.

As WOC was preparing for its 1978 gathering, the organizers decided, for the reasons noted above and others, that Baltimore would be the conference site, and they asked BTFWR to host the event. The local group responded whole heartedly and provided rooms, transportation, maps, registration teams, aspirins, phone numbers, and the myriad other forms of help necessary for a group of over 1,200 participants. After the crowd had dispersed and the local follow-up work had been accomplished, Rice and Mohler stepped out of their leadership roles and BTFWR soon disappeared.

By contrast, there are other local groups dating from the same time as Baltimore's and enjoying a longevity that has been either constant or sporadic. Many of the groups, like BTFWR, originated around general issues of women in society and church but quickly coalesced around the ordination issue. A Minneapolis group honors local predecessors by referring to itself as "St. Joan's" and is still very active with newsletters, lectures, discussion groups, prayer events, and communication with bishops and popes. One of its members, archaeologist Dorothy Irvin, stands as a marker of the group's span of years; she has labored for four decades in her scholarly work regarding women ordained in the early church.

Another local group of Chicago women has worked on issues of justice for women since before WOC existed. The energetic and creative leadership of Donna Quinn, OP, took them through the 1970s and beyond, addressing general issues of justice for women at first, then specifically working to end the church's ban against their ordination. This second phase has made the Chicago WOC a stop on the lecture circuit for international notables such as Ludmila Javorova, Ida Raming, and Iris Mueller. Some of its members have served on the national WOC board of directors (e.g., Deirdre O'Neill, Donna Quinn, Ginny Richardson, and Katy Scott Zatsick). The Chicago group has earned international recognition and emulation with its attention-grabbing billboard project and most recently has supported Zatsick in actualizing her call to ordination through RCWP.

The Cleveland WOC published and circulated its own impressive history,[35] which reveals the local group's strength from the earliest days of WOC. They, like the Chicago women, hosted Javorova in 1997; they have organized public lectures by nationally recognized theologians, educational workshops and retreats, letter-writing campaigns, and public witnesses with banners and signs. Three of their members have served on WOC's national board of directors: Evelyn Hunt, Dagmar Braun Celeste, and Mary Pilkington Hills Sylvania. At present their work is complemented and strengthened by that of Cleveland's FutureChurch movement, which came to being in 1990 with a broad agenda of church reform.

The San Francisco WOC emerged gradually after Ada Maria Isasi-Diaz's very early (1978) successes in seven California locales. After several low-key years of existence, the group came to national attention in 1995 with its regularly scheduled "Critical Mass," organized by liturgists Monica Kaufer, SC, and Victoria Rue. At first seeming to be a short-term endeavor, and despite Kaufer's later move out of state, the monthly events have continued, and Rue was ordained through RCWP in 2005. Simultaneous to the development of the San Francisco cadre of activists was the development of a more academically based group in Berkeley around the several graduate schools of theology located there. For several years in the early twenty-first century, theologian, author, and former WOC board member Marian Ronan organized small discussions and lectures that grounded the issue of ordination in serious study of Scripture and theology.

A different California group worked independently for years and then affiliated with WOC around 2007, organizing a celebration of "the newly formed group of WOC activists in Los Angeles," according to the WOC newsletter.[36] The same article referred to another group in Santa Barbara. These developments were no accident, for at the same time that they were emerging, California had come into its own on the WOC board with five members from the Golden State cities of Pismo Beach, San Luis Obispo, Watsonville, Richmond, and Temple City.

The Southeast Pennsylvania WOC (SEPA-WOC) flourishes against all odds in the Philadelphia area, where the Catholic Church does not enjoy a reputation as being reform-minded. Perhaps the archdiocese's very broad geographical range, and the extraordinarily large number of Catholics residing there and of Catholic theologians, religious orders, and colleges and universities make it impossible to rein in those who hold unorthodox beliefs. In any case, SEPA-WOC traces its roots to Leonard Swidler's decision to inaugurate in 1971 a lecture-and-discussion series called "Genesis II." A core group of area theologians—women and men—moved among several of the region's campuses lecturing on topics and aspirations flowing from Vatican II. After some years of that format, many of the same individuals became the nucleus for a new organization which they called the Philadelphia Task Force on Women in Religion (PTFWR), espousing women's ordination as a primary goal. In the 1990s PTFWR affiliated formally with WOC and changed its name to SEPA-WOC. The group's productive role is unusual in its unbroken chain of long life, as well as its origins in academia.

SEPA-WOC is unusual in several other respects as well. From its very earliest days, and under whichever name it used at the time, the little community has provided a home away from home for like-minded persons: Georgiana Putnam McEntee, the first U.S. member of the St. Joan's Alliance, came from New York to attend one of their meetings during the very early 1970s. Mary Lynch often did the same throughout her period of social work in Delaware before she succeeded Jeanne Barnes as head of the Deaconess Movement. In more recent years the group welcomed Marie Bouclin (WOW) and Patricia Fresen (RCWP). They have always formed a community of welcome, support, and collaboration with leaders in the movement, as well as for those who come to consult with them or to do public lectures for local Catholic colleges.

SEPA-WOC's annual, decades-long tradition of witnessing on Holy Thursday in front of the cathedral is public, and they thereby receive regional and national media coverage, raise awareness, and show fidelity to their cause. Their commitment to educate is clear through lectures and serious publications by such members as Regina Bannan, Gaile Pohlhaus, Marian Ronan, Virginia Kaib Ratigan, and Leonard and Arlene Anderson Swidler, as well as in the meaty content of their newsletter *EqualwRites*. Theirs is a far-reaching and serious contribution to the debate and is rooted in academic soil.

They embrace persons of varying and sometimes controversial theologies of ministry, priesthood, and church. Judith Heffernan's unheralded ordination in 1980 through simple acclamation by her worship community (Community of the Christian Spirit), and Eileen McCafferty DeFranco's extensively publicized RCWP ordination in 2006, both find understanding acceptance from other members who may themselves prefer to work for reform from within the institutional church framework. Nor is their work geographically confined to the Philadelphia area. Marian Ronan and Regina Bannan each served terms as national WOC board president, and Eileen DeFranco served as a WOC board member; DeFranco has been active on the national stage with RCWP; all of them write for *NWNC*; and the organization itself is a member of the national umbrella for Catholic Church reform groups, Catholic Organizations for Renewal (COR). Regina Bannan participates in its meetings as the SEPA-WOC representative.

While several other local groups in the United States exhibit some of the same qualities and strategies as SEPA-WOC, the latter is multifaceted and reflects in itself alone the entire spectrum found across the country. The serious and focused individuals who have served as the Core Committee of

SEPA-WOC for decades have included coordinator Bannan, Heffernan (former St. Joan's member), Alice Foley, editor Karen Lenz (deceased 2010), Pohlhaus, Ratigan, Ronan, Arlene Anderson Swidler (deceased 2009), and, most recently, Bernard McBride.[37] Their consistent work has ensured that the quality and variety of the regional group's activism continues.

OTHER STYLES

As complements to the organized group activism, there are poignant examples of the solitary style, usually chosen by necessity rather than by preference. On the date of a WOC-recommended prayer evening, one woman in Ville Platte, Louisiana, wrote to Isasi-Diaz in 1976 that hers was a small town of only one parish in the Diocese of Lafayette. She had no group to pray with so she asked permission to use the parish church, explaining why, and she sent a copy of her letter to the chancery. On the evening of the national observance, she spent the hour praying alone.[38] Far to the north of Ville Platte, Rene Buchanan has stood—often alone—in front of Boston's Cathedral while the clergy and hierarchy gather inside for the annual ordination of new priests. Though she speaks not a word, her prominent placard announces why she is there.

Between the model of group activism and solitary prayer lie many incarnations of the women's ordination movement across the country. In 1999, WOC publicized seventeen such groups in Berkeley, Binghamton, Boston, California's Bay Area, Chicago, Cleveland, Las Cruces, Long Island, Massachusetts (two groups), New Hyde Park (New York), New York City, Phoenix/Tucson, Rochester (New York), St. Louis, Southeast Pennsylvania, and Washington, DC. Other sources report additional groups in New Mexico (1977), Providence (Rhode Island; 1980), and Southern New Jersey (1983).[39] The 1995 WOC conference program listed a Cincinnati group, led by Ruth Steinert. Shirley Tung, a former WOC board member, and Eileen Pfeiffer organized Andrea Johnson's 1999 speaking tour for active groups in Scottsdale, Phoenix, Sun City, and Tucson of their home state of Arizona. From 2001 to 2004 *NWNC* reported activities of groups in Syracuse, Lexington (Kentucky), Detroit, Milwaukee, Pomona, and Virginia Beach. New groups have come into existence while some on earlier lists have merged with other local Catholic reform groups or have completely dissolved. Each geographic location has a different style from the others, a different cycle of peak activity, and a different personality; but common to all is the goal of bringing about a transformed church.

OTHER GROUPS AND ALLIANCES

Just as a desirable home design includes doors and windows, so WOC's commitment to communication and collaboration has a similar function, bringing light and energy into the organization. Either by intention or by happenstance, WOC and the movement at large have benefited from individuals and groups who have applied their respective talents to the issue of women's ordination in the Roman Catholic Church. It can be argued that the first priestly ordinations of Episcopalian women in July 1974 in Philadelphia functioned in that way: not by any intention of the ordinands or bishops to reform the Roman Catholic community but as an uncalculated "side-effect." The national news media covered the events extensively, and so conversation among Roman Catholics often touched on the topic. It is hard to imagine that Mary Lynch was uninfluenced by the Episcopalian ordinations when only four months later she sent her invitation to key Roman Catholic leaders to discuss how to advance the topic. As the decades went on, Episcopalian women priests served and influenced Catholics by more than simply the historical fact of their ordinations. They found themselves lecturing before groups of Roman Catholics, leading ecumenical retreats, teaching on campuses, and writing for broad, mixed readerships.

Somewhat later, scholarly research committees of the Canon Law Society of America (1995) and of the Catholic Theological Society of America (1997) worked with the intent to discern the evidence in their respective disciplines regarding women's ordination—whether positive or negative. The absence of definitively conclusive findings in either direction was an indirect encouragement to activists on both sides of the issue.

Support-by-indirection has been characteristic of some Catholic renewal groups, while others have chosen to be strongly explicit in their advocacy of Catholic women's ordination. The advocacy, of course, is strong or moderate, explicit or implicit, depending on the purpose and prevailing theology of the individual organization and the needs of its constituency. Several supportive reform organizations that sprang up shortly after Vatican II had productive life spans but disappeared for any of several reasons, e.g., burnout of charismatic leaders, diminishment of need, or merging with another group. Some continue and deepen their work, such as the Women's Alliance for Theology, Ethics and Ritual (WATER) under the leadership of Mary Hunt and Diann L. Neu. On the other hand, new needs have spawned new groups, such as Voice of the Faithful which arose in 2002 to specifically address the crisis of clergy sexual abuse of children in the Archdiocese of Boston. Their initial local crisis has ameliorated slightly, and their agenda has recently broadened to include additional topics of church reform.

In 1976, the U.S. bishops issued to the laity a Call to Action intended to give new life to the church. That episcopal summons gave rise to an organization of the same name (CTA) which has itself enjoyed a position of centrality in the arenas of church reform. In recognition of the fact that several reform groups with overlapping interests had formed in the years since CTA's founding, in 1991 they developed a regular in-person forum for the groups to share information, strength, and strategies. By 2010, twenty-four organizations were participating in this process called Catholic Organizations for Renewal (COR). There are many dozens more groups, both regional and national, that do not participate in COR but because of their proliferation are not recorded or described in these pages.

An uncommon pattern of development marks the organization called FutureChurch, founded in 1990 near Cleveland by Rev. Louis J. Trivison, a parish priest. His and his parishioners' primary concern was the growing likelihood that Catholics would soon not have access to the sacrament of the Eucharist because of the obvious priest shortage. Their proposed solution was to open ordination to women and married men, and after study and prayer several Ohio parishes created a network which has spread across the country. This network has gained global attention because of the leadership skills and theological background of the executive director, Christine Schenk, CSJ, who has served since the network originated.

FutureChurch's effectiveness is grounded in its parish origins and its continuing focus on the Eucharistic need of the people in the pews. Its day-to-day work serves that purpose, and its seemingly wide-ranging activities, as well, are actually directed toward that end. These include high-quality lectures by nationally noted theologians; a sophisticated newsletter (online and paper) providing data in easily understood charts and graphs; and online campaigns in which all can participate in preparation for synods or in response to developments in the Catholic Church. Schenk effectively initiated the rehabilitation of Mary of Magdala's reputation, which has had positive repercussions in piety and practices around the globe. Restoring the truth about Mary illustrates the conviction that, if errors and unfounded slander about her could be disproven then so could the error and slander promulgated about women in general as justification for not ordaining them. FutureChurch sees this as a way to increase the pool of candidates for ordination so that Catholics can be assured of a continued Eucharistic life.

AN AERIAL VIEW

With the founding of the U.S. Women's Ordination Conference in 1976, the movement designed itself a "home." In the design one finds elements of the movement's older homes: the responsible scholarship and professional approach of the St. Joan's Alliance (later seen in the Quixote Center's research and publications); Jeanne Barnes's commitment to regular, stimulating communication for the Deaconess Movement (evidenced later in *New Women, New Church*); and the conviction of Mary Lynch that working with clergy and bishops is crucial (reappearing in 1975 in Priests for Equality and in RAPPORT). In short order, WOC became a mobile home, geographically, strategically, and theologically; and like most homes it faces an unpredictable future full of remodeling and renovation.

NOTES

In her detailed and well-researched work, Mary J. Henold situates the women's ordination movement in the larger contexts of feminism and Catholicism in the 1970s and includes pieces of the founding and history of WOC until 2007. See *Catholic and Feminist: The Surprising History of the American Catholic Feminist Movement* (Chapel Hill: University of North Carolina Press, 2008).

1. Dolores Brooks, "News Release" (Sept. 1976), 1, Marquette University Archives (hereafter MUA) Series I, Carton 2, Folder 15.
2. "Brief History of WOC," MUA Series I, Carton 2, Folder 15.
3. Letter from Ruth Fitzpatrick to Rev. William Virtue (Aug. 9, 1977), MUA Series 1, Carton 3, Folder 3.
4. *We Are Called*, ed. Dolly Pomerleau (Rochester, NY: Women's Ordination Conference, 1978), 20.
5. Conversations between McDonough and author (New York, 1982–1983).
6. Maureen Fiedler et al., letter to constituents of WOC (July 29, 1983), MUA Series I, Carton 3, Folder 3.
7. *New Women, New Church* (hereafter *NWNC*; Winter 1985), MUA Series I, Carton 1, Folder 10.
8. Laurie Wright Garry, Appendix D: WOC Awardees, in "The Women's Ordination Conference (1975–1994): An Introduction to a Movement," unpublished doctoral dissertation (Milwaukee, WI: Marquette University, 2000), 249.
9. Arthur Jones, "WOC's Prelate, Fitzpatrick on Steady March to Ordination," *National Catholic Reporter* 30, no. 32 (June 17, 1994): 5.
10. Conversations between Fitzpatrick and author (1994).
11. "WOC to Have New Leadership in 2000," *NWNC* 22, no. 2:2, MUA Carton 23, Folder 6.
12. *NWNC* 28, no. 1 through *NWNC* 32, no. 2 (2004–2010), MUA Carton 23.
13. William V. D'Antonio, *American Catholics across Generations: Glimpsing the Future* (New York: unpublished lecture, 2010), especially pp. 14–15.
14. Aisha S. Taylor, "WOC Rises Like the Phoenix after Fire Destroys Office," *NWNC* 31, no. 2 (Spring 2008): 1.
15. Lawrence Cada et al., *Shaping the Coming Age of Religious Life* (New York: Seabury Press, 1979); Patricia Wittberg, *Creating a Future for Religious Life* (New York: Paulist Press, 1991), 24–35.
16. Maureen Dwyer, *New Women, New Church, New Priestly Ministry: Proceedings of the Second Women's Ordination Conference* (Fairfax, VA: Women's Ordination Conference, 1980).
17. Frances Lee McGillicuddy's letter to Mary Luke Tobin (June 4, 1978), Smith College Archives, Sophia Smith Collection Carton 13, Folder unnumbered.
18. Dwyer, *op. cit.*, 17–30.
19. Ibid., 148.
20. Ruth McDonough Fitzpatrick, "A History of WOC and the Movement to Ordain Women to a Renewed Priestly Ministry," unpublished paper (1989), 6, MUA Series I, Carton 2, Folder 15.

21. Dwyer, *op. cit.*, 7–9.

22. Author's group conversation with several participants: Rene Smith Buchanan, Nympha Clarke, Barbara Classen, Carol Crowley, Louise Cunha, Nancy DeRycke, Ruth Fitzpatrick, Rosalie Muschal-Reinhardt, Tara Seeley, Joan Sobala, Karen Swartz, Kathleen Vandenberg, Beth Rindler, and two women who choose to remain anonymous (Rochester, NY, June 1986). See also Rene Buchanan, "RAPPORT: A Project of the Women's Ordination Conference," *NWNC* 22, no. 1 (Spring 1999): 3.

23. Dorothy Vidulich, "Conference Marks 20th Anniversary," *National Catholic Reporter* (Dec. 1, 1995): 9–10.

24. Ibid.

25. Rosemary Radford Ruether, "Second International Women's Ordination Conference Exposes Rifts," *Agenda for Justice Newsletter* 1, no. 2 (Fall 2005): 4.

26. Evelyn Hunt, "Historic Collaborative Group Sponsors Boston Conference," *NWNC* (Summer 2008): 7.

27. Available to view at WOC website www.womensordination.org.

28. Over time, it became unfeasible to publish proceedings of conferences that were loosely structured or were based on discussions rather than on keynote speakers.

29. *Women's Ordination Conference Newsletter* 1, no. 1 (Dec. 1976). The newsletter was later known as *WOC News Bulletin*, and later as *New Women, New Church*.

30. Erin Saiz Hanna report (2010).

31. This survey was preceded by Andrew Greeley's survey of 1974.

32. Maureen Fiedler and Linda Rabben, *Rome Has Spoken: A Guide to Forgotten Papal Statements and How They Have Changed through the Centuries* (New York: Crossroad Publishing, 1998), throughout.

33. "Advisory Board: Accountability Report" (Nov. 1978–May 1979), MUA Series I, Carton 1, Folder 1.

34. Mohler-Rice Papers, St. Mary's Seminary, Baltimore.

35. *Keeping the Vision Alive, 1976–2001*, ed. Mary Englert (Cleveland, Ohio: Cleveland Women's Ordination Conference).

36. *NWNC* 31, no.1 (Winter 2008): 3.

37. Meeting of author with SEPA-WOC Core Committee (Philadelphia Catholic Worker House, Feb. 2, 2009).

38. *Women's Ordination Conference Newsletter* 1, no. 2 (April 1977): 9, MUA Series I, Carton 2, Folder 15.

39. COR members, as listed on its website August 2010: Association for the Rights of Catholics in the Church (ARCC), CTA Baltimore, CTA Northern Virginia, Catholics for a Free Choice, Catholics for a Free Choice/Canada, Catholics for the Spirit of Vatican II, Catholics Speak Out, CORPUS, Dignity USA, Ecumenical Catholic Communion, Federation of Christian Ministries, Fellowship of Southern Illinois Laity, FutureChurch, Good Tidings Ministry, National Coalition of American Nuns, New Ways Ministry, Pathfinder Community of the Risen Christ, Pax Christi Maine, Save Our Sacrament (SOS), Reform of Annulment & Respondent Support, Southeastern Pennsylvania Women's Ordination Conference, Spiritus Christi Church, Women's Ordination Conference, Women-Church Convergence.

Chapter Five

Cross

Clergy, Vatican Teachings, and Hierarchy

Few people are aware of the many instances and types of support given by Roman Catholic bishops, cardinals, priests, and the occasional pope to the aspirations of women seeking fullness of life in society and church. Even some of these men themselves have been and remain unaware that their simplest words and deeds have strengthened many women's commitment to the ordination movement. This influence was clearly acknowledged by St. Joan's Alliance members, by Mary Lynch, and by the roster of speakers invited to the earliest national WOC gatherings. In the United States, many Catholic women in the 1960s and thereafter often received encouragement from four different clerical sources. In the personal and pastoral arena many individual priests long acknowledged and affirmed women's priestly vocations. For other women, stimulus came from the spirit expressed in documents of the Second Vatican Council or from the several bishops like—but not restricted to—Maurice J. Dingman (Des Moines), William D. Borders (Baltimore), Charles Buswell (Pueblo, Colorado), and Carroll Dozier (Memphis) who wrote early pastoral letters on the equality of women and men in church and in society. Theologians as individuals (e.g., Carroll Stuhlmueller and Richard P. McBrien) and as professional groups (the Catholic Theological Society of America, the Pontifical Biblical Commission, the Canon Law Society of America) provided additional encouragement[1] to those advocating women's ordination. Papal inspiration for women's pursuit of ordination in the church has always been indirect (and almost certainly unintended)[2] but can be found in encyclicals, pastoral letters, and public speeches praising women's gifts, challenging the church to match the almost worldwide advancement of women's social status, and advocating new roles for women in the service of the church.

Increased access to education and to work experiences outside the home usually leads women to see new ways of exercising responsibility for their own lives and for the lives of their families and communities. This development is as true of the society we call "church" as it is of any other society. So the women's ordination movement would most likely have happened whether or not there had been a Vatican Council II or the social liberation movements of the 1970s. Conspicuous among Catholics in this development is the continuing growth over time in the leadership of women in the roles that were formerly filled exclusively by men: as spiritual companions, pastoral caregivers, and theologians in particular. But our exploration in this chapter is specifically of the surprising cadre of ordained churchmen at all levels who have supported the concept or encouraged women in pursuit of their goal. The purpose of this chapter is not to point out a discrepancy between words and deeds. Nor should it be interpreted as a naively rosy indicator that Vatican-approved ordination of Roman Catholic women can be expected at any time in the near future. These pages simply tell a piece of history.

In Catholic women's ordination circles, a frequent wry reminder elicits knowing groans: "When the Church finally does decide to ordain women, the official Vatican pronouncement will begin with the words 'As the Church has always taught.'" To a certain extent that phrase will be true, as the following pages demonstrate.

"AS THE CHURCH HAS ALWAYS TAUGHT"

Several pairs of contrasts are noticeable in the styles of teaching used by Catholic clergy and hierarchy on the subject of women's ordination: "explicit and implicit," "conscious and unconscious," "words and deeds," "secrecy and openness," social environments of "upheaval and stasis," and "open papacies and restrictive papacies." Consider each of these styles when examining the groups of "teachers" about to be described.

Priests

The role of the ordained clergy in another's vocational discernment varies from culture to culture, from age to age, and from personality to personality, but often a conversation between a woman and a priest has confirmed her belief that their strengths and weaknesses, aptitudes and shortcomings, and spiritual lives and sense of vocation are the same. Sometimes the ordained priest supported her explicit pursuit of ordination and offered opportunities for her to develop her sense of call by raising her visibility and responsibility in the worship life of the parish, suggesting or providing educational resources, or connecting her with other women who felt similarly called.

In our time and in our culture lay women and men often take on the responsibility of pointing out a person's gifts of spiritual leadership and inviting her or him to consider seeking ordination to church ministry. So today learning about one's vocation to the priesthood comes through diverse sources, not from the clergy alone. But it cannot be denied that the earlier model worked more effectively than anyone realized. And its success was wrought explicitly and implicitly, consciously and unconsciously, in words and deeds, secretly and openly, during open papacies and restrictive papacies, and in eras of social upheaval, as well as in times of social stasis.

Precisely because spiritual companioning such as the above has traditionally been private, there is little documentation of it. But listening carefully for decades to Catholic women seeking ordination provides evidence of the role some clergy have played in supporting the concept and the individuals who are grappling with the church's current practice. In the realm of the documentable, there have been some significant public instances of priests as individuals or as religious communities who have affirmed women's calls to ordination. Most have been as indirect in their wording as the documents of Vatican II were in 1965 because Popes John Paul II (in 1994) and Benedict XVI (in 2006) banned discussion of this subject. The ban has not changed minds, but it has changed behaviors and, in some cases, relationships with the Roman Catholic Church.

Yet two strongly expressed statements came from the Society of Jesus, in the documents of their worldwide 33rd General Congregation[3] held in 1995: "[Scriptural] sources call us to change our attitudes and work for a change of structures. . . . There is an urgency in the challenge to translate theory into practice not only outside, but also within, the Church itself." Shortly after that sentence is another particularly clear confession and firm purpose of amendment:

> We [Jesuits] have been part of a civil and ecclesial tradition that has offended against women. . . . We have often contributed to a form of clericalism which has reinforced male domination with an ostensibly divine sanction. . . . We wish to react personally and collectively, and do what we can to change this regrettable situation.

In recognition of the society's commitment expressed in this document, the Commission on Women in the Archdiocese of St. Paul–Minneapolis presented its Mary Kennedy-Lamb Award to the Jesuits in 2006.[4] Mary Kennedy Lamb had been one of the early members of the very active Minneapolis St. Joan's community, which established this annual award to keep alive the needed attention to the status of women in the Roman Catholic Church.

"Priests for Equality"

In addition to public statements made by such groups as the Jesuits, other priests (and bishops) have made known their support for the movement by individual, "private" acts of contributing modest amounts of money to or becoming members of WOC. Often caution or fear of ecclesiastical censure leads them to lend their support anonymously or under an assumed name. Yet, in uncharacteristically public actions, within eleven months of its founding over one thousand priests had taken membership in a movement called Priests for Equality (PFE).[5] Members "were asked to endorse a strong charter of gender equality and work to implement equality through their contacts at the local and national level." Priests were attracted to the organization by word of mouth, or by others who suggested their names to the Quixote Center (QC). "Gift memberships" were not accepted, for two reasons: in case the women's ordination views of the recipient had been misunderstood and offense given; and to require the priest to take a specific, though small, action of his own in order to confirm himself in his belief. Priests for Equality was the first project undertaken by QC staff William Callahan, SJ; Maureen Fiedler, SL; and Dolores C. Pomerleau in 1975, and its clear success was an energizing beginning for the center. By 1987, the number of members had grown to over 2,500 priests from thirty-five countries, and the membership rolls that year showed equal presence of members of the diocesan clergy and of religious communities.[6]

As Callahan described PFE members in a 1976 press release:

> These priests cover the entire spectrum of age and ministry. Members range in age from young priests and lay deacons recently ordained, to priests in their 60s, 70s and even 80s. Seminary professors, biblical scholars, pastors, associate pastors, curates, chancery officials, canon lawyers, high school and university teachers, retreat directors, charismatics, contemplative monks, campus chaplains, missionaries, superiors of religious orders, associates of the U.S. Catholic Conference of Bishops, local priests and those known nationally, these and many others are represented.[7]

Those priests initiated varied relevant activities on their home turf: creating dialogue events, raising the subject in media interviews, writing articles for the local press, and even mobilizing fellow priests to prepare and serve refreshments at women's ordination gatherings. One of the more dramatic local projects came from the Priests' Senate of Detroit. With the leadership of Joseph Nowlan, each priest of the Detroit diocese was sent a copy of the PFE charter to discuss with "his constituents" in preparation for a plenary vote by the senate members. At Nowlan's invitation, immediately prior to the voting in April 1976, Margaret Brennan, IHM, delivered a talk to them on the subject of women's ordination. That same day, following her presentation the priest-senators endorsed the PFE charter by majority vote of the whole senate and without any amendments or deletions.[8]

Callahan's commitment to transparency and assertive public relations is revealed in the inexpensive, direct, and regular reports sent to the members of PFE. The brief reports announced plans for the coming year, which in 1976 were

- to develop a research project called "Are Catholics Ready?" designed and coordinated by Maureen Fiedler and Dolly Pomerleau;
- to support and coordinate a study called "Who Are the Women Who Seek Ordination?" and to retain a professional psychologist (Fran Ferder, FSPA) to analyze and publish the data as a book, *Called to Break Bread*;
- to educate and organize Catholics for action toward passage of the Equal Rights Amendment;
- to increase membership;
- to create and promote materials related to sexist language (including body language) in liturgy and preaching ("Project Soapsuds"); and
- to develop a phased recruitment program to motivate U.S. bishops to join the movement.

The next year's report highlighted "Are Catholics Ready?" the national Gallup Poll which QC had commissioned to learn Catholics' opinions on women's ordination. It indicated, among other things, that there had been a 10 percent rise in acceptance during the six weeks after the Vatican declaration of its impossibility. Subsequent surveys revealed that the change of opinion among Roman Catholics had grown over the years: 29 percent in 1974, 58 percent in 1985, and 67 percent in 1992. Coordinated by Fiedler and Pomerleau, with the assistance of Callahan and Georgia Whipple Fuller, these results were announced at a June 1992 press conference at the University of Notre Dame where the annual meeting of the U.S. bishops was in progress.

For a three-person staff of extraordinary creativity, high idealism about social and ecclesial reform, and responsiveness to individuals involved in each of those arenas, the volume of work at PFE threatened to become overwhelming. It was a situation not unlike the slightly earlier development of the Deaconess Movement, when the voluminous response led Jeanne Barnes to call on Mary Lynch to take the movement to the next phase. So in 1982 Joseph Dearborn was hired as PFE's national secretary while its home base, QC, expanded and grew more complex. Animated by the documents of Vatican II, which thrust the Roman Catholic Church into the modern world, its members began to seek Scripture translations that would be alive to contemporary language usage and faithful to the original texts. Many knew that the Hebrew and Greek originals were often more gender-inclusive than the approved English translations then in use throughout the country. In response to the need, QC staff made a long-term commitment to produce an inclusive language translation of the Bible (both the Hebrew and the Christian Scriptures).[9] As a result, under the aegis of QC's Priests for Equality "department," Dearborn published *The Inclusive Lectionary* in 1999; and *The Inclusive Bible: The First Egalitarian Translation* appeared in 2009.

THE QUIXOTE CENTER

Clearly, support for the women's ordination issue was the catalyst project that led in 1976 to the official founding of the Quixote Center by Callahan, Fiedler, and Pomerleau; and women's status in society and church has remained a strong focus. Each of the three founders began the journey together with a deep social justice conviction grounded in her/his respective religious training, spirituality, and education: Callahan as a Jesuit priest, Fiedler as a Sister of Mercy (later as a Sister of Loretto), and Pomerleau as a former Sister of St. Joseph. As persons of their time, they were influenced by the social revolutions occurring all around them. Paradigm shifts could be found at every turn in the 1970s: communes, co-ops, radical egalitarianism, alternative lifestyles, the "back to nature" movement, intensified feminism, the peace movement, and the civil rights movement. It was a time of profound anger and fear for some and of exhilaration for others. It was a time of dreaming impossible dreams, as symbolized by Don Quixote de la Mancha, the fictional idealist who rode his nag across Spain in the seventeenth century, tilting at both real and metaphorical windmills. They realized what an appropriate icon Don Quixote was for their endeavors; so they named the newborn entity the "Quixote Center."

In the next phase, existing as well as new foci of the center were evident in the earliest staff members who joined the founders: in 1976, Jeannine Gramick, SSND, and C. Robert Nugent, SDS, who worked in ministries for gays and lesbians and their families; and in the following year Ruth Fitzpatrick, who took on the projects related to women's ordination. All six of the earliest workers lived with very thin permeable boundaries between the sacred and the secular, and though maturation and expansion of their ministries led Gramick, Fitzpatrick, and Nugent to move off the staff, their original pool of energy has flowed out to ecclesial and civil issues for more than three decades.

Adding to the center's abundance of research and publication on social justice issues that had already been completed or were under way, Bill Callahan and Francine Cardamon published in 1978 a guide to "deep prayer for busy people" called *The Wind is Rising*. In 1982, Callahan completed writing a widely well-received work of spirituality, the principles of which were the essence of his own activism: *Noisy Contemplation*. An enduring classic, the newspaper-insert style of its first appearance was upgraded with each new edition of the original; and in 2008 its timeless relevance and accessible content made a reappearance in book form.

In 1998 the center sponsored the work of Maureen Fiedler and Linda Rabben that led to the publication of their book *Rome Has Spoken*, published by the Catholics Speak Out project of QC. It was a perceptively conceived study of documents that had at one time been declared infallible, official church teaching and were then later abandoned.[10] They illustrated, of course, that if the infallibility of earlier church teachings was mutable, then one day in the future the teaching against women's ordination could be, too. Later, in 1997, QC and WOC and Catholics Speak Out collaborated in planning, funding, and hosting the stirring visit of Ludmila Javorova who had been ordained in the Czech Republic during the years of the underground church.

The mode of operation in the center has been decision-making by consensus in an egalitarian community. That work community increased in number and became, over time, diversified and complex as to skills, educational background, faith commitment, and age. It has been a clearinghouse for some projects, a seedbed for new ones, and an umbrella for still others, each of which is required to be financially self-sustaining. And while it is a challenge to describe what being "faith-based" might mean in 2009 compared to 1975, the center's staff and board of trustees has managed to agree on which quixotic reform movements it would address, both in Haiti and Latin America, as well as in the United States. Following Callahan's death in 2010 and several subsequent internal challenges, QC downsized, regrouped, and continued its quest for justice and peace in church and society. As William Callahan left the stage of human life, it was clear that for many he had become "The Man from La Mancha":

> And I know if I'll only be true to this glorious quest
> That my heart will lie peaceful and calm when I'm laid to my rest.
> And the world will be better for this.[11]

The Price Paid

While the world may, indeed, "be better for this" when a person acts for others on principles of justice, the irony is that in the short run a Quixote must often pay a painful price. Recall the physical abuse and imprisonment of the women in the early twentieth century as they struggled to gain the right for all women to vote. Recall, too, the murder of Martin Luther King Jr. who labored for justice toward his black sisters and brothers. Remember the ostracizing and harsh penalizing of Erin Brockovich, Crystal Lee Sutton ("Norma Rae"), and Karen Silkwood who in their respective lives "blew the whistle" on the big businesses that created unsafe working or living conditions. These outcomes are seen no less in churches than in civil societies, and may be physical, financial, mental, emotional, spiritual, or occupational.

Catholic clergy and hierarchy in the United States in the past one hundred years have addressed in different ways four major issues related to women: the right to vote, the Equal Rights Amendment, reproductive rights, and ordination. According to their lights, they have counseled in confessionals, preached in pulpits, debated at the dais, and published in the print media. But the following three ordained priests in recent decades have incurred heavy penalties for their unusual forms of activism on behalf of women's ordination.

William Callahan was a Jesuit priest in 1975 with a fresh doctorate in physics at the outset of his quixotic journey to work toward bringing about the ordination of women in the Roman Catholic Church. With his companions on the journey, he and they followed a rocky road filled with conflict, pain, confrontation, and public outcry, with no other desired outcome than that of justice for all. Inevitably, others disagreed with what constituted "justice for all," and some of them were persons in positions of either civil or ecclesial power. Predictably, QC's Maryland location so close to the nation's seat of power was a thorn in the side of the politicians who resented interference in certain national and international practices. And because of Callahan's stand concerning the ordination of women, the Jesuits' New England provincial administrator (Robert E. Manning, SJ) mandated that Callahan dissociate himself from Catholics Speak Out and PFE and, eventually, that he leave QC; the archbishops of Washington, DC, of Chicago, and of Boston each refused to accept him to work in their archdioceses; and the Jesuits' worldwide father general (Peter-Hans Kolvenbach, SJ) attempted to silence him concerning his work in opposition to "clear decisions of the Holy See." In his written appeal to Kolvenbach, Callahan affirmed:

> I have had great love and joy being a Jesuit for these 40 years. And I am also committed to the Gospel, to the Church's social teaching and to the adventurous ideals of the Jesuit order which have shaped my life, stirred my heart and led me to commit myself to the work of justice. . . . I cannot abandon my work for gender equality in the church or civil society; sexism is a sin of our church that is eroding the faith of millions. . . . What is needed now is not Jesuit timidity, but a gospel-inspired boldness that refuses to be silent and speaks out in a strong, loving voice to call the church to justice in its own life.

After several months of painful spiritual search and struggle far away from QC, Callahan ultimately decided in 1989[12] to "remain true to this glorious quest" rather than to accede to the Jesuits' more pedestrian hopes and plans for him, which resulted in their very painful and public parting of ways.

In much later years, when he was semiretired due to physical health challenges, Callahan focused again on his original quest and in 2009 developed a research project for himself, contacting many of the early members of PFE in order to stimulate their reflection. He intended to publish the results of his exploration into what those men had learned from their PFE experience, how they themselves had changed personally or in their ministries, and how their commitment to working toward the ordination of Roman Catholic women may have developed over the years.

James Callan was appointed to serve as the priest-administrator of Corpus Christi Church in Rochester, New York, in 1976. With his leadership, the parish became a vibrant worship community in service to a wide variety of human needs and Gospel justice issues. In doing so, it attracted new members and the congregation grew. Diversification came along with growth, and for twenty-two years Callan ministered in a model that included women, non-Catholics and same-sex couples. Most of the Corpus Christi parishioners embraced the ever-increasing varieties of behavior that reflected the varieties of the members.

As to women's participation in the worship of the church, Callan welcomed as associate pastor a lay woman, Mary Anne Whitfield Ramerman, to preach and to co-preside at Eucharistic liturgies for some years. She adopted ritual garb similar to the priests' and shared in the priestly functions during the liturgies. Other examples of the atmosphere of inclusiveness were "the blessing of gay unions, and the offering of communion to those who were not Catholic."[13] (It might be noted that these three issues are very closely related to the three specific areas that the Vatican later investigated regarding the Leadership Conference of Women Religious beginning in 2009.) In the summer of 1998, Bishop Matthew Clark received word from the Vatican that Callan, who allowed the three controversial practices, was to be removed from the parish; and during the autumn, Ramerman was also dismissed.

For two months after her dismissal from the parish staff, Mary Ramerman led Catholic weekly services at a nearby Presbyterian church for a very large group of alienated Corpus Christi parishioners, and Callan worked at his official new assignment in a nearby small city parish. After he returned in early December to lead a Eucharistic liturgy for Ramerman's worship community, Callan was suspended from the Roman Catholic priesthood for having done so. Over time he and Ramerman and other former Corpus Christi staff members found a permanent physical home for their church, Spiritus Christi, and established and now serve five additional, smaller communities in western New York State.

In November 2001, Mary was ordained to the priesthood by Bishop Peter Hickman of the Ecumenical Catholic Communion, which is "the nation's largest coalition of liberal, independent Catholic churches" and is of the lineage of the Old Catholic Church.[14] In 2003, he celebrated the ordination of a former staff member at Corpus Christi Church, Denise Donato. In 2009, she moved from Spiritus Christi to full-time service for Mary Magdalene Church, a community in Fairport, New York.

The price paid by Callan seems to have purchased a spiritual home for Catholics who prefer not to be "Roman" Catholics. The strong personalities involved in his decisions seem to have emerged unscathed, and all seem to have put the past behind them. But in the years of crisis, the elation of standing by their beliefs was counterbalanced by deep pain among the original congregants and among the leaders themselves. The larger Corpus Christi Parish community felt torn asunder and rejected by their leaders, and the leaders felt similarly rent within themselves and rejected by the Roman Catholic hierarchy.[15] The price paid by those acting in behalf of women's ordination was high.

Roy Bourgeois, MM, served as a Maryknoll priest for almost four decades and after 1983 focused his energy on working toward the closing of the School of the Americas at Fort Benning, Georgia, which is an "elite" U.S. training center for military officers. In addition to the questionable military techniques taught there, another moral flaw that he noted was the training of candidates from Central and South America who eventually returned to their countries to become actively engaged in oppressive and violent activities. One of Bourgeois's consciousness-raising strategies was to organize at the site of the school an annual public demonstration of protest, in which thousands of persons have participated each November since 1990. During those years, he could not help but notice the long-term fidelity of the many women among the protesters. Time and again they returned to join this advocacy event, incurring fines and sentences of imprisonment while seeking justice for oppressed people in the countries to our south.

Eventually Bourgeois came to believe that these strong and faithful women were, themselves, oppressed by the Roman Catholic Church. When invited by one of them, Janice Sevre-Duszynska, to be part of her Roman Catholic Women Priests (RCWP; see chapter 6) ordination ceremony in 2008, he accepted. His long commitment to addressing injustice in Georgia led to a decision to confront injustice to women in the church, knowing that it would be an ecclesially risk-laden action.

After having actively participated in the ordination ceremony of Janice and other women through RCWP, Bourgeois was officially reprimanded by the Vatican's Congregation [Office] for the Doctrine of the Faith and informed that he would be subject to excommunication unless he abjured his position of support for women's ordination. In response to that message he wrote back to the Congregation, "There will never be justice in the Catholic Church until women can be ordained." Inspired by Bishop Oscar Romero several years earlier, Bourgeois added, "Let those who have a voice speak out for the voiceless. . . . Let us speak clearly and boldly and walk in solidarity as Jesus would, with the women in our Church who are being called to priesthood."[16] In the summer of 2009, Bourgeois participated in a lecture tour called "Shattering the Stained Glass Ceiling," speaking throughout the United States on behalf of women's ordination. The excommunication threat had not been actualized, the Maryknoll community had not dismissed him, and his statements on behalf of the women's ordination movement had continued. In February 2012 Maryknoll's general council met to discuss the situation once again and to vote on the next action of the community regarding Bourgeois. Both the Maryknoll community and Roy Bourgeois are in a prolonged and painful attempt to clarify this difficult matter. At any moment, however, either or both the Vatican and the Maryknoll community may feel it necessary to enforce the ban on his activity and to publicly and irrevocably dismiss him from membership in their respective organizations. The price Bourgeois pays in the short run is the insecurity of not knowing what the eventual cost may be, and it is reminiscent of Theresa Kane's experience of delayed discipline after her public welcome of John Paul II in 1979. In the long run, the price Bourgeois will pay may be far more painful than his current uncertainty.

THE UNKNOWNS

In addition to the types of priests' support described above, there is a different, seldom-noted, usually unmentioned type of help given to the movement. Part of the process leading to a Catholic priest's official nomination is an inquiry among knowledgeable persons as to his adherence to doctrines and policies of the church. The non-ordination of women is not a doctrine—as is Jesus' divinity—but is, rather, a policy of long standing. Because of this inquiry there may be some unknown priests whose role in the women's ordination movement has been very private. They are the priests who have been informally mentioned for ordination to the episcopacy and have declined that invitation (or averted it beforehand) because they could not promise their allegiance to the policy of not ordaining women to the priesthood.

Conciliar and Papal Documents: A Design Emerges

The cynic may remark that official church teachings have not done much for women: In most cases, the person means that the teachings have not effected observable justice for women within the church, such as allowing them to be ordained or to be in high-level decision-making positions in church governance. There is no gainsaying the evidence presented by Deborah Halter in her volume *The Papal No*, but one can arguably maintain that in the twentieth century many of the official church teachings (when known and internalized) have contributed to Catholic women's understanding that they are equal to men. For many decades these documents have also contributed to women's trust that very soon appropriate actions would flow from the words. In addition to the effect of church teachings on large numbers of individual women, they are also self-created benchmarks against which the hierarchy and clergy themselves can measure their progress in acting on their own exhortations.

The members of the St. Joan's Alliance have spoken and written clearly of the energizing encouragement they felt upon studying the documents of Vatican II, particularly *Gaudium et Spes*. They were strengthened and motivated to work for women's ordination by such statements as "Every kind of social or cultural discrimination in basic personal rights on the grounds of sex, race, color, social conditions, language, or religion must be curbed and eradicated as incompatible with God's design." The St. Joan's members internalized these words from the council of bishops as exhortations to themselves as baptized persons, and they set about "curbing and eradicating" with spiritual and intellectual focus and energy. In addition, the council's encouragement of Catholics to read and study Scripture for themselves exposed them to such teachings as those in Paul's Letter to the Galatians: "There is neither Jew nor Greek, there is neither slave nor free, there is neither male nor female; for you are all one in Christ Jesus" (3:27–28). While those words from the teachings of Paul and of the Second Vatican Council did not explicitly advocate the ordination of women, they did strengthen and validate women's belief in their ecclesial equality with men.

But even before the council took place, Mary Henold notes[17] that Pius X's 1930 encyclical *Casti Connubii* escaped the bonds of its otherwise very traditional thinking and was the first papal writing to explicitly speak for "balance" in the spousal relationship instead of the prevailing model of obligatory wifely subservience. Though now considered to be a very small step, the pope's words indicated his growing awareness of women's rights and validated their changing roles.

By contrast, some thirty years later one of the most extensive official statements was that of Pope John XXIII in 1963 when he wrote, "The greatest cultural revolution of all times [will be] one which replaces a structure and culture that have been worked out by the male half of humankind over thousands of years by a structure and culture that will be the handiwork of the whole of humankind comprising the female, as well as the male."[18] It was crafted skillfully to appeal to the global community—secular, as well as religious—and was dramatic in its language. In the same document he stated, "Human beings have the right to choose freely the state of life which they prefer, . . . and also the right to follow a vocation to the priesthood or the religious life."

Twelve years after Pope John's statement, in 1975 Pope Paul VI spoke to a committee studying the church's response to the UN, which was sponsoring International Women's Year: "We must recognize and promote the role of women in the mission of evangelization and in the life of the Christian community. . . . What is most urgent . . . is the immense work of awakening and of promoting women at the grass roots, in civil society, as well as in the Church."[19] The "awakening" was not such an immense task, for the women were ready; but the "promoting" has been slower in its actualization because the church hierarchy were not. Thirty-one years after this message of Paul VI, it was reported in the *Tablet*[20] that women represented "in 2006 only about 15 percent of staff positions in major departments of the Holy See, none of them in major decision-making roles. Three major tribunals . . . have no women at all, and the Congregation for Catholic Education has only one woman on its staff of 23."

In a move that was different from simply writing statements about women, Pope Paul VI had fed their hopes in 1976 by establishing the Pontifical Biblical Commission to study the scriptural basis for withholding ordination from women. After a year of study, the commission's members concluded that there was no basis for withholding the sacrament from them. Oddly enough, almost immediately after the results arrived in the pope's hands, he issued *Inter Insignores*, the "Declaration against the Ordination of Women," asserting that "women cannot image Jesus in the priesthood because scripture and tradition do not permit it." His disregard of the work of extraordinarily competent scholars whom he himself had appointed seemed to be out of character and was unfathomable to many. However, just as there are "sins of omission" in life, there can be countervailing "virtues of omission" as well. In careful reading of the declaration, one can note that it specifically bans only ordination to the priesthood, omitting any mention of ordination to the diaconate.[21] Thus, it seems to many women that there is hope of gaining a toehold by pursuing ordination to the diaconate (see chapter 7).

Only two years later (1978), Karol Wojtyla was elected to serve the worldwide Catholic Church as the pope, and he took the name John Paul II. There was widespread hope that he would emulate John XXIII's enthusiastic openness, as well as Paul VI's generally reserved reasonableness, but his long papacy of twenty-seven years became one of active retrenchment from the spirit and teachings of Vatican II and of an inability to dialogue with feminists. While he published a conspicuously large number of letters, statements, and exhortations in praise of women, his actions (or lack thereof) were at variance with his words. Catholic activists note the irony that he was eager to meet and pray with his would-be assassin, Mehmet Ali Ağca, after his attempt of May 1981, but consistently refused to meet with Theresa Kane, RSM, who, in his presence in 1979, had publicly requested inclusion of women in all ministries of the church. Yet in 1988 John Paul II wrote in *Mulieris Dignitatem*:

> The Church is determined to place her full teaching, with all the power with which the divine word is invested, at the service of the cause of women in the

modern world. . . . The seriousness of this commitment requires the collaboration not only of the entire college of bishops, but also of the whole church.

And in the third chapter he notes that an equal relationship between man and
woman was God's plan in creation. In the fourth he summarizes: "In Christianity the mutual opposition between man and woman—which is the inheri-
tance of original sin—is essentially overcome. 'For you are all one in Jesus
Christ.'"

On the other hand, a few years after the appearance of *Mulieris Dignitatem*, John Paul issued in 1994 *Ordinatio Sacerdotalis: On Reserving Priestly
Ordination to Men Alone* in which he announced that the exclusion of wom-
en from the priesthood must be "definitively held by all the church's faithful," and that there was to be no further discussion of the subject.[22] This
mandate certainly curtailed any overt forward movement of the issue by
bishops and severely limited them as individuals or groups from even participating in discussion on the topic. Yet with a subtle teaching technique, Archbishop Francis T. Hurley issued a public statement to the people of the
Anchorage diocese that clarified what the pope had said. In his article he
strategically included several non-polemic allusions to the results of Paul
VI's biblical commission study and to the growing numbers of women who
feel called to ordination, based on their experience as pastoral leaders in the
parishes.[23] His ostensible purpose was to teach about the ban; yet at the same
time he was providing Catholics with the information they needed to make
their own decision about its rightness or wrongness, without coming down on
either side himself.

On June 25, 1995, John Paul II inspired many with the following unexpected words in his *Letter to Women*: "Unfortunately, we are heirs to a
history which has conditioned us to a remarkable extent. In every time and
place this conditioning has been an obstacle to the progress of women. . . .
And if objective blame, especially in particular historical contexts, has belonged to not just a few members of the Church, for this I am truly sorry."

Ten years later, the election of his successor, Pope Benedict XVI (Joseph
Ratzinger), ensured continuity of John Paul's thinking, though manifested in
a very different personal style. A thought-provoking item written by Ratzinger before his election is often quoted by reform-minded Catholics: "The
Church is not the petrification of what once was, but its living presence in
every age. The Church's dimension is therefore the present and the future no
less than the past."[24] This assertion seemed to support those in the church
who felt that contemporary arguments against women's ordination based on
the Christian Scriptures ignored serious, relevant scholarship of the day.

This necessarily very brief collection of papal statements and church
documents may help the reader to understand why many Catholic women

harbor an unfathomable hope that the future will be brighter than the present regarding their vision of an inclusive Roman Catholic priesthood.

Bishops

Whereas the actions of priests in supporting an inclusive priesthood usually have been concrete, personalized, and deliberate, the encouraging teachings of popes on this issue have always been theoretical, general, and unintentional. Bishops, however, stand in an ecclesial middle place, and the encouragement of several of them has manifested itself as a combination of the priestly and the papal styles. Some bishops with an academic bent have researched, written, and lectured in service to the movement. Many have been extraordinarily successful in building helpful pastoral friendships with women who feel called to ordination. Still other bishops have worked within established structures of the National Conference of Catholic Bishops (NCCB) and other church bodies to raise or support the issue.

Among the hundreds of bishops and theologians shaping, embracing, and authorizing the documents of the Second Vatican Council, a few, like Cardinal Josef Suenens (Belgium), were most probably *conscious* that some of the documents could lead, ultimately, to the question of women's ordination. Upon returning from the first session of Vatican II, ecumenical theologian Gustave Weigel, SJ, stated privately, with a combination of awed simplicity and utter surety, "It's going to be a whole new church!"[25] Yet even though the vast majority of the men debating and voting on these documents could not possibly have foreseen specifically where the promulgation of the teachings would lead, by their votes even they were contributing unconsciously to the future roles of women in the church.

In subsequent decades, bishops who have been animated by the spirit of the council have, at times, acted publicly and explicitly in support of women's ordination. As early as 1971, Leo C. Byrne argued at the International Synod of Bishops in Rome that "women are not to be excluded from any service to the Church, if the exclusion stems from questionable interpretation of Scripture, male prejudice, or flawed adherence to merely human traditions that may have been rooted in the social position of women in other times."[26] In April of the following year, the NCCB released the results of a three-year study, the "Roman Catholic/Presbyterian and Reformed Consultation," in which Bishops Byrne and Ernest L. Unterkoefler were the officially appointed cochairs of the Worship and Mission Subcommittee. The public final report of the group[27] recommended that qualified women "be given full and equal participation in policy and decision-making, and voice in places of power, in the churches on local, regional, national and world levels." It urged that seminaries "in all the churches" be open to women, that qualified women be admitted to ordination, and that study and action be initiated for those churches in which women's ordination was a problem. That the leadership of two Roman Catholic bishops resulted in these conclusions indicates that open discussion of women's ordination was accepted within NCCB structures at that time.

A creative strategy of Archbishop Rembert Weakland was to include in every confidential *ad limina* report to the Vatican a section on the state of the question of women's ordination in the Archdiocese of Milwaukee. Preparatory to his report one year, he held open hearings for the people of the archdiocese and reported to the pope that Catholics there had initiated serious discussion about the ordination of married men and of women as solutions to the rapidly growing priest shortage.[28] Weakland was committed to keeping the issue before the eyes of the pope and used a formal, obligatory, and long-established process of the Vatican itself to do so.

A different type of support came from Bishop Maurice Dingman, who invited, encouraged, and financially assisted Mary Lynch's work to such an extent that she was able to achieve rapid, successful growth in the advancement of the Deaconess Movement. In addition to his unusual support of Lynch, he consistently worked to educate the people of the Des Moines diocese, by gathering leaders of its various programs "in which rich dialogue took place concerning openness to the idea of women in the ordained ministry."[29]

Around the same period of time, other bishops wrote public pastoral letters to their dioceses concerning women in the church and society: Leo T. Maher (1974), Carroll T. Dozier (1975), William D. Borders (1977), John S. Cummins in "Statement on Women in Ministry" (1981), Peter Gerety in "Women in the Church" (1981), and Matthew H. Clark in "American Catholic Women: Persistent Questions, Faithful Witness" (1982), among several others. In most cases, they did not explicitly advocate women's ordination but made such statements as "Modern woman cannot be expected to treasure institutions which have limited her freedom, growth, and opportunity in life. . . . Woman's determination to assert her equality and competence must be recognized and respected. Otherwise, the inevitable cost will be women's indifference."[30] Borders, in his letter, called on the NCCB to initiate a study of the possibility of ordaining women to the diaconate. Yet in 1975, Charles A. Buswell was the only bishop to express an encouraging message that was read publicly at the first national Women's Ordination Conference (Detroit). Though not in attendance himself that year he was a faithful participant at subsequent national WOC conferences and was joined at one or more of them by P. Francis Murphy, auxiliary bishop of Baltimore.

In addition to writing pastoral letters, several bishops took to different venues to express their support. Three bishops were quoted in a Washington interview appearing in 1978.[31] The three were Thomas C. Kelly: "The declaration is not infallible and of course it's reformable"; Joseph A. Francis:

"I'm very sympathetic [to women's ordination] and find no theological problem with it"; and Charles A. Buswell: "For 2000 years we haven't had women priests, but otherwise there's no problem with it, if people would accept it."

Despite the growing body of supportive statements by bishops, the experience of Bishops Rembert Weakland and Richard Sklba provided a cautionary tale. In 1979, Sklba was nominated by the Apostolic Delegate in the United States, Jean Jadot, to be auxiliary bishop to Weakland and almost did not see his ordination come to pass. After giving their initial approval of him, the Vatican notified Sklba that his ordination to the episcopacy was to be cancelled unless he recanted in writing his earlier support of women's ordination. "Sklba had chaired a committee of American biblical scholars who issued a document saying that, from a strictly biblical point of view, the ordination of women could not be decided one way or the other. The committee added a codicil stating that a positive answer would be more in keeping with the biblical evidence." This upset Pope John Paul II to the extent that he threatened to rescind his approval of Sklba for the Milwaukee post. With Rembert Weakland accompanying Sklba to Rome and aiding in rewrites, the pope finally approved their multiply-revised statement, and the ordination did take place in Milwaukee—with only three days to spare.[32]

Even Cardinal John J. O'Connor, commonly perceived as rigidly orthodox, found himself in the spotlight on the issue following his 1987 interview with a staff writer from the *New Yorker*. When asked about the ordination of women, he responded that the current pope [John Paul II] would never allow that to happen, "But a future pope *could* announce that he is going to do something unexpected [concerning that issue]." The reporter led him to be more explicit by asking, "So it is conceivable that sometime in the future women may be ordained?" O'Connor responded, "Yes, it is conceivable. But, I remind you, not in the lifetime of this pope."[33] O'Connor's openness to this change in the future church led to another remarkable conversation, this time with author Phyllis Zagano, who was at that time on O'Connor's staff in the New York archdiocese. Over lunch one day, she raised with him the subject of a writing project that she wanted to undertake concerning ordination of women to the diaconate. He reminded Zagano that if she proved that women had been ordained deacons then she would also be proving that they could be ordained to the priesthood, and then he urged her to do her research and writing.[34]

In 1991, Bishop Howard J. Hubbard was interviewed by a reporter and pointed out the contradiction between church practices that discriminate against women and the bishops' "call for women's more direct involvement in the life of the church." He also said explicitly that he felt positive about the possibility of ordaining women deacons: "Research indicates that women served as deacons in the early church, and there is no reason why they can't do so again."[35] In Bishop Kenneth Untener's case, his scholarly research resulted in a published refutation of the *in persona Christi*[36] argument against the ordination of women. The Latin phrase means "in the image of Christ." In the debate about women's ordination, some interpret that to mean the physical (male) image of Christ; others, like Untener, understand it to mean a spiritual image. Both the title and the content of his 1991 article speak for opening the door: "The Ordination of Women: Can the Horizons Widen?" Two years after Untener's article, Bishop William A. Hughes noted in a public talk that the church ought to at least consider restoring the ordination of women and of married men. Regarding women's ordination, he said that the challenge is twofold: "On the one hand is the difficulty the church faces if it deprives itself of the gifts and talents of these individuals. The second is the potential loss to the church as they [women] see they cannot become full members. . . . I am only pointing out that this issue cannot be ignored. And a deep study of the question of women's ordination will be called for as we approach the next century."[37]

Quite unexpectedly, in November 1989 William E. McManus became the first bishop to explicitly raise the advisability of women's ordination on the floor of the annual meeting of the NCCB.[38] Bishop Raymond A. Lucker noted in June 1992 when commenting on the ill-fated bishops' pastoral on women: "We have come to recognize that there is sexism within the church, that we have not treated women equally and have not applied our own teaching to the internal life of the church. The most critical issue then is the participation of women in ministry in the church and especially the discussion on the ordination of women." Lucker's personal academic credentials (doctorates in theology and in education) and his professional writings put him at the forefront of the "Vatican II bishops" and gave credibility to his analysis of church history and politics. He believed in empowering by educating. For addressing conflicts about Vatican pronouncements, his clear, simple, useful chart "Levels of Church Teachings"[39] is invaluable.

There have often been dispirited comments on the failed attempt to produce "the bishops' pastoral on women," but the journey toward its nonexistence was not without value. In 1982 Bishop Michael F. McAuliffe suggested that the bishops in the United States write a pastoral on women's concerns, in recognition of growing criticism of the hierarchy for its unequal treatment of women. Year after year saw draft after draft of this document go through rewrites, critiques, and discussions by committees and the body of bishops until in 1992 they failed to pass the fourth and final draft. Several values were realized from this ten-year journey. Strenuous dialogue with women opened the ears and eyes of many bishops; some who had not considered it an important topic became convinced of its centrality; and many women felt that their voices were heard. A key point voiced by many women that eventually affected the downfall of the project was that pastoral letters are usually written to address a problem, and that women are not a problem. They told the bishops that sexism in the Catholic Church is the problem and should be the subject of the hierarchy's attention. But perhaps most significant of all was the fact that for those ten years the subject of women in the church was regularly and explicitly on the table at the annual bishops' meetings.

In 1993, Bishop William A. Hughes noted in a public address to Future-Church members, "The questions of women's ordination and a married clergy should be up for discussion."[40] And two years later, a bishop from the western United States wrote privately to RAPPORT members, "I am very thrilled about the fact that you are getting interested in the diaconate. I think a new approach to that offers reasons for both hope and optimism."[41] In addition to publishing a pastoral letter about women and church, Bishop Matthew H. Clark raised the question in his article "The Pastoral Exercise of Authority" in 1997: "Why is the diaconate . . . reserved to men alone? . . . Why does the *magisterium* seem to say that all are called to holiness but only men may symbolize that holiness to the community?"[42]

According to one *National Catholic Reporter* writer in 1994, other bishops known to have been supportive over the years of women seeking ordination have included Thomas Costello, Thomas Gumbleton, Francis Quinn, Peter Rosazza, John Snyder, and Joseph Sullivan.[43] The traces of others' footsteps have been covered over by more recent travelers on the path, but their contributions to the movement were strong and clear; Juan Arzube, Joseph P. Delaney, Edmond J. Fitzmaurice, John J. Fitzpatrick, Frank J. Harrison, James R. Hoffman, Joseph L. Hogan, Joseph L. Imesch, Michael H. Kenny, John McGann, Amedee W. Proulx, Ricardo Ramirez, John R. Roach, and John Snyder are a few of these contributors.

In the end, despite the abundance of material and of goodwill produced by the bishops as individuals and as a group, the church members at large see and experience a wide discrepancy between their words and their actions, as witnessed in the "Bishops' Report Card Project" of 2006–2007.[44] Sponsored by the Women's Justice Coalition out of QC, the project was reminiscent of a similar, much earlier one organized by Margaret Mohler and Thekla Rice in Baltimore three decades earlier.[45] The nonscientific 2006 assessments were compiled from surveys done in twenty-three dioceses over a period of several months and rated practices in education, liturgical life, representation, and employment as to their justice toward women. According to the survey analysts, the bishops' final grade was C–.

RAPPORT

An almost textbook case of the tension between bishops' words and deeds developed later in the group of Catholic women of WOC who call themselves Renewed and Priestly People: Ordination Reconsidered Today (RAPPORT). They came as individuals from many parts of the country to the 1985 St. Louis WOC gathering, which was called "Ordination Reconsidered." Shared dissatisfactions with the conference agenda drew together about forty of the participants whose vision and energy led them to develop a covenanted community that has lasted into the twenty-first century. Early on, during their twice-yearly meetings they realized that relationships with supportive bishops would be essential to achieving their long-range goal of ordination. Ruth McDonough Fitzpatrick was at that time a member of RAPPORT and also the national executive director of WOC. Through the latter position she had become well acquainted with several of the U.S. bishops and believed that P. Francis Murphy would be the most willing and the most effective bishop to help the group strategize.

From his first participation in a regular RAPPORT meeting in the late 1980s, Murphy proved himself to be a valuable resource to the group, as well as a kind and compassionate brother in the women's ordination movement.[46] His visit occurred during the early days of the U.S. bishops' work to produce a public pastoral letter on women, and he identified forty-seven bishops whom he knew to be particularly open to the ordination of women. All of them knew that it was essential to prepare themselves for their task in the bishops' body through dialogue with women who were intensely involved in the Roman Catholic Church. The fact that each of the RAPPORT women felt a vocational call to the ordained priesthood was an added value to these bishops, in Murphy's mind, for they would be free to talk, pray, and socialize in a confidential, safe environment concerning a topic banned by Pope John Paul II. As an example of just how privately they held their opinions on the subject, Raymond Lucker revealed that at an early RAPPORT meeting he had never known that the bishop he saw across the room that afternoon felt the same way as he himself did about women's ordination. The women realized that assuring an atmosphere of confidentiality would draw more of the bishops to participate, and so they offered the explicit promise to never reveal (until death) the identities of those who met with them.[47] In fact, several of the women in the group have needed the same protection, lest they be dismissed from their ministries in certain parishes and dioceses.

Over a period of several years, the women of RAPPORT brought into their meetings theologians (among them, Mary Aquin O'Neill and David Powers), canon lawyers (James Coriden and Thomas Doyle), bishops who had ordained the first group of Episcopalian women (George Barrett and Robert L. DeWitt), an ordained Episcopalian priest (Marilyle Sweet-Page), and experts in church reform movements (Jan Blaha, Dan Daley, Maureen Fiedler, Ludmila Javorova, Anthony Padovano, Dolly Pomerleau, Chris Schenk, and others). Among the now-deceased bishops who participated in some of these events were Joseph Breitenbeck, Charles Buswell, John J. Fitzpatrick, Michael Kenny, Raymond A. Lucker, William E. McManus, P. Francis Murphy, and Kenneth Untener. Because of these retreat-like events, social times, and educational experiences, many in this subgroup of bishops became somewhat confident in speaking and writing successfully against the passage of a proposed NCCB document about women's concerns written by a group of celibate men. Some even increased their commitments to writing, speaking publicly, and counseling on the issue.

Two bishops in particular must be highlighted: Charles A. Buswell of Pueblo, Colorado, and P. Francis Murphy of Baltimore, Maryland. Study abroad has traditionally been the indicator of those whom the Vatican has marked for a future of leadership in the church. Both were very well educated in theology, Buswell at the University of Leuven (Louvain, Belgium) and Murphy at the North American College in Rome. Their modes of later involvement in the women's ordination movement differed slightly, reflecting their respective ages, personalities, and hierarchical ranks, but each held a common passion for the issue. Buswell's commitment to it preceded Murphy's by a few years and showed itself in the national arena for the first time when he was the only U.S. bishop to publicly acknowledge and support the first national WOC conference in 1975 in Detroit. From that time on, Buswell happily and unobtrusively became the confidante of many women seeking ordination; he supported efforts within the national body of bishops to advance women in the Catholic Church, and he regularly participated in RAPPORT's activities and donated money to help defray their cost. Buswell participated openly in interviews with members of the press and did not hesitate to express his belief in favor of the ordination of Catholic women. As early as 1977, he told an interviewer for the *National Catholic News*, "We should continue to be involved in women's issues and to study the possibility of admitting them to full participation in the Church. . . . At the present time the Doctrinal Congregation does not see the possibility of ordaining women to the priesthood. I don't think that closes the door on the matter.[48] Twenty-three years later, he was still advocating: "I really think we're guilty of some sort of sexism if we refuse to allow women to be ordained. . . . There's nothing in the scriptures that says women cannot be ordained. One of our basic tenets is that women are equal to men. Therefore they have the same rights to leadership."[49]

Buswell's assertive yet low-key public behavior and statements reflected the self-confidence that the head of a diocese can afford to show; Murphy's reflected the stance of an auxiliary bishop, whose actions are evaluated by his "supervisor," the local ordinary (another title for the bishop in ultimate charge of a diocese). P. Francis Murphy's youth and inexperience as a bishop led him to such a cautious stance that he did not attend the second WOC national gathering—even though (or, perhaps, because) it was held in his own diocese of Baltimore.

After a forward-looking action or statement by one among them, the reform-minded auxiliaries and ordinaries would tease one another with "Well, you'd better get to like your current post, because now you're never going to be moved up or out." Michael Kenny of Juneau, when asked by RAPPORT members to ordain them, responded in mock seriousness, "Maybe I *am* the one to do it. Who else would they find to go to Alaska?" Once Murphy found his voice on some issues that were "taboo" according to the Vatican, it signaled that he had made his peace with living the rest of his life in Baltimore.

During those decades in Maryland, P. Francis Murphy served as episcopal vicar of the western sector of the archdiocese, an area geographically removed from the seats of power in both civil and ecclesial circles and thus an oft-neglected region. For a man of less spiritual commitment, the appointment may have been "the kiss of death," removing him from the mainstream and reducing his influence on the regional and national church, but the opposite happened. His self-chosen episcopal motto was "To listen to God speaking in human words," so Murphy listened hard, and he learned from his listening. He learned from western Maryland's poor persons, its disaffected Catholics, its homeless citizens, its hearing-impaired adults, and its clergy of other faiths. He learned the personal first, then extrapolated to the theoretical and finally the political. That progression of learning gradually took him into nonstructural positions of leadership among the reform-minded bishops of the U.S. Church, and to his close, long relationship with the women of RAPPORT.

Buswell was a Bostonian by birth but grew up in Oklahoma, far away from his New England roots, and he served the church in a modest-sized diocese still farther away in Colorado. Conversely, Murphy was born and raised in the small western Maryland town of Cumberland, attended the undergraduate seminary in Baltimore, and served a very large, extraordinarily diverse, and predominantly urban population.

Charles Buswell's leadership of the Diocese of Pueblo, Colorado, extended from 1959 to 1979, at which time he retired from the office of bishop but not from the work of actualizing the spirit of Vatican II, as he continued to advise, counsel, grant interviews to the media, and encourage women to pursue ordination for the good of the church as a whole. "Charlie," as most of his acquaintances called him, died in June 1998 at age ninety-five. He was followed soon after by his younger counterpart, "Frank," whose premature departure from this life at age sixty-six in September 1999 was caused by cancer. After Murphy's death, there was a measurable leadership lacuna among the reform-minded bishops, as indicated by the sudden lessening of their involvement with RAPPORT. Without Murphy there to motivate them to attend, to gather them for lunch beforehand, and to discuss their insights afterward, the bishops sympathetic to women's ordination gradually stopped coming to RAPPORT's gatherings.

Other factors came into play simultaneous to the deaths of Buswell and Murphy: the very long papacy of John Paul II and its tendency to reinterpret the teachings of Vatican II and the continuation of that same type of leadership by Benedict XVI; the lack among educated Catholics of a "next generation" of any significant size; and the fatigue of many Catholics who were weary of the entrenchment they experienced and chose to spend their energies in social reform. The death and diminishment of "progressive" clergy and bishops has taken its toll as well. Of those forty-seven bishops named by P. Francis Murphy on his original list to RAPPORT in the 1970s, by 2011 the following had died: Juan Arzube, Joseph Breitenbeck, Charles Buswell, Joseph P. Delaney, John J. Fitzpatrick, Joseph Francis, James R. Hoffman, Michael H. Kenny, Raymond A. Lucker, James W. Malone, Leroy Matthiesen, Michael McAuliffe, John McGann, Murphy himself, John R. Roach, William McManus, and Kenneth E. Untener. That represents slightly over one-third of the supportive bishops, and the remaining cadre includes several who are ill, elderly, or disabled.

SUMMARY

Though there is a difference in status, rights, and responsibilities between priests and bishops, there are several commonalities among them surrounding the issue of women's ordination. After several years, the members of RAPPORT realized that most of the sympathetic ones are torn in mind and heart: how to claim to be an inclusive church in the light of a publicly discriminatory key policy; and how to encourage women to remain in the church, without asking them to accept the second-class position it requires of them. These inner conflicts of the bishops and priests are compounded by their immense gratitude to the institutional church for much in their own lives: their education, spiritual development and growth, comrades in ministry, and overall knowledge that they are part of an enterprise larger than themselves.

Even the bishops who believed deeply that Roman Catholic women should have the opportunity to be ordained each admitted to the RAPPORT group that he did not have the inner strength to ordain women because of the repercussions from the Vatican that would ensue. To be excommunicated from the Catholic Church—as they surely would have been during the late twentieth and early twenty-first centuries—would remove them from their teaching roles in service to the body of U.S. bishops, from their social reform work that ranged from local to international, and from their healing relationships with individuals who had been wounded by many and varied church teachings and actions.

One of the most painful "incompatibilities" in the life of a human being occurs when one's deepest convictions, values, and beliefs are at odds with one's life experience. The Vatican has not forced priests and bishops to change their belief regarding women's ordination, but it has severely limited their expression of those beliefs. So there are many among them who do support the movement yet do not externalize their support. For them, the challenge flows from the incompatibility of their values. A symbol for "incompatibilities" is a cross, after all is said and (not) done: two pieces of wood in opposite alignment with one another.

NOTES

1. Over time, RCC professional organizations of theologians, Scripture scholars, and canon lawyers advanced from their earlier membership composition of all-clergy and/or all-male.

2. Deborah Halter, *The Papal No* (New York: Crossroad Publishing, 2004).

3. "Jesuits and the Situation of Women in Church and Civil Society," *General Congregation of Jesuits* 33 (1995), paras. 367 and 370.

4. "Province Update," *Newsletter for Jesuits of the Detroit Province* (Oct. 2006).

5. *Quixote Center Chronicles* (Hyattsville, MD: Quixote Center Archives [hereafter QCA], 1987), 6.

6. William Callahan, "Progress Report" (Hyattsville, MD: QCA, June 27, 1976).

7. William Callahan, "Press Release" (Hyattsville, MD: QCA, Apr. 28, 1976).

8. Quixote Center Chronicles 1975–1985 (Hyattsville, MD: QCA), 3.

9. *The Inclusive Bible: An Egalitarian Translation* V–VII, ed. Joseph Dearborn (Hyattsville, MD: QCA, 2010).

10. *Rome Has Spoken: A Guide to Forgotten Papal Statements, and How They Have Changed through the Centuries*, ed. Maureen Fiedler and Linda Rabben (New York: Crossroad Publishing, 1998).

11. "The Impossible Dream," words by Joe Darion, music by Mitch Leigh (New York: Andrew Scott Music and Helena Music Company, 1965).

12. "Jesuits Threaten Dismissal of Bill Callahan," *Catholic New Times* (Hyattsville, MD: QCA, May 14, 1989), 2.

13. See www.spirituschristi.com (2010).

14. David Haldane, "Faithful, Yet Not Traditional Catholics," *Los Angeles Times* (June 4, 2006), B1.

15. Conversations between author and Denise Donato (1998–2002).

16. Roy Bourgeois's letter sent by WOC to its members and others (May 2009).

17. Mary Henold, *Feminist and Catholic: The Surprising History of the American Catholic Feminist Movement* (Chapel Hill: University of North Carolina Press, 2008), 360.

18. Pope John XXIII, *Pacem in Terris* (Vatican City, April 11, 1963), par. 9.

19. "Pope Paul [VI] on the Role of Women," *National Catholic News Service* (April 15, 1975), MUA Carton 9, Folder 41.

20. Christine Schenk quoting Robert Mickens in "Vatican Shows a New Openness to Women," *The Tablet, National Catholic Reporter* (Nov. 3, 2006): 19.

21. *Encyclopedia of Catholicism*, ed. Richard McBrien (San Francisco: Harper Publishers, 1995), 397.

22. The ban ignored Paul VI's earlier statement (1971) called *Communio et Progressio*: "If public opinion is to emerge in the proper manner, it is absolutely essential that there be freedom to express ideas and attitudes. In accordance with the express teaching of the Second Vatican Council, it is necessary, unequivocally, to declare that freedom of speech for individuals and groups must be permitted, so long as the common good and public morality be not endangered. In order that men may usefully cooperate and further improve the life of the community, there must be freedom to assess and compare differing views which seem to have weight and validity. Within this free interplay of opinion, there exists a process of give and take, of acceptance or rejection, of compromise or compilation. And within this same process, the more valid ideas can gain ground so that a consensus that will lead to common action becomes possible."

23. Francis T. Hurley, "Ordination of Women," *Catholic Commentary, Diocese of Anchorage* (Alaska, June 12, 1994): 2.

24. Joseph Ratzinger, "The Dignity of the Human Person," in H. Vorgrimler, *Commentary on the Documents of Vatican II*, 5 (New York: Herder and Herder, 1969), 116.

25. Gustave Weigel, SJ, private conversation with the author (Mercy High School, Baltimore, Jan. 1963).

26. "Synod of U.S. Bishops," *The Bulletin*, U.S. SJA newsletter (Sept. 1977): 11. MUA Carton 18, Folder 12.

27. William Ryan, "Churches Urged to Accord Women Full Right of Participation," United States Catholic Conference, press release (Washington, DC, April 28, 1972), old.usccb.org/seia/re3.pdf.

28. Rembert Weakland, *A Pilgrim in a Pilgrim Church: Memoirs of a Catholic Archbishop* (Grand Rapids, MI: William B. Eerdmans, 2009), 320.

29. *The Journey* 4, no. 2 (Summer 1973), MUA Series 2, Carton 3, Folder no. 2.

30. Carroll T. Dozier, *Woman, Intrepid and Loving* (Memphis, TN: Catholic Diocese, 1975).

31. George Cornell, "Bishops Pressed on Male Priesthood Issue," *Pittsburgh Post Gazette* (Nov. 18, 1978), MUA Carton 3, Folder 1.

32. Rembert Weakland, *op. cit.*, 239, 256, and 259.

33. Nat Hentoff, "I'm Finally Going to Be a Pastor," *New Yorker* (March 23, 1987), 63–65.

34. Phyllis Zagano, "Ecclesial Need for Ordained Female Clergy," Loyola College, Baltimore (March 24, 2004).

35. Howard Hubbard, as reported in the *Catholic Review* (Baltimore, May 10, 1989), A-5.

36. Kenneth Untener, "The Ordination of Women: Can the Horizons Widen?" *Worship Magazine* 65, no. 1 (St. John's Abbey, Minnesota, Jan. 1991): 50–59.

37. William A. Hughes, "The Future Church," *Focus on FutureChurch* (Cleveland, Ohio, Winter 1994): 1.

38. Conversation between author and RAPPORT members (Washington, DC, 1989).

39. Catharine A. Henningsen, "The *American Catholic* Talks with Bishop Raymond A. Lucker," Shedding Light on Church Teachings, www.womenpriests.org/teaching/lucker.asp (Jan./Feb. 2001).

40. *Focus on FutureChurch* (Cleveland, Ohio, Winter 1994).

41. RAPPORT archives, anonymous (Baltimore, Nov. 30, 1995).

42. Matthew H. Clark, "The Pastoral Exercise of Authority," *New Theology Review* 10, no. 3 (Aug. 1997): 6–17.

43. Arthur Jones, "Women React in Anger and Pain," *National Catholic Reporter* (June 17, 1994), 1.

44. Emily Holtel-Hoag, "A Report Card for the Catholic Bishops: Do They Make the Grade?" *EqualwRites* XVI, no. 1 (June–Aug. 2007): 7. See also www.womensjusticecoalition.org.

45. Mohler-Rice papers, "Parish Surveys" (Baltimore), folder unnumbered.

46. RAPPORT minutes (Baltimore, Nov. 1988).

47. Following the same principle, in this book the author has named as supportive of the ordination of women only those bishops and clergy who have spoken or written publicly in favor of it.

48. Staff interview of Charles Buswell, *The New World* (Chicago, Feb. 4, 1977).

49. Judith Brimberg, "Ordination of Women: Still a Live Issue," *Denver Post* (June 1, 1994), 9A.

Chapter Six

Centripetal Lines

International Influences on the U.S. Movement

The design element that emerged in the previous chapter was that of lines crossing, two elements going in opposite directions. Many clergy and hierarchy have felt conflicted in themselves over the issue of women's ordination because they feel pulled between fidelity both to church law in one direction and to the search for wisdom in another direction. There are also examples in those pages of individuals whose decisions to act from one of those two positions resulted in conflict between themselves and another person or group. And lastly, even the broadly phrased formal teachings of the church since the early twentieth century have seemed to be in conflict with the church practices during the same time.

In exploring the role of international influences on the Catholic women's ordination movement in the United States, a centripetal design suggests itself: energy flowing from many sites around the world toward the United States. From Australia, Bangladesh, Brazil, Canada, the Czech Republic, India, Ireland, Japan, Turkey, Uganda, and points in between, individuals and groups have acted and spoken and written for decades in support of ordaining Roman Catholic women. Each time this has happened the U.S. Catholic Church has felt some impact, as has the church around the globe. Thus it would be shortsighted of the movement's supporters (and detractors) to ignore the documentable pioneering roles played by like-minded individuals and organizations throughout the world. Many opponents of women's ordination have dismissed the notion as a U.S. phenomenon among "uppity" white Catholic women of means (and of a certain age), yet exploration of the facts uncovers the breadth and depth of the global Catholic women's ordination movement.

EARLY MEDITERRANEAN CHRISTIANITY

The scriptural basis for Christian church teachings on any subject is often shaky, due to the wandering mind and hand of manuscript copiers, the physical condition of the source manuscript, and the translation challenges inherent in pronunciation, grammar, and meaning, especially with texts that are centuries old. In our own day we experience the challenge in a very modest way when reading materials written in British English ("lift" and "bonnet" are two simple examples) or even English as used in different parts of the United States or in different eras. Not all words or usages mean the same thing across the lines of geography, class, race, age, and time, even words in our own language. In the case of ancient texts, there have also been occasional deliberate alterations from the earlier text at hand (changing originally female names to male names, for example, or omitting the name of a woman who had an equal role to the man mentioned) in order to reflect the copier's or the community's biases.

Though trite, the truism is valid that "one picture is worth a thousand words." Verifiable pictures and visual symbols can often reveal the inaccuracies and gaps in some ancient texts, whether religious or secular. Hence there is great significance to the archaeological and epigraphic evidence from the Christian communities of AD 125 to AD 820 uncovered by Dorothy Irvin in her scholarly onsite archaeological studies since 1966. Irvin has identified many early sites surrounding the Mediterranean Sea in which women functioned as ordained deacons, priests, and bishops.[1] Some of the visual clues to one's state of life emerge in the universally accepted professional conventions of any active field archaeologist: the subject's clothing, hairdo, colors, and surrounding symbols, as well as activities depicted, animal symbolism, and placement of visual elements. Using these interpretive tools of her trade, along with scientific methods of dating, accurate photo reproductions, and knowledge of Mediterranean cultures and languages, Dorothy Irvin has collected and disseminated considerable evidence of what were once rather common practices in Christianity.

Gravestone inscriptions, representational frescoes, and symbolic art in churches and catacombs near the Mediterranean indicate some of the Christian communities that ordained women in Lyon (France), Amay (Belgium), Salona and Cappadocia (Croatia), Umbria-Rome-Naples-Tropea (Italy), Centuripe (Sicily), Hippo (Algeria), Corinth and Thera (Greece), Cilicia (Turkey), Ephesus-Constantinople-Iconium (Turkey), Moab (Jordan), Jerusalem, and Alexandria (Egypt). The women from those areas who are pictured and described were named Chrodoara, Maria Venerabilis, Flavia Vitalia, Olympias, Grata, Aleksandra, Leta, Vitalia, Maria, Timothea, Basilissa, Phoebe, Giuilia Runa, Kale, Epikto, Maria, Sophia, Apollonia, Artemidora, and Theodora. Though knowledge of these women and their ordaining communities emerged only in the twentieth century, they are the earliest known women to have been ordained in the Christian tradition, and a growing number of Catholics have become aware of them.[2] They are, indeed, the earliest international influences on the U.S. ordination movement.

Shortly after Irvin first published her archaeological findings in 1980, in 1982 Giorgio Otranto approached the ordination issue from the perspective of original Latin documents of early Christianity, especially a letter written by Pope Gelasius I: "In sum, we may infer from an analysis of Gelasius' epistle that at the end of the fifth century, some women, having been ordained by bishops, were exercising a true and proper ministerial priesthood in a vast area of southern Italy."[3] Because Otranto wrote the article in the Italian language from Latin documents and for academicians of Christianity's very early history, it did not have broad readership at first. Scholars received it with esteem, but the wider world was unaware of it. Almost a decade later another widely published Latin scholar who is also fluent in Italian, Mary Ann Rossi, translated Otranto's article into English in 1991 and brought it to public awareness. This attention resulted in a lecture tour of the United States sponsored by the Catholic University of America, Gordon-Conwell Seminary, and others.[4] On November 8, 1992, the BBC's *Everyman Programme* featured a relatively lengthy interview with Rossi called "Women's Ordination: The Hidden Treasure," presenting what Rossi had found in Otranto's original work and describing her own subsequent research. Because of the international accessibility of television, the interview gained widespread recognition, and the ministering women of antiquity moved into a very contemporary spotlight.

EARLY INFLUENCE FROM FRANCE

As mentioned in chapter 1, the French Revolution (1789–1799) led to an unforeseen result: that of women as women pursuing *egalité* across a broad spectrum of issues, including church-related matters. Though the Roman Catholic Church had been deposed by the citizens from its power in civil society, its adherents merely went underground for a time and then re-emerged in the nineteenth century as a somewhat chastened entity. Seeds of a "women's revolution" had been sown, and the nineteenth century saw the flowering of some of those seeds in unlikely places. Social changes of the day squeezed under the doors and into the windows and over the solid walls of family dwellings and even into the gardens of cloistered monasteries of women.

While the effects of the French Revolution may seem unrelated to "the role of women in the Church" as that phrase is used today, one unlikely nineteenth-century French woman, Thérèse Martin, has acquired an influence within the women's ordination movement that would have surprised her greatly. Born in 1873, she became a Carmelite nun at age fifteen after personally going to the pope with her father in order to plead for exemption from the minimum-age rule that prevented her from entering Carmel immediately. Her audacity worked. During her few years as a nun, her spirituality was characterized by simplicity and child-like trust in God, which she called "the little way." In 1897, when dying of tuberculosis, she remarked that she would be pleased to die that year because she had always wanted to be a priest and would be of ordination age at her death. It seems that she looked upon her death as a type of ordination. That attributed sentiment was reinforced when her sister, Céline Martin, stated under oath at Thérèse's beatification process in Rome: "The sacrifice of not being able to be a priest was something she always felt very deeply."[5] Because of the overwhelming, worldwide spiritual devotion to her that sprang up after her death, as well as the miraculous events attributed to her and the value of her spiritual writings, Thérèse Martin of Lisieux was canonized in 1925. In 1944, Pope Pius XI named her "co-patron of France" along with Joan of Arc: the cloistered nun of the little way walking alongside the warrior woman.[6] Pope John Paul II named her a "Doctor of the Church" in 1997 thus wedding the unsophisticated, concrete, "little way" with the abstract writings of the other "Doctors of the Church."

Coincidentally, Thérèse Martin's lifespan (1873–1897) closely overlapped with the French anticlericalist movement, "one of the most significant political issues in French politics between 1870 and 1914." Fifty years later, after the waning of the most virulent forms of that issue, scholars began to notice that "one of the anticlericalists' most serious allegations was that the Church oppressed women." This, they contended, was accomplished through conscience-formation done in the confessionals and through the predominance of schools run by communities of women religious: "Without the secularization of girls' education, women were doomed to remain the slaves of the Church."[7]

Some today feel that the conspicuous honor accorded Thérèse Martin by the popes and other clergy of that time is precisely a sign that she was considered by them to be "safe": a nonthreatening woman, the imitation of whom would keep Catholic women humble, passive, and out of the spotlight. Little did Catholic officialdom know that Thérèse's stated desire to be a priest would propel her into the role of a patron of women's ordination. Many individuals and groups invoke her for this radical cause precisely because the church with which they seek dialogue perceives her to be safe. Since the nonthreatening Thérèse wanted to be a priest, and is admired by both sides of the tension, the women hope that there can be a start to reconciling the opposing points of view.

ACROSS THE CHANNEL: ENGLAND

In London, May Kendall and Gabrielle Jeffery engaged in a physically strenuous and dangerous social revolution, earning universal suffrage for women.
The two then turned their attention to the Roman Catholic Church and the
matter of women's ordination. Their founding and leadership of the Catholic
Women's Suffrage Society (later known as the St. Joan's Alliance) in 1911
was an echo of their French predecessors' motivation over a century earlier
as, once again, a specific revolution in secular society led to the pursuit of a
related revolution in the religious realm. As was the case with very many
organizations for reform throughout the world, the alliance members necessarily redirected their energies to different pursuits during World War I and
World War II. The years of armed conflict on their own soil were followed
by periods of intense focus on rebuilding the lives of individuals and the
nation. Church reform was not the main concern of the day.

Having survived the physical, emotional, spiritual, and economic fallout
from two world wars, or perhaps because of this, the St. Joan's Alliance
became a seedbed of theologians seeking to develop an academically responsible approach to the neuralgic issue of ordaining women. One of the most
richly complex international leaders in the cause of women's ordination was
Joan Morris. "Bridging" is the clearest metaphor for what she accomplished
in her lifespan. She was born in England in 1901, ten years before the formal
emergence of the women's ordination issue; and she died in 1988, when the
movement had taken root around the globe. Morris spent her earliest professional years in the study and production of visual arts, which eventually led
her to the formal study of liturgical art, to publishing in that field, and to
designing and painting religious spaces. Along the way she met the UK
branch of the St. Joan's Alliance and became an energetically productive and
creative member.

Subsequently, Joan Morris moved temporarily to the United States to earn
(in 1954) a master of arts degree in liturgical studies at the University of
Notre Dame and spent ten years there in various related pursuits as lecturer,
journalist, film producer, and theologian. After the 1973 publication of *The
Lady Was a Bishop*, she returned to the United States for a book tour at
several Catholic colleges. Accompanied on the tour by Mary Lynch, she
enthusiastically responded to Lynch's description of Jeanne Barnes's newly
founded Deaconess Movement (see chapter 1). Through Lynch, too, she
became connected to Leonard Swidler's Philadelphia Task Force on Women
in Religion (which later morphed into SEPA-WOC), even to the extent of
contributing financially to the seminary education of one Sister Francesca
and to "Jeanne Barnes in her organization for the Diaconate Movement."[8]

In addition to earlier publications on church art, Joan Morris produced
several articles and books focusing on the medieval evidence of women's

authority roles in the Catholic Church: "Women and Episcopal Power" appeared in *New Blackfriars* (1972), followed by *The Lady Was a Bishop* (1973) and *Pope John VII: An English Woman* (1985). Of the three, it is the last mentioned that has caught the most widespread and enduring interest of the "people in the pews." A frequently heard question after a presentation on women's ordination is not "What about the theology underlying the issue?" but "Have you ever heard of Pope Joan?" Though the legend of a female pope may be spurious, there is no denying the very real impact it has on the contemporary imagination. To lead others to imagine a different way of seeing is a great contribution of a scholar, and Joan Morris is among those who have succeeded at the task.

Of this human bridge between the UK and U.S. branches of the St. Joan's Alliance, between the early ordination movement and the later one, and among church history and theology and art, Morris's peers in the St. Joan's Alliance wrote after her death:

> Her longstanding membership and leadership of the St. Joan's International Alliance have been responsible for its ongoing vitality. She has bonded it together by her long years of editorship of *The Catholic Christian*, until in 1986 ill health forced her to resign. Joan was a militant feminist, but one who stayed firmly within the Church, and who saw the ordination of women as an important objective. [9]

Joan Morris spanned yet another chasm, perhaps the widest one of all: militant feminism and the Roman Catholic Church.

THE NETHERLANDS

Ten years after the St. Joan's Alliance was established in England, an organization called The Grail arose in the Netherlands in 1921, flowing from the insight of Jacques van Ginneken, SJ. It was his belief that women, especially well-educated women, had never been allowed to influence society or the church in proportion to their great skills, and he inspired the female students at the Catholic University of Nijmegen to organize to change that reality. In this they were forty years ahead of the so-called women's liberation wave that began to animate Western nations in the 1960s, and The Grail ideology spread to Great Britain, Australia, and Germany. As near-neighbors of Germany, however, their activity was dramatically restricted at the rising of the aggressively encroaching regime to their east. In 1940, two leaders of the movement left the Netherlands for the United States only steps ahead of the enemy, and relocated their worldwide educational and community center in a rural area of Ohio. Eventually, there sprang up across the United States nine

Grail centers (reduced by 2010 to three); and by 1998, there were sites in seventeen countries around the globe. [10]

While the elusive Grail of literature and legend is an apt symbol for Catholic women's ordination, that issue has not been the primary focus of the organization, for it has been true to the mission of the first group of Dutch students at Nijmegen in 1921: preparing single Catholic lay women to leaven society and church in a nontraditional living environment by means of extraordinary educational activities, opportunities for serious spiritual development, and commitment to service of the human community. Because of its origins in a Catholic milieu, the spirit and mission of The Grail was imbued with that particular culture for several decades. Indeed, in 1972 the Ohio center held a workshop titled "Women Doing Theology" and led by Elizabeth Schüssler Fiorenza, one of her earliest and most significant appearances outside formal academia. The workshop has been called "one of the birthplaces of feminist theology." The Grail does not focus on the women's ordination issue but has provided high-quality theological and sociological programs, retreats, publications, and experiences of prayer in a nontraditional environment that inescapably has led many of its members to question the church's policies for themselves. [11] In more recent times, changes in The Grail reflect society's changing understanding of religious commitment, of interfaith and ecumenical life, and of community.

SWITZERLAND

Because of church regulations prohibiting women from earning graduate degrees in Catholic theology, Gertrud Heinzelmann instead regretfully chose to earn a doctorate in law and politics at the University of Zurich, completing her work there in 1943. Her path back to theology came precisely through her work in the fields of civil law and politics, as the content of her work forced her to face the "general absence of political rights for Swiss women"— including the right to vote. [12] In devoting her professional work to the civil rights of women in Switzerland, the similarity of women's situation in the Catholic Church became evident to her, just as it had in the lives of May Kendall and Gabrielle Jeffery several decades earlier when they established the St. Joan's Alliance. Gertrud Heinzelmann, an active member of St. Joan's, saw the patterns and acted on her convictions.

Consequently, when Pope John XXIII called for all Catholics to engage in the preparations for Vatican Council II, Heinzelmann wrote and published a paper and sent it to the Preparatory Commission of the council in 1962. In it she identified the ban against women's ordination as oppression, traced its roots in Thomas Aquinas and its fruits in canon law, and announced the necessity for women to be ordained to all the ranks of ministry. [13] Her national leadership in secular organizations working for women's suffrage, combined with her well-honed sense of political opportunity, allowed her to publish the Vatican-destined paper in the journal of the Zurich suffrage organization where it was widely disseminated. Heinzelmann's paper for the Preparatory Commission was thereby the first to publicly assert that the policy against women's ordination must change.

Just as Giorgio Otranto's work would not have become widely known without Mary Ann Rossi's translation and further research, Gertrud Heinzelmann's significant contributions to the ordination movement would have been unknown in the United States were it not for Rosemary Lauer, then on the theology faculty of St. John's University in New York. In 1963 she wrote an article called "Women and the Church"[14] which included a supportive, lengthy summary of Heinzelmann's proposal paper, as well as Lauer's own insights tracing seemingly supportive statements of Pope Paul VI, Cardinal Leo Suenens, and Bishop Georges Hakim. The article appeared in *Commonweal Magazine* and was the first of its kind in the U.S. Catholic press: explicitly supportive of women's ordination and openly critical of the church regarding women in general.

Until the end of her life in 1999 Gertrud Heinzelmann continued to publish articles and books advocating the reform of church policies toward women. As her writings spread broadly from Germany throughout the world, they have stimulated, even to this day, tidal waves of others' writings concerning the topic. In her final article before death she asked, "How many generations of women must become old or must die before a real progress will take place, concerning women in the Roman Catholic Church?"[15]

GERMANY

Born and educated eighteen years after Gertrud Heinzelmann, Ida Raming experienced a somewhat improved academic environment in Europe: at least she was allowed to study Catholic theology and—not to be outdone by the clergy—she earned a doctorate in that field. Like Gertrud, Ida was born and raised in an observant Catholic family and cites happy instances of her religious and spiritual development, beginning with childhood play that imitated religious rituals and other pious practices. As an adult, Ida received energy for her education work with women from her membership in the St. Joan's Alliance, as had Gertrud for her legal work. In 1963, Ida and her colleague Iris Mueller advanced a theologically grounded proposal to the Vatican advocating women's ordination, just as Gertrud had done before them. Seven years later, Ida earned her doctoral degree from the University of Freiburg in 1970 with the dissertation topic "The Exclusion of Women from Priestly Office: God-Given Tradition, or Anti-woman Discrimination?"[16] Her very presence as a student in the theology department was pioneering, and the topic of her research was groundbreaking.

As Heinzelmann had done in the secular sphere, Raming and Mueller have done in the ecclesial arena: writing articles, lecturing, organizing, participating actively in events for Catholic women, and even founding one group: *Maria von Magdala.* In 1986, Raming contacted a small number of like-minded women in Aachen (Germany) and gradually led them to organize by 1987 and to officially register with the state by 1993. The original group grew in numbers, and the movement has spread throughout Germany. They have published two booklets covering such topics as "inclusive language, the ordination of women and the situation of women theologians in the Catholic theological faculties of Germany."[17] They function in Germany similarly to WOC in the United States with a very high priority being theological education, though WOC tends toward theologically grounded public activism.

"Vocational homelessness" is the term Ida Raming has used over the years to describe the result of ecclesial and social obstacles to her developing professorial career and to her deepening call to the ordained priesthood. Echoes of Mary Lynch's hunger for ordination and/or a nontraditional living community resonate in Ida's early adulthood. And, like Lynch with Aileen Murphy, Raming found new energy with a colleague and close friend, theologian Iris Mueller. She also found, in Iris, a certain new perspective as Mueller (deceased 2011) was a theologian who had been educated in an Evangelical Lutheran tradition where women have been ordained. Despite knowing that she would lose this possibility, Iris had converted to Roman Catholicism. As well, Iris had completed her doctoral course work in 1970 with Ida. One can imagine the heat and light of their lively conversations on matters theological.

Later, the relative ease of improved travel brought Raming and Mueller to the attention of the U.S. public, as the Quixote Center and WOC sponsored their lecture tour in 1995 and made sure that there was abundant coverage of it in the secular press. Seven years later, the worldwide media surrounded them as they were ordained priests in June 2002 in the first Roman Catholic Women Priests (RCWP) ordinations. Raming had become an accomplished and highly regarded theologian who matched her beliefs with her action, which led her to pursue an unorthodox ordination. The following December, Raming, Mueller, and the five other women ordained with them were excommunicated by the Vatican.

ROMANIA

Romania might garner a small part of the credit for Elizabeth Schüssler Fiorenza's contributions to the theology of women's ordination, as she was born there in 1938. However, at a very young age she fled with her parents to West Germany to escape World War II. There she later (1963) earned a licentiate (master's degree) in the standard seminary courses of theology at the University of Wurtzburg. Her master's thesis posited a new model for the Catholic Church, a model in which women and men would function as equal partners in all arenas. It was published in 1964 as *The Forgotten Partner* while she was working toward her doctorate in biblical and early Christianity at Wilhelms-Universität, Münster. In 1971, she emigrated from Germany to the United States where she has taught at the University of Notre Dame, Episcopal Divinity School, and Harvard Divinity School. There and in national and international settings, Schüssler Fiorenza has consistently challenged the women's movement in the church to work toward a church which would be a "discipleship of equals." This focus, it must be admitted, begs the question of why ordination is necessary at all.

BELGIUM

On Easter Sunday in 1972 two women religious in Belgium founded a small organization they called the *Amicale des Femmes Aspirant au Ministère Presbyteral* (AFAMP). Valentine Buisseret, SB (Belgium), and Beatrix Dagras, OP (France), served the movement for women's ordination out of a desire to find kindred spirits to feed and be fed by.[18] As a simple strategy, they developed a mailing list of like-minded friends which grew until it reached all the way across the Atlantic to Mary Lynch. The newsletter of the *Amicale* came out regularly and included lengthy stories from all over the world of individual Catholic women's calls to ordained priestly ministry. It also publicized upcoming relevant events in other countries. Lynch eventually met the organization and its founders in person during a trip to Europe for work in Rome at the bishops' synod. She came back home heartened by their zeal and friendship, and eager to integrate some of their AFAMP practices into the U.S. Deaconess Movement. Lynch even changed the name of the latter to the Association of Women Aspiring to Priestly Ministry, which reflected the U.S. women's shifting focus from pursuit of solely the diaconate to work toward the priesthood.

OTHER INTERNATIONAL VOICES

In addition to the pioneering international theologians described above, there have been well-known male clergy and hierarchy around the globe who have supported the ordination of women in their writings and teaching. Most avoided mentioning the phrase "women's ordination" but came at the issue indirectly. Their contributions were in the realm of the theoretical and were valuable worldwide in providing a comprehensive framework for serious discussion of the issue.

Some of these theologians, however, raised the topic head-on and early, such as Haye Van der Meer, SJ, at the University of Innsbruck (Austria) who (like Raming and Schüssler Fiorenza) wrote his doctoral dissertation on the subject in 1962 with Karl Rahner, SJ, as his advisor: "Theological Reflections on the Thesis: The Male Alone Is Fit for Ordination." Van der Meer's conclusion was that there is no proof in the Scripture that ordaining women is allowable and that there is also no proof nor acceptable scriptural basis against it. Long after its completion, in 1974 Arlene Anderson Swidler translated the dissertation into English and disseminated it as *Women Priests in the Catholic Church*. The year after Van der Meer's dissertation was completed in Innsbruck, Jose Idigoras, SJ, at the Catholic University in Peru successfully completed his doctoral dissertation "Woman in Relation to Holy Orders."

During the 1967 Congress of the Laity and the 1971 International Synod of Bishops in Rome, members of the St. Joan's Alliance who were following both events perceived the following international bishops and cardinals to be supportive of "women's issues": Samuel E. Carter (Jamaica), Roger M. Etchagaray (France), George B. Flahiff (Canada), John W. Gran (Norway), George Hakim (Israel), Gabriel A. F. Marty (France), Guy M. Riobe (France), and Valfredo B. Tepe (Brazil), along with Theodore Van Asten (Tanzania) who was the superior general of the White Fathers. At the same time, one of the German St. Joan's members surveyed the twenty-two bishops in her country and reported that eleven of them were in favor of women's ordination to the diaconate.[19] "At this same synod, the Canadian bishops presented an unexpected resolution declaring their support for women's rights. Subsequently, both the NCCB and the Vatican established committees on women's changing roles in church and society. A few years later the conference of Indian bishops approved the concept of ordaining women, and some decades later the Australian bishops' conference did the same.[20]

A German bishop particularly known as "an advocate for women," Ernst J. Gutting, was a product of the University of Tübingen (as were Irvin and the Swidlers). The press release on Gutting's ninetieth birthday noted the 1987 publication of his book *An Offensive against Patriarchy*, which, among other acts of his, strengthened his reputation as "a feminist bishop." His episcopal motto, "Only love counts," reveals an unusual and attractive approach to his hierarchical role. Consistently since the 1970s, Remi de Roo, bishop of Victoria, British Columbia, has spoken out in favor of women's ordination as an issue of justice and of necessity for the life of the church. Another Canadian bishop, Maurice Couture, RSV, took his cue from his diocese's laity at their synod in 1995: They passed a resolution demanding that the pope be asked "to re-examine the issue" of women's ordination, and Couture announced that he considered it his responsibility to not only take it to the pope but to discuss it with other Canadian bishops.[21] A few years later, Ernest Kombo, SJ, bishop in the Republic of Congo, formally urged the bishops' synod to "make women religious lay cardinals" and in 1998 publicly advocated the ordination of women.[22]

Interspersed with the public and official statements of bishops, cardinals, and theologians, one finds individuals' cheering personal statements that have indicated support of women's ordination. In 1976 Mary Lynch received the following note from Msgr. G. Thils who was a professor at the University of Leuven in Belgium: "Dear friend Mary Lynch, I was delighted to receive your letter. I cannot say what a precious strength it is to know that yourself and several American women agree with us in pursuing the ordained ministry."[23] At a later date, the mailbox contained a creative gesture from Bishop Louis LaRavoie-Morrow of India: enclosed was a prayer tract he had written to Thérèse of Lisieux for the ordination of women, and he asked that Lynch circulate it worldwide.[24] Some thirty years later, Morrow's successors in the Indian episcopacy decided at their biennial plenary session to reserve for women 35 percent of the positions in church structures of all types.[25]

Some years later in 2001, Giuseppe Casale, a retired Italian bishop, joined two colleagues in promoting the full inclusion of lay women and men in the College of Cardinals, which includes selection of the pope among its responsibilities. The theologian speaking with him, Caterina Iacobelli, noted that what is needed is "a global re-thinking of the ordained ministry, priesthood included. . . . a reformed ministry, open to men and women, providing real ministry to people, rather than being a privileged caste."[26] Two years later the international press picked up the story of one of the cardinals who has spoken repeatedly on the ordination subject, Belgian Godfried Daneels. During a public interview[27] Daneels noted, "Two of my substitutes [in my work] are women. I therefore cannot see why a woman could not lead a Catholic congregation. Today the power structure within the church is male, but it does not necessarily have to remain that way."

In recent years, one man has made a worldwide impact on those who seek to understand the women's ordination movement: Johannes Wijngaards of the Netherlands. Born in 1935, he was ordained a Mill Hill missionary priest in 1959 and strode along the usual path for those deemed by his superiors to be "most likely to succeed." He was sent to Rome for his doctorate (licentiate) in biblical studies and returned to a prodigious and prolific career in theological writing and teaching, being eventually elected to serve his international community of men as vicar general.

The topics of Wijngaards's books and articles have been primarily in Scripture and in ministry; and with his 1997 book *Did Christ Rule Out Women Priests?* he emerged as one of the theologians doing serious research on women's ordination. Among his more than twenty published books are at least four on that topic. Eventually, because of his deep conviction that the Catholic Church must allow genuine dialogue on this and many other policies, he left the Mill Hill community, resigned from the priesthood in 1998, and married. "I saw colleagues being forced to swear oath to things they don't believe in and I decided enough is enough. I couldn't represent an institution that was telling people they couldn't be part of the church if they believed in ordaining women."[28] But that is far from the end of his story.

Riding the wave of the earliest days of popular computer usage, Wijngaards had the foresight to move his in-person teaching career to the Internet in 1999. In ten short years John Wijngaards's website grew immensely, providing four thousand relevant documents in sixteen languages (including Japanese, Korean, and Malay), which can be downloaded or studied online. The documents cover relevant theological writings both ancient and modern, history, influential persons, organizations around the globe, and ongoing developments. He has retained professional visual designers and illustrators throughout; use of the site is ever-increasing, and in the early years of the twenty-first century[29] there were over five hundred thousand visits annually and millions of pages downloaded. At the outset, John Wijngaards announced, "I aim at making this the fairest, most complete, most detailed, academically tested and interactive site on the ordination of women." It was an ambitious goal, and by achieving it, he has had immeasurable influence on the ordination movement far beyond the Netherlands.

Related closely to the U.S. movement in time and in geography is the experience of Edward Cachia, pastor of St. Michael's Parish in Ontario, Canada. When publicly asked if he supported the Ottawa RCWP ordination of women in 2005, he indicated in the affirmative and was quickly penalized for that statement and was obliged by his bishop to take a one-month leave from the parish "to pray and reflect and then retract his comments."[30] After the month away, he was permanently removed from his parish and from the priesthood and was excommunicated. The haste and severity of his punishment seemed, to many, to be disproportionate and received wide coverage in the U.S. media.

ITALY

This episode in Cachia's life is but a single example of the Vatican's commitment to keep its teaching authority intact around the globe. A local bishop interpreted the church teaching and applied it to the particular circumstance, aware that the penalty would not be considered excessive by his superiors. Earlier chapters of this book describe similar disciplinary actions of other bishops and of papal documents banning not only the actual ordination of women but even the discussion of it. In this respect, the Vatican itself has been and is currently a major negative international influence on the U.S. women's ordination movement. On the other hand, all the surveys and studies of those U.S. women seeking ordination reveal that it is precisely their deep devotion to the Roman Catholic Church that motivates hundreds upon hundreds of them to remain in a profoundly conflicted situation: being qualified, being desirous, and being rejected. The strength of their commitment to the Roman Catholic Church cannot be denied, and in that respect, too, the Vatican can be called a positive international influence on the movement. In addition, tracking done by the Quixote Center and by WOC indicates that there is an increase in the number of women's ordination supporters following each punitive episode or sexist statement from members of the hierarchy. So in that respect, too, the Vatican can be called a contributor to the movement.

THE CZECH REPUBLIC/CZECHOSLOVAKIA

Before the experiences in the underground church of then-Czechoslovakia could be said to have an influence on the ordination movement in the United States, they had to be dug out delicately, heard respectfully, and captured in writing accurately. A secular culture of mistrust and secrecy developed over the decades of war and repressive regimes and was necessarily a part of the church, as well, in that country. In times of danger and persecution, habits of hiding one's activities and beliefs become necessary for survival and are difficult to shed long after the time of peril has passed. Given those painful realities, it is remarkable that the story of Felix Maria Davidek, Ludmila Javorova, and the underground church have emerged at all. What is just as remarkable in this process is the entwined involvement of dozens of persons and organizations already mentioned in these pages: the Second Vatican Council, Pope Paul VI, the Quixote Center, Dolly Pomerleau, Maureen Fiedler, WOC, Ruth Fitzpatrick, Andrea Johnson, Bishops P. Francis Murphy and Raymond Lucker, and RAPPORT members.

Ordained a priest in 1945, Felix Davidek had been perceived in the Brno diocesan seminary as a questioning nonconformist, convinced that the Catholic Church had long estranged itself from its original mission and ministry to the world. For seven years he fulfilled routine assignments to two successive rural parishes, but his intellectual and ministerial energy outstripped the parish work expected of him. So during those same years Davidek also completed medical studies, was licensed for medical practice, and earned a doctorate in psychology. His theological reflections, along with his pursuit of the medical profession, reveal that he believed the authentic priest to be "a worker priest," which was a popular concept lived out by many French priests in the 1940s. Worker priests earn their living by something other than church ministry, immersing themselves in the world's workplaces and doing explicitly church ministry only on the side. Though that ministerial model has not become a major trend in the U.S. Church, there are many ordained priests here and around the globe who, because of various factors, do fit the early definition of a "worker priest." The non-churchly work of many priests is exercised even in the most conventional of ministries: among them are professors, accountants, businessmen, engineers, farmers, and lawyers. Some of them work for Catholic institutions, and some for a "secular" employer, but their main work is performed outside the ecclesial context.

Because of the Russian occupation of 1948 and the imposition of a particularly rigid communism, the schools and universities in Czechoslovakia deteriorated quickly, which stoked Davidek's creativity. His dream was to improve society by improving the quality of education, and so he opened a small underground university (the Catholic Atheneum of Chrlice) for that purpose, including theology courses as a substitute for the government-controlled seminary system. In 1950 the authorities imprisoned him as a person subversive to the welfare of the state. Subsequently Davidek served fourteen years in prison, during which time he applied his lifelong intensity to updating his own theology, devouring the Vatican II preparation documents, and secretly discussing their new theology with his fellow prisoners. Based on these teachings, he developed a detailed model for the future church of his diocese, in the form of small faith communities. Upon his release from prison, the birthing and strengthening of these groups (collectively called *Koinotes*) was his pastoral passion; and in 1967, he sent one of the *Koinotes* priests to Germany to be legitimately ordained as a bishop. The priest, Jan Blaha, then returned to Brno, ordained Felix Davidek as a bishop, and both their episcopal ordinations were eventually recognized by Pope Paul VI.[31]

Turn now to Ludmila Javorova, for the rest of the story. Her family and Davidek's had been very close friends since her childhood, with her father—a well-educated and pious man—serving as a mentor to Felix. Originally planning to enter a religious community, Ludmila was thwarted by the political and ecclesial upheavals of the time and place. Her studies and personal inclinations led her to the education of children, and yet she continually fed her contemplative side. Equally intense in her commitment to a new church vision as Davidek, she was a leader in the egalitarian Catholic community that he had founded and eventually took up the responsibility of serving as its vicar general. The bishop planned to hold a synod of the *Koinotes* members (laity and clergy alike) in December 1970, focusing particularly on the role of women in church and society. Part of the agenda was the discernment of whether they should begin to ordain women, and upon that point there was inalterable division among the participants. Half of them walked out of the discussion. Those who stayed did so for two reasons: deep conviction about the Vatican II vision of equality in the church and the serious need to find sacramental ministers for the hundreds of women in prison. If women were priests, their sacramental purposes could be disguised when visiting women prisoners, whereas men were not even allowed to visit them. The pastoral need and the principle of equality convinced Davidek to go ahead immediately with ordaining some theologically prepared women to the priesthood and some to the diaconate. Ludmila Javorova was ordained a priest on December 28, 1970, with Felix Davidek's brother, Leo, as witness.

Sometime after the fall of communism in the country (1991), the Vatican began to review the secret ordinations and to invite the male married priests to apply for "re-ordination" to the diaconate only. Several, including Javorova's brother, Josef, did accept that arrangement and functioned as deacon for several years. The female deacons and priests were ignored, and Ludmila, for one, was explicitly forbidden in writing by the Vatican to act upon her ordination or to discuss the letter with anyone. She has continued to observe both prohibitions for decades and has taught in religious education programs for her parish and the Diocese of Brno in the Czech Republic.

For several decades after his death, the work Felix Davidek had done to preserve and vivify the Catholic Church in Czechoslovakia was dismissed as that of a mentally unbalanced man and was not taken seriously. However, Ondrej Liska's history of the underground church appeared in January 2003, containing a positive, appreciative tone in prefaces[32] written by Cardinals Miloslav Vlk and Karl Lehmann.

The impact of Bishop Davidek's decisions on the U.S. ordination movement is due to the collaboration of many. A member (anonymous) of RAPPORT happened upon a brief article in the *New York Times* of August 10, 1991, and took a copy of it to the next RAPPORT meeting in November 1991. It stated that a Bishop Felix M. Davidek had ordained a woman, Ludmila Javorova, to the priesthood in the Roman Catholic Church. Ruth Fitzpatrick, at that time a member of RAPPORT, as well as the national director of WOC, put actions to words and, together with Dolly Pomerleau of the Quixote Center, effected a 1992 visit to Javorova in the Czech Republic. After a few more visits from Dolly; Ruth; Carolyn Moynihan; Maureen Fiedler, SL; Martha Ann Kirk, CCVI; and Andrea Johnson, Ludmila hesitantly agreed to do a lecture tour in the United States in 1997. She brought with her Magdalena Zahorska, who was an ordained deacon and friend, and brought Magdalena's sister, who had been one of the underground church leaders. Pomerleau had arranged for a Czech translator at each location on the tour, so Javorova spent one of her days with RAPPPORT in Washington, DC, and that evening at the Quixote Center in Maryland. During the earlier part of that day, the RAPPORT members dialogued privately with her and three U.S. bishops, among whom were P. Francis Murphy, Raymond Lucker, and one bishop who must remain unnamed.

After her return to the Czech Republic, Ludmila agreed to Pomerleau's urging that she write her autobiography. With Miriam Therese Winter, MMS, as Ludmila's "scribe," and Pomerleau as her agent and funding coordinator, *Out of the Depths* appeared in the United States in 2001 and garnered the Catholic Press Association's top honor in the 2002 category "Popular Presentation of the Catholic Faith." As the details of her ordained ministry became widely known in the United States, Ludmila Javorova became an icon, of sorts, for many in the ordination movement. Testifying to that fact were over 1,700 signers of a letter of support for her that challenged the Vatican to recognize her priesthood and that of the several other women and married men who had been ordained in similar circumstances at the same time.[33]

BANGLADESH, BRAZIL, AND UGANDA

Though the 1992 groundbreaking field interviews, research, and writing of Francis B. O'Connor, CSC, were described in chapter 3 of this book, they deserve mention more than once and so reappear here under consideration of international influences on the U.S. women's ordination movement. As O'Connor herself has said: "In refutation of Rome's assumption that women's desire for full participation in the church is only a North American 'problem,' this book reveals the striking similarities between the experiences and the unfulfilled hopes of women on the four continents of Asia, Africa, South America and North America." Over time, Australia, Bangladesh, and Japan had developed "strong, alive" women's ordination movements active in Women's Ordination Worldwide (WOW) and other projects related to women in the Roman Catholic Church.

IRELAND

During the same year that O'Connor's work reflecting a global view was published, local and regional work was taking place in individual countries. In Ireland the group called itself, aptly enough, BASIC (Brothers and Sisters in Christ) and began their work in 1993 coordinated by Colm Holmes and

Soline Vatinel. BASIC burst upon the church reform scene with a written petition sent to each of Ireland's bishops "for all ministries and offices in the church to be equally open to both men and women, and for all sexist structures and regulations to be abolished."[34] The fact that twenty-two thousand individuals signed on to the petition indicated widespread support for women's ordination and energized the members to organize lectures and seminars, to publish periodic newsletters and the formal proceedings of its events, and to commission a now well-known painting representing an egalitarian image of the *Last Supper*. Eventually they accepted the invitation to organize and host in Dublin the first international conference of WOW. The unusual aspect of BASIC has been its own role as a model for collaboration among females and males, and laity and clergy, both in leadership and membership.

THE EUROPEAN SYNOD

At the same time that Catholics in Ireland were organizing BASIC, their counterparts in Austria were hard at work preparing for a landmark ecumenical synod of European women to be held in 1996 in Gmunden. There had been regional women's synods on the continent in the past, but the burgeoning of the secular "European community," the projected adoption of a common currency in 1999, and the vision of a continent without boundaries all called for an event that would incarnate in microcosm the surrounding secular movement toward unity. Thus the European Women's Synod was the first of its kind, and the unity underlying the diversity was strong. Among the 1,074 participants were non-European "observers" from such far-flung and unexpected nations as Australia, Egypt, Ghana, Kenya, the Philippines, the Republic of South Africa, South Korea, Surinam, Taiwan, Uganda, and the United States.[35] Plenary scholarly lectures, small group discussions, and special caucuses (e.g., the Roman Catholic women religious in attendance) addressed the four themes of the week: political life, economics, spirituality, and personal development. One full day dealt with each proposal that came from individuals and groups, resulting in a series of resolutions toward action. ("Observers," too, were given equal voting rights.) Coming to agreement as a diverse group of over one thousand made each resolution the more significant. In fact, the resolution calling for the Roman Catholic Church to allow women's ordination revealed the widespread feeling of insult and injustice of very many non-Catholic women in the face of this practice.

Another significant moment of consensus at Gmunden occurred during the caucus held for leaders of the ordination movement around the globe. When Andrea Johnson, then-executive director of WOC, formally proposed the establishment of a global umbrella organization, the consensus was immediate and its name emerged soon after: Women's Ordination Worldwide

(WOW). Upon its founding, Johnson was WOW's first international director and was succeeded in 1998 by Myra Poole, SND (UK). Subsequently, members of BASIC and *Wir Sind Kirche* (Austria) took separate, brief stints of leadership-service for WOW until 2001 when Marie Bouclin (Canada) accepted the invitation to serve as coordinator. Upon the ending of Bouclin's term, Jennifer Stark (UK) accepted the responsibility in 2006; and from June 2007, a leadership team of Colette Joyce, Erin Saiz Hanna, Saiorse Bann, and There Koturbase took office.

ALL NATIONS

After WOW developed its organizational structure, its leaders and members began plans for a worldwide conference on the ordination of women in the Catholic Church. They chose Dublin as the site because of the energy and skills of BASIC, whose leaders volunteered to host and coordinate the event. Had things gone only as planned, the gathering would still have merited a good deal of media coverage simply for what it was: the first large (over 345 participants) international meeting of Roman Catholics whose specific purpose was to openly advocate the ordination of women in the Roman Catholic Church, in opposition to the church's well-known official policy.[36] However, the Vatican's reaction to plans for the event guaranteed that the resulting publicity would only escalate public awareness of the issue and provide activists for women's ordination with unimagined opportunities to educate the public. Because the participants represented twenty-seven countries around the world, the news of the unforeseen crises spread broadly around the globe to local media outlets.

And what were the crises? They centered around three women with significant roles in the event: Aruna Gnanadason; Myra Poole, SND; and Joan Chittister, OSB. Each of them was told by the Vatican that her participation in the conference would have serious repercussions, even Gnanadason (India), who is not a Catholic. She is a theologian who has been head of the World Council of Churches (WCC) planning and administration division, and a Vatican representative informed the WCC that her participation would be offensive to the Vatican and perhaps would set back the cause of ecumenism. She complied and sent her written remarks to Dublin for another to read.

Myra Poole, SND (UK), a leader in WOW, had been the coordinator of the conference, and she learned six weeks beforehand that the Vatican had told her community administrator to expel her from the community if she insisted on attending the event. She stopped in for the international panel and briefly at other times. No action was taken against her by the community or the Vatican, and Poole, shortly after the Dublin conference, served as initial chair of WOW.

Joan Chittister, OSB (United States), an internationally known theologian and lecturer, was the most globally known of the three women, and her Benedictine prioress had been told to prevent Chittister from speaking at the conference. The prioress, the community, and Chittister worked together on how to respond to the Vatican, but the matter was not settled by the opening day. No subsequent action has yet been taken against her or her community by the Vatican.

The significance of these three cases resides in the fact that the Vatican experiences the discussion of women's ordination as seriously problematic and deserving of severe punitive threats. At the same time, the fact that each of the three was from a different part of the world illustrated that the issue is a global matter. To further drive home that fact, the editors of the conference's proceedings included an inventory of then-known organizations working on this aspect of church reform in Australia, Austria, Brazil, Canada, France, Germany, Hungary, India, Ireland, Japan, New Zealand, Portugal, South Africa, Spain, the United Kingdom, and the United States. In the years since then, additional groups have organized, as indicated on the WOW website.

Equally significant was the panel of international women which took place on the stage in Dublin. Apollonia Lugemna (Uganda), Naoko Iyori (Japan), Kornelia Buday (Hungary), and Yury Pueblo Orozco (Brazil) described the women's ordination movement as it had developed in their respective countries. Lugemna was particularly direct as she focused on the related questions that arise on this topic in her own culture and on the Vatican's responsibility to provide understandable answers. "Until ample explanations are given on [these] questions," she said, as if speaking to the hierarchy itself, "it will be very difficult for Catholic women leaders to discuss comfortably the equality of Catholic women in our church. I await your enrichment on this matter."[37]

To coordinate and host a conspicuously successful event was exhilarating and exhausting for the members of BASIC. By the time the event was accomplished and wrapped up, successive tidal waves of sexual abuse scandals in the 1990s washed over the Catholic Church in Ireland. For twenty exhausting years the demoralizing reports continued to emerge, and many longtime church reformers turned their energies to that crisis, or withdrew from the church in grief and anger, or muted their work in respect of the innumerable personal tragedies that engulfed the nation.

Meanwhile, Catholics in Austria were experiencing similar anger and disillusionment with the hierarchy concerning a pedophilia scandal in Vienna and elsewhere. They took their protests to the streets at home and at the Vatican, organizing into a broader church reform movement *Wir Sind Kirche* (We Are Church) in 1995. The concept of addressing multiple areas of needed reform appealed to many Catholics around the globe who learned of the movement on websites, in online discussion groups, and, of course, in the traditional media coverage of *Wir Sind Kirche* events and public statements. As a result, there are large and small groups around the globe who work toward the same goals as *Wir Sind Kirche* and call themselves by similar names.

During the early years of *Wir Sind Kirche*, two women in particular raised the issue of women's ordination as a necessary focus of the group: Christine Mayr-Lumetzberger (Austria) and Gisela Forster (Germany). They planned and implemented a three-year, individualized training program for interested women; they searched for and found a bishop (Argentina) willing to ordain the women; they ensured interviews of the candidates with the bishop; and they oversaw the committees established to actualize the ordination event. In June 2002 seven women were ordained in a large tour-boat on the Danube River near the city of Passau, Germany. The elements of this occasion deserve some elucidation because of its complexity and the worldwide attention it has garnered.

The women who were ordained on the boat came from Austria, Germany, and the United States: Pia Brunner, Dagmar Celeste, Gisela Forster, Christine Mayr-Lumetzberger, Iris Müller, Ida Raming, and Adelinde T. Roitinger. Most of them had completed some amount of standard theological study before entering the pre-ordination training program, which was geared to pastoral subject matters such as sacramental practices and homiletics—"applied theology," as it were. All of them were middle-aged white women with experience in the world of work; some were married, some single, and one was a vowed member of a Franciscan religious community.

The planners decided to situate the event on a boat between Germany and Austria as a tactic for muddying the waters regarding which (if any) diocese would have juridical authority over the event. The decision was pragmatic for another important reason: security and privacy are easier to maintain when away from eyesight and earshot on shore. Using a boat had its symbolic and poetic values as well, among them that one traditional name for the Catholic Church has been "the barque of Peter" and that water is the element associated with birth, as also with cleansing, with baptism, and with pleasant refreshment.

It was and it remains very important to the women ordained in RCWP that any bishop who would ordain the first group of them should be legitimate in the eyes of the Roman Catholic Church. They believe that they found such a man in the person of Romulo Antonio Braschi of Argentina,[38] and they describe him as being "in good standing with the Catholic Church." Others feel that the descriptor is misleading, in view of his own history as an ecclesial dissenter who in 1978 had publicly separated himself from the Vatican and is not accepted as a bishop by the pope. Still others[39] believe that too much weight has been placed on the lineage of an ordaining bishop because the line of succession from St. Peter has been murky, at best, in the whole of church history. That Braschi presided over the ordination ritual of the seven women is not disputed, but his relationship to the Roman Catholic Church is problematic for many: though legitimately ordained a priest, his ordination to the episcopacy in the Catholic Apostolic Charismatic Church which he founded seems separatist by self-definition. In fact, his automatic excommunication by the Vatican in 1978, well before the 2002 Danube ordinations, was noted in the preface to the women's excommunication document. It should be recalled here that there was no such ambiguity about the legitimacy of Felix Maria Davidek, the bishop who ordained Ludmila Javorova. He had been ordained to the episcopacy by Bishop Jan Blaha, whose legitimacy and good standing is uncontested.

Shortly after their ordinations to the priesthood, two of the women (Forster and Mayr-Lumetzberger) were ordained bishops by some male bishops whose names have not been revealed. Those two women and each of the other five ordained to the priesthood together on the Danube received "writs of excommunication" from the Vatican's Congregation for the Doctrine of the Faith. In May 2008, the congregation issued a decree that automatically excommunicated anyone involved in the ordination of women priests, applicable to those in the past.[40] It was not clear whether or not the same penalty would be incurred by the ordination of women deacons.

Despite the theological, canonical, and strategic questions raised by the ordinations, the RCWP movement has grown in both Europe and the United States. In 2003 the two women bishops ordained Patricia Fresen as priest and then bishop. In rapid succession she, Mayr-Lumetzberger, and Forster ordained women to the priesthood and diaconate semipublicly in groups or singly in Barcelona (2003); Ottawa (2005); Lyon (2005); Switzerland (2006); Pittsburgh (2006); Quebec (2007); Toronto (2007); New York City (2007); Santa Barbara, California (2007); Portland, Oregon (2007); Minneapolis, Minnesota (2007); Lexington, Kentucky (2008); Boston (2008); St. Louis (2007); and Sarasota, Florida (2010). In addition to these semipublic celebrations, Andrea Johnson has noted that there are eight male bishops "in good standing with the Roman Catholic Church" who have presided at private, secret, "catacomb ordinations" in various countries.

And what of the women's lives after ordination in the RCWP community? Their style is, by necessity, similar to that of "the worker priests" of France in the 1940s and of Felix Davidek in the 1960s. They cannot be hired by any Catholic-affiliated institution, parish, or agency, so most of the women support themselves financially by continuing in their previous paid position (social worker, counselor, lawyer, theologian, etc.). They make themselves known in reform-minded circles near them and build their own worship congregations, which meet as house-churches or in borrowed or rented worship space. At this moment, there are over seventy RCWP women or-

dained to the Catholic priesthood in the United States and over nine in
European countries. In the training process are women in Austria, Colombia,
Germany, Holland, Scotland, and the United Kingdom. Undeniably, the initial energy around this development came from Austria/Germany and has
proved contagious in the United States and elsewhere.

It must be noted, too, that some Roman Catholic women have been ordained in other ways and consider themselves to be thoroughly in the tradition of Roman Catholicism, for example: Mary Ramerman and Denise Donato (both in Rochester, New York) by the hands of Bishop Peter Hickman of
the Old Catholic Church; and Judith Heffernan (Philadelphia) by the affirma-
tion of the small local Community of the Christian Spirit. In addition, very
many Catholic women around the globe quietly function exactly as male
priests do, though in the "worker priest" model: leading the celebration of
sacraments, engaging in pastoral counseling, and addressing all other pastoral needs. In many an idle conversation among women in the movement there
has been recurring, informed speculation for some years that several of these
women have stayed "beneath the radar" and have been legitimately ordained
by local bishops under the justification of "desperate pastoral need" in their
area churches.

THE DIACONATE REVISITED

One of the first organizing principles around women's ordination in the U.S.
Roman Catholic Church was that ordination to the diaconate was a worthy
goal: toward that end Jeanne Barnes founded the first "home-grown" organization, the Deaconess Movement, in 1970. Three years later, Mary Lynch's
leadership broadened the focus to include ordination to the priesthood as well
as to the diaconate. Somehow, by inference the outlook developed that the
diaconate was a "lesser" option for women, and its pursuit fell by the way-
side in most of the relevant organizations. During those middle years there
were, however, a few consistent voices reminding the listener that every
mainline church that had the order of deacons had ordained women to that
order before ordaining them to the priesthood or full ministry of their tradition. The point was also made that to ignore that fact revealed an unrealistic
approach and doomed the Catholic movement to failure. Energy for organized work toward the ordained diaconate waned, but some women have
pressed on for what they perceive as their vocation.

Light from the East?

As time went on, with all their emphasis on ordination to the priesthood,
most U.S. Roman Catholics missed the fact that in October 2004, the Greek
Orthodox and the Armenian Apostolic Orthodox Churches quietly made the

decision to resume and/or revivify their practice of ordaining women to the diaconate. These decisions, made separately by the two churches, have inescapable implications for the Roman Catholic Church, flowing mainly from the fact that the Orthodox Churches and the Catholic Churches enjoy mutual recognition of each other's "apostolic succession" and validity of ordinations. For example, if a Roman Catholic priest wishes to become an Orthodox priest, he is not required to be re-ordained, and vice versa. In addition, they share an early history of ordaining women, accept the Bible as the foundation of their faith, have similar sacramental structures and formats, and have highly developed traditions of liturgical ritual. (They were, after all, one church until 1054.) Those points of connection might well be ignored, but for the fact that since Vatican II the Roman Catholic Church has specifically been trying to revive the relationship, engaging in dialogue with the Orthodox Church and exploring possibilities of a new future. But by the end of the pontificate of John Paul II, strain had crept back into the dialogue, with neither party willing to accept a position of subordination to the other.[41] Benedict XVI, however, decided early in his papacy that healing the divisions would be a priority for him. Since then, seemingly small steps on both sides have improved the atmosphere for future work together.

Those who consider the Eastern Orthodox decisions concerning women deacons to be a predictor of change in the Western Church note that the long-standing agreement of mutual recognition of the validity of one another's ordinations means that the Western Church might be expected to recognize and accept the Eastern rite women deacons as validly ordained. They also point out that the refusal to do so would conflict with the agreed-upon and long-standing acceptance of ordained Orthodox males. In view of that agreement, and in view of the Roman Catholic Church's own earlier history of ordaining women to the diaconate, a refusal to resume such ordinations would appear to be based solely on a belief that women are not equal to men.[42]

SUMMARY

The centripetal design of the women's ordination movement in the U.S. Catholic Church means that there have been streams of energy moving from around the globe into the thought and actions of American women and men. It was a design whose time had come, in terms of the ease of communication and travel among countries and cultures. Dorothy Irvin, Mary Lynch, Francis McGillicuddy, Francis Bernard O'Connor, Mary Ann Rossi, and Arlene Anderson Swidler and Leonard Swidler enjoyed lively international work even before the days of easy air travel and the Internet, crossing the Atlantic in person often enough to import news and insights from abroad. Fresen, Javorova, Morris, Mueller, and Raming traveled easily and rapidly to bring their respective energies to their U.S. supporters. Those in the U.S. movement traveled in the opposite direction to Austria, Bangladesh, Brazil, the Czech Republic, Germany, Ireland, and Uganda in order to learn and to return enlivened.

Relevant dissertations, articles, and books circulate ever more easily, to the point that in the early twenty-first century many materials can be studied on electronic readers and by way of the Internet. By the same means, news from everywhere on the globe is almost immediately available in word and picture from the comfort of home. John Wijngaards created a globally accessible (in technology and in language) library of thousands of relevant documents and links available at the touch of a button. There is no doubt that information on and awareness of the current status of the women's ordination issue continues to spread rapidly in both directions: from and to the United States.

NOTES

1. Dorothy Irvin, *Calendars of 2003–2007* (St. Paul, MN: privately published, 2007). View online at www.womenpriests.org. See also the introductory twenty-five-minute video of Irvin's presentation at www.godtalktv.org during a program hosted by Brigid Mary Meehan.

2. Dorothy Irvin, "The Ministry of Women in the Early Church: The Archaeological Evidence," *Duke Divinity School Review* 45 (1980): 76–86.

3. Giorgio Otranto, "Note sul sacerdozio femminile nell'antichità," *Vetera Christianorum* 19 (1982): 342–60.

4. Willmar Thorkelson, "Women Served as Priests in Early Days, Scholar Says," *Washington Post* (Oct. 19, 1991), B07.

5. Christopher O'Mahoney, *St. Thérèse, by Those Who Knew Her* (Dublin, Ireland: Veritas Publishers, 1975), 80–81.

6. Incongruously enough, Jeanne d'Arc's identity as a woman of courage and adventure was "tamed" in the 1930s and 1940s when advertisers in the United States used her image to promote domestic items such as vacuum cleaners, laundry detergent, bath soap, etc. (SCA unnumbered).

7. James F. McMillan, "Clericals, Anticlericals and the Women's Movement in France under the Third Republic," *Historical Journal* 24, no. 2 (1981): 361–76.

8. Letter from J. Morris to M. B. Lynch (undated), University of Notre Dame Archives, Joan Morris Papers Carton 1, Folder 16.

9. St. Joan's Alliance, "Women Priests Book of Honor: Joan Morris," www.womenpriests. org/honour/morris.asp.

10. The Grail, www.grail-us.org.

11. Conversations and e-correspondence, especially that of March 1, 2010, with Marian Ronan (longtime Grail member).

12. Ida Raming and Iris Mueller, "Gertrud Heinzelmann," trans. Mary Dittrich (Sept. 1999), www.womenpriests.org.

13. Ibid.

14. Rosemary Lauer, "Women and the Church," *Commonweal Magazine* (Dec. 20, 1963), 365–68.

15. Gertrud Heinzelmann, as quoted by Raming and Mueller in death announcement (Sept. 1999), RAPPORT archives, Baltimore.

16. Ida Raming, Gertrud Jansen, Iris Mueller, and Mechtilde Neuendorf, eds., *Called to Be Woman Priest*, trans. Mary Dittrich (Thaur, Austria: Druck und Verlagshaus Thaur, 1998), 78–89.

17. Ibid., 2.

18. Unknown author and title, UNDA CMBL Carton 2, Folder 3. Mary B. Lynch developed a translated acronym which she used for the U.S. group, also called the Deaconess Movement: Association of Women Aspiring to Priestly Ministry (AWAPM).

19. Frances L. McGillicuddy, ed., *The U.S. St. Joan's Bulletin* (June 1973), UNDA CMBL Carton 1.

20. *The Catholic Citizen* 2 (2000): 34.

21. Christine Schenck, "Infallibility and Equality in Catholicism," *FutureChurch Newsletter* (Nov. 27, 1997): 1.

22. Luigi Sandri, "A Bishop and Two Theologians Propose a Radical Reform in College of Cardinals," *Christianity Today* (June 1, 2001), www.christianitytoday.com/ct/2001/juneweb-only/6-4-27.0.html.

23. Letter from G. Thils to Mary B. Lynch (Aug. 9, 1972), MUA Carton 13, Folder no. 1.

24. *The Bulletin* (Fall 1976), UNDA CMBL Carton 3, Folder 12.

25. "India's Bishops Strive for Gender Equality in [RCC] Church Bodies," *National Catholic Reporter* (March 7, 2008), 12.

26. Luigi Sandri, *op. cit.*, 1.

27. Godfried Daneels, *Katholiek Nederland* (Sept. 2003).

28. John L. Allen, *National Catholic Reporter* (May 28, 1999), 8.

29. See www.womenpriests.com.

30. Dorothy Irvin, *Collected Calendars of 2003–2007* (St. Paul, MN: Privately published, see 2007), 45–46.

31. Christine Pongratz-Lippitt, "Davidek: Mad or a Genius?" *Tablet* (March 8, 2003): 10.

32. Ibid, 8.

33. "An Open Letter," *National Catholic Reporter* (May 31, 2002).

34. Frances Bernard O'Connor, *Like Bread, Their Voices Rise: Global Women Challenge the Church* (Notre Dame, IN: Ave Maria Press, 1993), 16.

35. Eamonn McCarthy, ed., *Now Is the Time: Proceedings of First International WOW Conference* (Dublin, Ireland: Joneswood Press, 2002), 109.

36. *Cymbals and Silences: Proceedings from the First European Women's Synod* (London: Sophia Press, 1997). There were fifteen U.S. participants, among them S. Cancio, M. J. Daigler, R. Drury, M. Fiedler, A. M. Johnson, R. Nobleman, F. B. O'Connor, D. Pomerleau, S. Roll, and S. Tung.

37. Apollonia Lugemna, "Should the Church Ordain Women or Not?" in *Now Is the Time,* ed. Eamonn McCarthy (Dublin, Ireland: Johnswood Press Ltd., 2002), 55.

38. Eamonn McCarthy, ed., *op. cit.*, 103–12, and table of contents.

39. Ferdinand Rafael Regelsberger of Austria assisted Braschi at the ordination ceremony on the Danube and has the same ambiguous standing in the RCC as Braschi, each having been legitimately ordained to the RC priesthood and each omitted from the official roster of RC bishops to be found at www.catholic-hierarchy.org/. See also Rose Marie Berger, "Rocking the Boat," *Sojourners Magazine* (March 2007), www.sojo.net/index.cfm?action=magazine.article&issue=soj0703&article=070322.

40. William Levada and Angelo Amato, "General Decree regarding the Delict of Attempted Sacred Ordination of a Woman" (Vatican City, Congregation for the Doctrine of the Faith, May 30, 2008), 1.

41. Interview with Andrea Johnson, Severna Park, Maryland (March 3, 2010).

42. Christine Schenk, "Women Deacons: Why Now?" *Focus on FutureChurch* 12, no. 4 (Cleveland, Ohio, Winter 2005): 1.

Chapter Seven

An Upward Spiral

Longstanding Challenges

The history of the women's ordination movement is simultaneously a revelation of the past and a hint of the future. In these two functions, one might compare human history to a complex piece of weaving: all the threads are entwined, and pulling one snags others with it, altering the design. The following pages will examine significant issues that have arisen continuously over time in the movement in the United States and yet remain unresolved, as they are in many social reform groups and, indeed, in U.S. society in general. The imperfect resolution of these several challenges does not represent a flaw in the individuals who have advanced the goal of women's ordination in the Roman Catholic Church. It simply reflects the human condition which often falls short of complete success but must await a *kairos*. Meanwhile, people of good intent continue working to improve their small spot on the planet.

Commentators and analysts of the movement's life from 1911 to today offer remarkably similar predictions of issues that need to be addressed now and in the future. In a paper delivered at the 1978 WOC conference, Sheila Collins pinpointed racism as such a matter.[1] Shortly after that, Rosemary Radford Ruether[2] noted that the 1978 conference included dialogue on racial and class issues, as well as the conflict in the movement between those who want to be ordained in the Roman Catholic Church and "those who wish to construct a radically new Church."[3] In the year 2000, Laurie Wright Garry nuanced the issues still remaining to be successfully addressed[4] as the exclusivity of the movement, the existing gap between professional theologians and professional practitioners, and operative theologies that are radically at odds with one another.

159

Ten years after Garry's analysis, the members of RAPPORT, who are longtime practitioner-theologians, discussed this topic at their April 2010 meeting and identified issues from their shared perspective and personal experiences.[5] The root challenge, they noted, is that "the Roman Catholic Church is based on and embraces power" which expresses itself in its communication style, its rules, and its manner of relating with contemporary society. The hierarchy's commitment to retain power, they said, leads to (among many other things) its institutionalized and personal fear of women. In turn, the fear leads to anger toward and demeaning of women. The group's members reflected, too, on their observations that many in the current hierarchy and many of the younger clergy and seminarians (who will be the next generation of hierarchy) are committed to retrenchment from the spirit and teachings of Vatican II, rather than to their advancement.

The RAPPORT women, whose theological studies inform their thinking, listed a growing phenomenon specific to the U.S. Church. While the Second Vatican Council's theology advocated a priesthood and liturgical life that would embrace the best of the surrounding culture and language, the ever-increasing practice of "priest poaching" (recruitment of ordained men from foreign cultures profoundly at variance with the United States) in the twenty-first century suggests a rejection of the council's teachings and is very often a grave problem in ministering to and with the people of God.

In this same discussion, the women of RAPPORT spent time discussing ongoing challenges particular to the women's ordination movement and related to the picture of the church at large. Based on their pastoral experience, the primary issue is that so many Catholics—women and men—continue to lose interest in choosing a ministerial life that would position them as "the public face" of a church that is perceived to be very unhealthy. Thus there is a real possibility that in the future there will be no critical mass of energy toward reform. In the face of this broad reality in the U.S. Church, another question they raised was whether the movement can or will integrate the theology that informs several women's (and a few men's) decision to be ordained in the Roman Catholic Women Priests (RCWP) group.

The challenges laid down in recent decades by these and other individuals provide a possible design for future work. By and large they are issues partially addressed at several moments in the history of the women's ordination movement, and they call out for resolution in the years ahead.

A NEXT GENERATION?

Their Catholic Identity

It is not a question of whether there are "enough" young Catholics to maintain the women's ordination movement, but a question of what sort of Catholics they are or will become. After all, the church's demographics reveal a sizeable cadre of members between the ages of twenty-three and thirty-one.[6] The operative questions are, rather, their type and level of education, to what extent they own "the Catholic culture," and which version of the Catholic culture they are likely to own. Sociologists of the Life Cycle Institute at the Catholic University of America have conducted a longitudinal study of American Catholics from 1987 through 2005, and have arrived at some conclusions relevant to the future of the Catholic Church and, therefore, of the women's ordination movement.

The youngest Catholics studied in this research survey, called the "Millennials," were born between 1979 and 1987. The vast majority of them indicated an acceptance of the "core beliefs" of Roman Catholicism (the life, death, and resurrection of Jesus), but they do not include in that core "any of the teachings on human sexuality, or on clerical celibacy or women priests, or how parishes are run, or the importance of celebrating the sacraments regularly." The trends suggest a continuing decline in identity and commitment.[7] While the data on that one age cohort are revealing, taken in isolation from the other cohorts' data, they would not be reliably predictive. But because the study found a clear and consistent decline in identity and commitment from the oldest Catholic cohort to the youngest, it can be presumed that the next generations to be studied will continue that downward trend. Anecdotal comments, such as Robert Egan's, further specify one area of disenchantment for young adults: "Increasingly, in my experience, most Catholic undergraduate students find the exclusion of women [from ordination] strange and embarrassing."[8]

Some twenty years after Vatican II, St. Joan's Alliance president Virginia Sullivan Finn described other factors that raised similar questions in the alliance's U.S. branch.[9] She urged the few remaining members to support the organization's activities, noting that only three (herself, Bernice McNeela, and Verna Mikesh) had attended the national meeting, making it difficult to do business without a quorum. She expressed her understanding that many members were ill, aged, disabled, or otherwise prevented from traveling to the meeting, and prodded them to recruit new members to the organization. This dynamic, described so simply by Finn, is a poignant reality shared with other Catholic reform groups and religious communities of women and of men. The reality of fewer members results in fewer projects being initiated; having fewer projects means the organization's visibility is reduced; and reduced visibility of the organization results in still fewer (if any) new members.

Despite the success of WOC's Young Feminist Network, including its intergenerational dialogues with theologians, its mission to challenge and support younger women, its international awareness and experiences, its periodic retreats, and its members who serve as national WOC leaders, the demographic future of the overall movement may replay that of the St. Joan's Alliance, as expressed by Virginia Finn above. The Life Cycle Institute's conclusions, the ministry of the RAPPORT women, and the experience of the St. Joan's Alliance (among many other indicators) raise the question of whether there will continue to be enough sufficiently invested Catholics to do the hard work of changing the practices of the church, including those concerning the ordination of women.

Their Education

The passion of Catholic Church reform groups (of both the right and the left) seems to stem from many members' earlier strong immersion in the church's culture, which in the recent past has been conspicuously imbued in students during education in its schools and colleges. The reality, however, belies the common impression held by even Catholics themselves that most Catholic students attended these denominational schools. The fact is that only about 50 percent of them did so—even in the schools' heyday.[10] Still, one looks to the educational environment of the Millennials and their descendants as one predictor of the church's future.

U.S. Catholic schools and universities in the hundreds have closed since the 1970s for lack of funds to pay women and men to replace the Sisters who had been staffing the system for little or no salary. Parishioners have been financially unable or unwilling to sufficiently support the parish schools; in addition, non-parochial private Catholic schools were necessarily pricing themselves out of existence. The Sisters' departure from the field of education was due to several factors, among them that large numbers of women were leaving the religious communities and very few new members were arriving. Compounding these hard realities was the fact that the ever-fewer women religious who were available to work needed to serve in positions that would bring some money into the community treasuries to support their members' basic needs and a few community-sponsored ministries.

As the Catholic educational institutions have closed, many families have perforce sent their children to public schools or faith-based schools of other religious denominations because of the financial or geographic inaccessibility of a Catholic school. This development has virtually erased the strong and visible Catholic culture that was the seedbed of varied types of service, from reform activities to religious vocations. In addition to functioning as conduits of the culture, secondary schools and colleges often provided the environment in which to discuss Catholic teachings on contemporary issues. Today, however, those students who do attend Catholic schools at any level often find that their teachers or professors have become reluctant to speak in favor of controversial church-related issues, especially women's ordination, homosexuality, birth control, and married clergy lest they lose their jobs by the action of a bishop, a president, or a principal. Exacerbating these educational realities is the fact that these age cohorts were born so long after Vatican II (1962–1965) that the excitement, enthusiasm, and hope which animated and propelled reform movements in the 1970s is missing from both their church lives and the society surrounding them.

Thus, the great majority of Catholic Millennials and their successors in the near future lack a religious education foundation for engaging matters of consequence to the church at large.

Their Feminism

In the 1960s and 1970s, "feminism" was a polarizing term. As women used their new skills and behaviors, North Americans reacted strongly, some perceiving women's advancement as a long-overdue good and some as an evil that portended the disintegration of church, family, and society. Of course, women's struggle for their rights was not really a new thing, even in the 1960s and 1970s, and precisely because of the successful labor of their foremothers, the Millennial generation seems to believe that the struggle for equality is over and that they can easily achieve whatever they set their minds to. They do not appear to spend much time or effort working for women's rights, either social or ecclesial. Is there a likelihood of finding among them a new form of energy for women and passion for the church?

WOC's Young Feminist Network is quite successful in its work, but its members are not young, by most standards. Many of them, in fact, are the ages of the national and local leaders of the ordination movement in the 1970s, who were at that time in their late-thirties. Today Joy Barnes, Stephanie Barnes, Erin Saiz Hanna, Carmen Lane, Kerry Danner-McDonald, Laura Singer, Aisha Taylor, and Theresa Trujillo are prominent in younger Catholic feminist circles and are women of privilege because of their college and university degrees. By their ages, educations, experiences, and other similarities to the original leaders of WOC, the members of the Young Feminist Network offer a degree of hope for the movement, but they cannot carry the weight of it alone.

Their Financial Status

Very many young adults are, in addition, necessarily preoccupied with tasks of their stage of human development, which today involves developing lifetime relationships, starting families and, for some, repaying unprecedentedly large college loans. These societal facts of life may attract them to easily practiced traditional forms of Catholic piety, and direct social-service volunteerism, which usually seem to be simpler and more doable than participating in a complex, time-consuming, spiritually innovative activist movement for systemic reform. The ordination of women may be, to them, an issue of justice and logic, and a matter of deep conviction, but they are unable to work toward its actualization. Added to those realities is a long-lasting and widespread global financial crisis that has reduced most Americans' spending ability. The U.S. movement, therefore, runs the risk of becoming elitist, if mainly the rather financially secure and/or highly educated are able to fill its membership ranks and participate in its activities.

UNAVOIDABLE CLASSISM?

If indeed the women's ordination movement does by necessity gradually fill with the privileged, the dynamic would be the opposite of that seen in the suffrage movement (1848–1920) in this country,[11] which began among relatively well-to-do women and eventually democratized. Within the segment of the U.S. women's ordination movement that is represented by WOC, democratization came first, with the thousands of "rank and file" who appeared at the doors of the 1975 Detroit gathering. On the other hand, even that egalitarian event saw very few (if any) long-term, chronically impoverished women in attendance. The participants were largely middle-class and white, despite the best efforts of the planners, some available financial aid, and a modest degree of ethnic and cultural diversity of speakers and content. In this, WOC reflected the situation in the United States at the time, where descendents of the earlier immigrant Catholic population in that century had risen from the lowest socioeconomic class to the middle.

In addition, the upward mobility of Roman Catholics has been accompanied by higher levels of education, and for some time now most of that education has been taking place on non-Catholic campuses. This context leads students to experiences outside the earlier Catholic constraints: attending lectures by scholars with very different beliefs from theirs, reading books that would have been listed in *The Index of Forbidden Books* (in effect from 1559 through 1966), and viewing films that would have been banned by the "Legion of Decency" (1933–1966). Their experiences with persons of various religious beliefs or none became more comfortable after the Second Vatican Council relinquished the former Catholic teaching that "outside the church there is no salvation." Consequently even those who preceded the Millennial generation have felt free to devise their own path to salvation, "cutting and pasting" their beliefs and practices, without fear of eternal damnation as the consequence of their choices.[12] Sometimes this results in an extremely rich, multifaceted spirituality and sometimes in a *laissez-faire*, minimalist practice. For all of them the shifting of socioeconomic class causes ripples even in their spiritual lives, beliefs, and religious practices.

One of the effects of those ripples may be one's drifting away from strong identity with the church, thus reducing its pool of potential change agents.

Another way to examine classism within the movement is through the absence of impoverished women from its decision-making roles. Though an economically poor woman may find satisfying ways to be involved in the activities of her geographical area, the money required for travel and accommodations for national gatherings or for service on the board of directors is prohibitive. In addition, if she is employed outside the home, there is a great cost to her for taking time off from work or providing family care while she is away. The result of classism is that her voice and experience is missing from dialogue and decision-making about ordaining Roman Catholic women.

There are those who hold that yet another type of classism is to be found in the very structure of the ordained ministries themselves: that hierarchy is simply an elaborate arrangement of power groups (classes) from bottom to top. This outlook underlies a frequent challenge to women who work for ordination: "Why would you want to be ordained into the power structure that is the church today?"

DIVERSITY: RACIAL, ETHNIC

Always revisiting and never able to resolve the organizational issues surrounding diversity of race and ethnicity, WOC has devoted considerable resources and much creative energy to addressing them. Like the older St. Joan's Alliance, WOC's aggregate membership has mirrored its surrounding culture and the U.S. Catholic body of priests and hierarchy. While there is no documentation of the St. Joan's U.S. branch's work on these matters in the United States, they have a strong record of focused projects and advocacy for indigenous women's rights in developing nations. However, WOC's abundant history on the matter is quite well recorded, from 1975 to current times. [13]

At the 1975 Detroit conference, Shawn Copeland, OP, and Maria Iglesias, SC, "expressed their isolation as members of minorities within the Church." [14] In response, Rosalie Muschal-Reinhardt and M. Roger Thibodeaux, SBS, convened an initial meeting for March 6, 1976, barely three months after that landmark conference. Ada Maria Isasi-Diaz; Muschal-Reinhardt; Sylvia Sedillo, SL; and Thibodeaux were among the participants, and they established an *ad hoc* committee to surface names of minority women to nominate for membership on WOC's Core Commission. Meanwhile, Isasi-Diaz was becoming a voice for greater diversity in the organization, communicating her observations to Mary B. Lynch in a letter. [15] Thibodeaux and theologian Jamie Phelps, OP, of the Black Sisters Conference, engaged in numerous and extensive conversations with Hispanic and African women, inviting them to greater involvement in WOC, and reported that "the general response is that black women prioritize racism over sexism, or that ordination of women is not an issue with them."[16] Nonetheless, Muschal-Reinhardt continued her search among the members of the Black Sisters Conference for those who would write articles and join a cross-cultural group to "eradicate racism with sexism and classism."[17] In 1980, as a member of the WOC staff, Isasi-Diaz planned a minority women's conference, and in addition to "routine" work in that area, awareness workshops were held for the board of directors (October 2001) for the Leadership Team and for the Young Feminist Network. In February 2006, Aisha Taylor, executive director, presented a proposal paper expressing WOC's antiracism vision, strategy, institutional commitment, and plan of action. The board did accept the proposal, and by 2008 an eight-member antiracism team was functioning, with Erin Saiz Hanna as the liaison with the WOC board. This list of WOC actions is not all-inclusive but rather highlights a few events that have occurred over a long period of time as the backdrop for the day-to-day, less dramatic evidence of the organization's values. The more recent work may even create the atmosphere for a more richly diverse approach to the task to which they are committed.

WOC's commitment and actions notwithstanding, the issue remains a very complicated one in value-laden organizations as in society at large, beginning with the definition of what constitutes a person's "minority" status. Is it defined by place of birth or economic status or educational level or skin color or familial culture? Is it defined by how society has treated people who look or speak like you? Is it entirely up to self-identification? Does minority status "wear off" after a certain number of generations? Sociologists struggle with the complex task of defining minority status, so the answer will not be found in these pages. Here, generalizations must suffice.

Only a very small percentage of individuals concerned about any issue can be predicted to become activists for that cause. This fact alone may explain why so few women of diverse racial and ethnic origin are members of WOC: they are by birth the minority in the U.S. Church. Demographers, however, predict that Hispanics will soon arrive at majority status in this country. This development is likely to affect the agenda for WOC's future, as it will for the whole U.S. Catholic Church.

The societal factors of age, class, and race/ethnicity described above are vast in their causes and extraordinarily demanding in their resolution. The leaders of WOC have exhibited no illusions that they can reform the entire U.S. society but have addressed the issues in-house over the decades as a public reminder that each of these ills is "incompatible with God's design."

VARYING THEOLOGIES

Theological principles evolve over time, and the primary task of a Catholic ecumenical council is to reflect on believers' current experience of God and of church, to put that experience into words, and to design some behavioral "best practices" flowing from both. For this reason the participants in the Second Vatican Council (1962–1965) articulated and affirmed theological principles different from those formulated by the First Vatican Council (1870): people's experiences of God and of church had changed profoundly due to two world wars and radical alteration of social patterns. Because experiences, hearts, and minds change at varying paces, the articulation of a universally shared theology at any one point in time is virtually impossible. So it is within the women's ordination movement, which, in this respect, is a microcosm of the Catholic Church.

Theologians have held and expressed many varying theological principles during the life of the movement. Some of them are opposed to the official teachings of the Vatican and have incurred censure or punishment. The existence of the diversity of thought in itself witnesses to the effect of one of Vatican II's teachings: that there are many paths to salvation.[18] This new (in 1965) teaching refuted Catholicism's almost two-thousand-year teaching that "outside the Church there is no salvation."[19] This change of a previously taught major belief has raised doubt among many Catholics that absolute belief in and obedience to all church teachings and practices is necessary: "Since the church was wrong on past teachings, it can be wrong on this one, too," many reason. Furthermore, the possibility of excommunication because of certain beliefs or actions does not seem so dire when one knows that another Christian community can equally well be their "path to salvation." Though the actual numbers who have taken such action is undocumented, based on this author's acquaintances alone it is clear that many qualified Roman Catholic women have accepted ordination in the Lutheran, Methodist, Episcopalian, and other churches with clear consciences.

In addition to the church's changed outlook on religious denomination as predictor of salvation, women's entry into serious theological studies has equipped them with additional knowledge to utilize in professional debate of women's ordination. These scholars have actively sought opportunities to teach the same principles to the broader population by writing, lecturing, discussing, and advising. One thinks of the dramatic increase in Catholics' interest in and devotion to the Judeo-Christian Scriptures since the 1960s. In their studies, they learned of "prophetic disobedience" as a long-standing tradition in the lives of passionate, faith-filled individuals or groups, including the Jesus of the Gospels. Today "prophetic disobedience" is very often invoked as the explanation for ordination-related statements and actions that may seem unthinkable to the onlooker, such as ordination through the RCWP movement (see chapter 6), public witnessing at the national meetings of bishops, leading house-church liturgies, or "fasting" from liturgy for periods of time or special feast days.

The commonly mentioned and often debated concept of "the discipleship of equals," advocated by Elizabeth Schüssler Fiorenza and Rosemary Radford Ruether, is another stream of theology flowing from the post–Vatican II resurgence of Scripture studies among Catholics. They hold a vision of returning to the spirit and practices of the early Christian church, as described in the New Testament, and their lectures, writings, and teachings have influenced many in the movement from 1976 until present times. This vision includes a completely egalitarian approach to the life of the church and precludes ordination as a prerequisite for sacramental leadership of the community. In theory, anyone could serve in any of the ministerial functions with which Catholics are familiar. This vision's desired priestless goal is in tension with those in the movement whose goals are solely the elimination of sexism in the Catholic Church and increasing the availability of the Eucharist for believers.

During theological studies, very many women have chosen to specialize in canon law. Along the way some of them have appropriated and have brought into fairly common discourse in the ordination movement the philosophical principle of *epikeia* as it is housed in canon law. Theologian Daniel Maguire explains the principle thus:

> An important virtue given to us by the ancient Greeks is *epikeia*. This virtue frees us from the letter of a law and binds us only to what could be seen as the mind of a reasonable lawmaker. Law, again in the Thomistic tradition, is a dictate of reason and law of its essence is also *ad bonum commune* so that the unreasonable law that does not serve the common good is no law at all. It is, as Saint Thomas Aquinas says, "iniquity rather than law." There can be abundant application of this in nations [and churches] where the most conservative religious positions on moral matters have been ensconced in law.[20]

In the universes of theology and philosophy there are, of course, differing views on how to interpret and apply *epikeia*, but among the women seeking ordination who hear of it, there has been widespread embrace of the principle. They continue to educate Catholics about it, and they have been reminding bishops for decades that the current particular crisis in the availability of the Eucharist justifies invoking the principle of *epikeia* for the ordination of women.

Some Results of the Varying Theologies

The variety of the theological points noted above illustrates a dilemma which the ordination movement faces for the future: how to advance a movement that seems to have seriously limited resources (human energy, creativity, money, and time), profoundly divergent foundations of belief, and fragmented focus. Surely some of the differences can be held in one embrace, but can its members agree to forever disagree on certain basics, such as whether ordination is necessary? Can advocates of *epikeia* collaborate with those who strongly believe that only a change of the specific canons of church law will do? Can the leaders plan events, publish articles, and commission writings simultaneously for those who hunger for ordination now and for those who reject ordination of both women and men as the ultimate classism? Historian Mary Henold names the challenge "sustained ambivalence"[21] and holds out little hope for the likelihood of lasting success until a degree of resolution and focus is reached.

From the 1970s until today, conflicting beliefs within the movement have stirred up many questions. Some call for radical social egalitarianism and for complete inclusivity in every sphere of life, affirming anyone who wishes to serve in any role whatsoever in the Catholic Church. Some raise the questions mentioned above as to whether ordination in itself is just, perpetuating a classist religion. Others believe that ordination of women must be the goal so that the church can be a witness to the equality that it espouses in words, but they question the justness of a system or preparation that eliminates so many persons from ordination. Yet a third group aims for ordination to specific pieces of the priesthood, basing ordination on preexisting strong skills of the candidate: a skilled counselor or spiritual director could be ordained to the ministry of reconciliation, an effective persuader could be ordained to the ministry of evangelization and baptism, and so on. Subscribers to this school of thought understand these ordinations to be not mere commissioning but "true" ordinations, though the distinctions they make between commissioning and ordination are not clear. Then there is the RCWP phenomenon in which the women invest abundant energy in witnessing to what ecclesial ministry could be like, patterning their preparation, spiritual development, ministerial activities, and governance structure precisely to fit many current practices of the male clerical state (except that RCWP does not assign the women to their ministries).[22]

RESPONSES TO AMBIVALENCE

Emboldened by the loopholes they see in the current state of Catholic theology and law, and impatient with the slow pace of even minor change in the Catholic Church, women previously involved in the movement have resolved their own ambivalence by various means.

Some have become disillusioned by what they believe is the church's deliberate discrimination against women, thrown up their hands, and left the entire enterprise, including their membership in the Roman Catholic Church. Their ministries on campuses and in parishes, families, hospitals, and diocesan offices are the poorer for their decision and their departure.

Not wanting to let their ministerial gifts lie fallow, another set of women has left the Roman Catholic Church and been ordained in a different Christian and/or Catholic Church (e.g., Lutheran, Episcopalian, Old Catholic). Their new spiritual homes have welcomed them into Christian ministry and confirmed them in what they knew all along: that they are women called to servant-leadership in the Christian community.

A less familiar choice of some women has been to accept a call to spiritual and ritual leadership in a small Roman Catholic community where the regularly, licitly, validly ordained male priest has retired or died and his diocese or religious order has not provided a replacement for him. For lack of a more common term, its proponents call this "ordination by acclamation"; it is similar to bishops' and popes' "election by acclamation" in earlier centuries. The ministry in these communities is very similar to the Latin American ecclesial development called *comunidades de base*. In fact, this practice was common in the house-churches of the young Christian community before the church instituted a formal process for ordination as it is understood and implemented today.

This ordination by acclamation also somewhat resembles the RCWP phenomenon in its day-to-day workings. The women in both groups must support themselves financially in non-church-related work because there is no parish structure through which they can earn a living. Following their ordinations, both RCWP and "acclamation priests" find or develop a small worshipping community, or they reenter their former one in their new role as priest. By way of contrast between the groups, many of the women ordained by acclamation have initiated their own theological education and pastoral experience, whereas the RCWP women are required to prepare for ministry according to requirements of the program.

One requirement in civil law and church law alike is that participants in certain activities be appropriate to the activity, that they be "fit matter" for the activity. For example, canon law of the Roman Catholic Church disallows the marriage of infants as "unfit matter" due to the absence of the use of reason appropriate to the action. Likewise, in civil courts a tree cannot own a barn, nor can a rose copyright its scent. They are all "unfit matter" for the proposed activity. Each legal system establishes its own parameters for fitness and unfitness, and the Roman Catholic Church's legal system defines fit matter for ordination to the priesthood as *vir baptizatus*—a baptized male. In the belief that one day the church will change that definition of fit matter for the sacrament, RCWP strives intentionally to illustrate women's fitness for the ministry of priesthood. The group's requirements include formal theological study, ministerial experience and reflection, baptism and membership in the Roman Catholic Church, and participation in regular spiritual companioning. They precisely replicate the current preparatory stages of male candidates, even to the structure, texts, and rituals of their ordination ceremonies. Their ministries echo the historically validated peripatetic types of priests throughout the history of the Catholic Church.

Many U.S. women now working for ordination will be satisfied only when a Roman Catholic bishop in good standing steps forward to ordain them sacramentally, either in public or secretly. This was the strategy chosen by the members of RAPPORT, and they have been vigorous in the attempt to find such a bishop. Upon learning of Bishop Felix Davidek's decision to ordain women in the Czech Republic in 1970, it seemed reasonable to them to hope that one or two bishops in the United States would find a way to do the same, using *epikeia* as their starting point, perhaps. As far back as Mary Lynch's work with the U.S. bishops in the early 1970s, some women in the movement have consistently taken it as their goal to make the acquaintance of bishops and motivate them to act in prophetic disobedience to the Vatican. Many believe (based on rumor, not on documented proof) that this type of ordination has already occurred in several countries around the world, dictated by acute pastoral need.

Not the least of the strategies with a long history of debate (and an even longer history of actualization) has been that of working for licit and valid Roman Catholic ordination to the diaconate. Some of the women in the early Christian communities were ordained as deacons, and Dorothy Irvin's archaeological research verifies that the practice continued for at least eight hundred years. In 1963, the international leaders of the St. Joan's Alliance sent to the Vatican a proposal requesting women's ordination to the diaconate. In 1969, theologian Ansgar Christenson, OCSO, brought the subject to public discourse by his article "The Deaconess Movement: A Catholic Appraisal." This article was followed in 1974 by Josephine Massingberd Ford's "The Order for the Ordination of a Deaconess";[23] in 1975 by Peter Hünermann's "Conclusions Regarding the Female Diaconate";[24] and in 1976 by "The Place of Women in the Ministerial Offices of the Church, as Witnessed by Ecclesial Tradition and Rites of Ordination," the doctoral dissertation of Marie Walter Flood, OP. Historical and theological writing on the subject of ordaining women to the diaconate seemed to be pouring out everywhere.

So it is no wonder that diaconate ordination was explicitly espoused by Jeanne Barnes when she published her galvanizing letter in the *National Catholic Reporter* and subsequently organized the Deaconess Movement throughout the United States. Mary Lynch followed in Barnes's footsteps at first, and in the early period of their work she sought to restore the ancient practice of ordaining women to the diaconate. By the mid-1970s, however, the influence of the very strong international women's liberation movement throughout society had shifted attention away from diaconate ordination to priestly ordination. Part of that shift was due to the perception of the diaconate as a limiting type of ordained ministry, one that would perpetuate stereotypical "women's work" and that was, therefore, antifeminist and against the best interests of women as a whole. In addition, those holding the theology of the "Discipleship of Equals" (especially Elizabeth Schüssler Fiorenza and Rosemary Radford Ruether) do not support the quest for diaconate ordination because it simply perpetuates the classist structure of the church. As for the first-mentioned objection, a RAPPORT report[25] notes, "We see that the circumstances of the time shape all ministries in the Church, and that circumstances of the early Church dictated the differences in male and female deacons' roles. Recall, for example, the 'Mass priests' of the Middle Ages, who were ordained *only* to 'say Mass' in private chapels or at side altars for those who had paid for such a service."

At the same time that the U.S. movement was shifting its attention away from the diaconate, however, the Pontifical Biblical Commission published its 1976 report, opening the door slightly for consideration of women's ordination in announcing that there is nothing in the Scriptures that either prohibits or mandates the ordination of women to the diaconate. This seemingly minor statement has strengthened the conviction of those who focus on diaconate ordination: those who know that they are called to the diaconate, not to the priesthood, and those who seek ordination to the diaconate as a probable door to priesthood. Even some of those who do not seek permanent diaconate ordination for themselves accept the second stance as a basis for strategizing, knowing that every other mainline Christian church that has ordained or installed women to full ministry has first opened the diaconate to them.[26] It is true, as well, that some so-called permanent deacons in the Roman Catholic Church have been ordained to the priesthood upon changes in their life situations (usually the death of their wives).

At the 1978 Baltimore WOC gathering the participants passed the following resolution: "We recommend that the Women's Ordination Conference call upon the officials of the Roman Catholic Church to recognize God's call to some women to be Permanent Deacons."[27] In 1980, the WOC leadership indicated its commitment to pursuing ordination to the diaconate as a valid goal by publishing a study guide on the topic and sending it to all members. In 1982, the organization established a Permanent Diaconate Committee, chaired by Catherine Stewart-Roche to study the issue. In view of all those actions, the outcome of the committee's six months of work with Mary Hunt, Marsie Silvestro, Elizabeth Schüssler Fiorenza, and Rosemary Radford Ruether (coordinated by M. Fidelis McDonough, RSM) was startling: the committee rejected diaconate ordination for women[28] and recommended, instead, pursuit of the cardinalate. Some years later, the diaconate discussion warmed up again with the publication of several pieces of research.

The Canon Law Society of America concluded its examination of the church's body of canon law and issued a statement (1995) that echoed the earlier Pontifical Biblical Commission's decision concerning its examination of the Scriptures: The current code of canon law neither mandates nor forbids the ordination of women to the diaconate.

That ordination to the diaconate is once again a lively part of the public debate among women seeking ordination is also due to the emergence of Phyllis Zagano's groundbreaking scholarly work, published in 2000. Titled *Holy Saturday*, it is a collection and analysis of the Catholic Church's major documents on the subject and the history of its practice of ordaining women to the diaconate.[29] A few years later, Zagano's research led her to conclude, "The judgment that women cannot be ordained priests does not apply to the question of whether women can be ordained deacons."[30] Though not intended as such, this volume can function as a complement to Dorothy Irvin's archaeological work, which was also coming to public attention around the same time.

Then in 2008, designed to coincide in timing with the synod of bishops in Rome, representatives of Women's Ordination Worldwide created and presented to the Vatican a petition "requesting restoration of the female diaconate" supported by twenty-six international organizations and more than 1,700 individuals.[31] The following year, in December 2009, Pope Benedict XVI issued a statement "clarifying Canon Law on the distinction between the diaconate and the priesthood." The pope's clarification "appeared to be a technical step, but it could pave the way for women to be admitted to the permanent diaconate," observed theologian and Vatican-watcher Zagano.[32]

Meanwhile, two of the Eastern Orthodox Churches that are particularly close in dialogue with the Catholic Church were unostentatiously proceeding through similar theological debates and studies. The two Eastern churches—the Greek Orthodox and the Armenian Apostolic Orthodox—had never explicitly and officially banned women's ordination to the diaconate; but by the twentieth century there had been very few such ordinations. In 1984, Primate Archbishop Vatche Hosvopian ordained a young woman to some of the "minor orders" in the Armenian Orthodox Church.[33] Four years later, the participants in the Inter-Orthodox Consultation with Women (at Rhodes) called for full restoration of the order of women deacons.[34] Shortly after that, the World Council of Churches sponsored an Eastern Orthodox women's meeting in Istanbul, and its participants recommended "full participation of Orthodox women in the life of their Church . . . and women's ordination."[35]

As a result of decades of such dialogue and theological reflection, in the early twenty-first century the Greek Orthodox and the Armenian Apostolic Orthodox Churches made the decision to reinstitute and to rejuvenate, respectively, their practice of ordaining women to the diaconate. This decision has inescapable implications for the Roman Catholic Church, which shares the Orthodox history of ordaining women in earlier centuries and then discontinuing the practice. Even more significantly, prior to their 2004 decisions about female deacons, the ongoing dialogue among the three churches had resulted in their mutual recognition of one another's ordained ministries as valid through clear apostolic succession. This challenge to traditional ways of thinking about women's ordination to the diaconate is fraught with complications for the Vatican in the light of its earlier-developed stand of acceptance of male ordinations in the Eastern Orthodox Churches. Will the Vatican acknowledge the Orthodox women's diaconate ordination as valid in the line of succession?

CONCLUSION

The very thesis of this book, found in the words of the Vatican II document called *Gaudium et Spes* (see frontispiece) hints at the realities discovered in the U.S. Catholic women's ordination movement. The fuller context of the quotation makes clear that the incompatibility is between certain human behaviors (discrimination based on gender, for example) and godliness. But the term "incompatible" can be applied as well to strictly human interactions and suggests the existence of tension, conflict, and fractured relationships; of differences so profound that reconciliation cannot be a reasonable hope. Similarly, the convictions of those seeking to change the institutional church's position on the ordination issue are themselves sometimes nearly incompatible with one another. This tension results in a sort of schizophrenia in the women involved: they are considered to be "on the cutting edge" by some, and passé by others. Some of them describe it as "the good girl, bad girl syndrome" and find it distracting from their purpose to be cast as both hero and villain simultaneously, not only by the Roman Catholic Church but also by coworkers in the movement.

For any individual or group working toward radical change in an institution, tension and ambivalence—though very painful at times—can keep them on their toes and often help set the agenda for their future efforts. Certain personalities can be more comfortable with life's ambivalence than other personalities can, and reform organizations need a certain percentage of participants who can creatively cope with the ongoing lack of clarity. Despite Henold's skepticism about the ability of a movement or organization to function well for very long in a state of "sustained ambivalence," such a state can provoke thought and debate and can, along the way, help people to see where they really stand. Those great goods may not be the long-term goal, but they are valuable, in themselves, in any human endeavor.

From the very beginning, the leaders of the U.S. ordination movement have repeatedly acted on their commitment to address racism, classism, "reverse-agism," and conflicting theologies. Regina Bannan captured the situation clearly in 1999: "We are in the middle of every dichotomy: between those who see ordination as irrelevant and those who see it as essential; between those who want to support women's ministries now and those who want [to work on] only this one; . . . I think our genius has to be to continue balancing on our point, never leaning too far one way or the other."[36]

OVERVIEW

As this account of the movement for the ordination of Catholic women in the United States draws to a close, the reader may feel that the sheer mass of historical data has been overwhelming; yet even the non-historian reader knows that the whole story needs to be recovered and has lain buried for too long. That burial covers the roots of the current harvest of many women's anger or indifference toward the Roman Catholic Church. Susan Hill Lindley's significant contributions[37] to the scholarship on this topic are important and very specific: proof of the universality of the issues across religions, cultures, and time; illustration of the inevitability of changes in religious groups, though they are made at varying paces; and documentation of the consistent pattern in which the changes are effected. For example, in all major religions and spiritual groups, women's leadership was at first limited to the home; then to modeling fidelity to the faith and its moral code; then to faith-related charitable work, and later to home missions, foreign missions, and membership on church committees and boards; then to preaching; and lastly, to ordination. Chronologically, some religions have faced the issue of women's ministry earlier than others, but it arises eventually in each of the groups in an amazingly similar pattern of progression. Careful examination of history reveals an eye-opening consistency and persistency of very similar developments in one faith community after another. Among the major religions found in the United States, five still exempt themselves from this progression, however: Eastern Orthodox, Orthodox Judaism, Roman Catholicism, and Missouri Synod Lutheranism (though some of the Eastern Orthodox and of the Missouri Synod Lutheranism churches do ordain women to the diaconate). In Islamic communities, there is no "ordination" as such, but a few women do function as imams.

The metaphor of the "domino effect" comes to mind: one can study the map of the United States, imagining a tremendously long winding path of upright domino tiles falling, one after the other, across the country over the centuries. One after another those tiles fall, upon the impact of the ones standing next to them. There is suspense, there are obstacles (perhaps the mountains will prevent this one or that one from toppling), but in the end all those tiny walls fall.

NOTES

1. Sheila Collins, "Sexism, Racism and the Church: A Social Analysis" (New York: St. John's University, Summer 1978).
2. Rosemary Radford Ruether, "Next Steps for the Women's Ordination Conference" (undated, but internal evidence indicates 1979–1985), MUA Cartons 14 and 15, Folder 52.
3. *Op. cit.*, 2.
4. Laurie Wright Garry, "The Women's Ordination Conference (1975–1994): An Introduction to a Movement," unpublished dissertation (2000): 179–82, MUA.
5. RAPPORT members' dialogue from River's Edge Center (Cleveland, Ohio, April 12, 2010), RAPPORT Archives.
6. William V. D'Antonio, "American Catholics across Generations: Glimpsing the Future," unpublished paper delivered at St. Ignatius Church, New York (2010), 14ff.
7. Ibid., 14.
8. Robert J. Egan, "Why Not? Scripture, History & Women's Ordination," *Commonweal Magazine* (April 11, 2008): 17–27.
9. Letter from the SJA president to all members (Sept. 4, 1988), SCA Carton 11, Folder unnumbered.
10. Timothy Walch, *Parish Schools* (New York: Crossroad Herder Press, 1996), 32.
11. Karen Kennelly, "Ideals of American Catholic Womanhood," in *American Catholic Women: A Historical Exploration*, ed. Karen Kennelly (New York: Macmillan, 1989), 14–16.
12. D'Antonio, *op. cit.*
13. *New Women, New Church* 1, no. 1 (1976 to present).
14. "Coordination of Ministry Response," memo to WOC Core Commission from Rosalie Muschal-Reinhardt and M. Roger Thibodeaux (June 25, 1976), MUA Series 2, Carton 5, Folder 1.
15. Letter from Isasi-Diaz to Mary B. Lynch (March 11, 1976), UNDA CMBL Carton 2, Folder 48.
16. Memo to Core Commission (June 25, 1976), *op. cit.*
17. Letter from Muschal-Reinhardt to Antonia Ebo (June 5, 1980), MUA Carton 17, Folder unnumbered.
18. Second Vatican Council, *Lumen Gentium*, par. 16.
19. Saint Cyprian was the first to use the phrase *Salus extra ecclesiam non est* in his Letter LXXII.
20. Daniel C. Maguire, "*Sex, Ethics, and One Billion Adolescents*," Religious Consultation on Population, Reproductive Health and Ethics, www.religiousconsultation.org/sex,_ethics_&_one_billion_adolescents.htm.
21. Mary J. Henold, *Catholic and Feminist* (Chapel Hill: University of North Carolina Press, 2008), 197–232.
22. For a contemporary critique of this approach, see Marian Ronan, "Living It Out: Ethical Challenges Confronting the Roman Catholic Women's Ordination Movement in the Twenty-First Century," *Journal of Feminist Studies in Religion* 23, no. 2 (2007): 149–69.
23. Josephine Massingberd Ford, "The Order for the Ordination of a Deaconess," *Review for Religious* 33 (1974): 308–14.
24. Peter Hünermann, "Conclusions Regarding the Female Diaconate," *Theological Studies* (1975): 325–33.
25. Annual RAPPORT meeting (Baltimore, 2002), RAPPORT Archives.
26. Susan Hill Lindley, *You Have Stept Out of Your Place: A History of Women and Religion in America* (Louisville, KY: Westminster John Knox Press, 1996), 133–34.
27. Mary Lynch, "Women and the Diaconate" Series Study Guide (Rochester, NY: Women's Ordination Conference, 1980).
28. Virginia Kaib Ratigan and Arlene Anderson Swidler, eds., *A New Phoebe: Perspectives on Roman Catholic Women and the Permanent Diaconate* (Kansas City, MO: Sheed and Ward Publishers, 1990).
29. Phyllis Zagano, *Holy Saturday* (New York: Crossroad Publishing, 2000).

30. Phyllis Zagano, "Catholic Women Deacons: Present Tense," *Worship* 77, no. 5 (Sept. 2003): 386–408.

31. Unknown, "Newsnotes: They've Got a Little List," *Tablet* (Oct. 15, 2008): 19.

32. Phyllis Zagano, "Inching towards a Yes?" *Tablet* (Jan. 9, 2010): 10–11.

33. Vazken Movsesian, "Women in the Armenian Church," Lay Leaders Retreat, Santa Barbara, California (1986), 2.

34. Unknown, "Address of the Ecumenical Patriarch Bartholomew to the Inter-Orthodox Conference for Women" (Istanbul, May 12, 1997).

35. Unknown, "Orthodox Women Issue 'Very Strong' Recommendations" (Geneva: World Council of Churches, May 28, 1997).

36. Regina Bannan, "An Uncompromised Voice," *New Women, New Church* 22, no. 1 (Spring 1999): 7.

37. Susan Hill Lindley, *op. cit.*

Afterword

At a certain point in many individuals' lives, they recognize that they are the only ones in the family who have personal memories of great-aunt Clotilde, of the widening of Delaware Avenue, or of the now long-gone corner deli. That point arrived for me in recent years concerning those Roman Catholic women and men who have labored for the ordination of women to the diaconate and the priesthood in their church. In my concern that the work and relationships of these persons would soon be lost in the mists of time (or incense), this seemed to be the moment to set down as much of the story as possible.

Incompatible with God's Design, now reissued in paperback, reflects repeated requests for a softcover edition, most from "people in the pews," faculty members in universities and secondary schools, and persons who are interested in related topics such as the history of religions, social movements, and gender discrimination. Since the appearance of this book's first edition, there have been significant developments in the lives and works of various persons mentioned.

Popes

On February 28, 2013, due to infirmity and old age, Pope Benedict XVI resigned—the first Pope to have done so since Pope Gregory XII in the year 1415. Many observers imagine that his physical deterioration was hastened by two enormously mismanaged crises in the Roman Catholic Church: the Vatican Bank scandals and the almost worldwide crimes of sexual abuse perpetrated by Roman Catholic clergy.

Within two weeks of Benedict's retirement on March 13, 2013, Jorge Mario Bergoglio was elected by the Cardinals of the Church to be Benedict's successor. Upon his election, he chose to be called "Pope Francis." As a canny administrator, he immediately began to change certain visible, concrete traditions that were almost certain to be received calmly by most Catholics. These include such relatively simple changes as what he wore, where he lived, what he drove, and where he visited. Soon after this innocuous introductory period, Pope Francis initiated the reformation of the Vatican Bank, which necessarily affected many of its current employees—both lay persons and priests. In the process, he called in more outside finance experts as consultants to help oversee the changes required to place the Church's financial affairs in order and on a more morally sound footing.

Simultaneously Francis has since made notable progress in the visible, well-publicized, human aspects of his work: washing the feet of prisoners (females and males) as part of the Holy Week rituals; embracing babies and adults alike; musing aloud about the impossibility of assessing others' spiritual state. (He captured that difficulty in his now well-known "Who am I to judge?" question.) He also considers outreach to victims of clergy sexual abuse to be essential and has made some overtures to affected individuals. But the needed healing among survivors, the treatment of perpetrators, and the reformation of the clerical system alike will be lengthy and complex. It will surely be more painful than the resolution of the current bank crisis.

Amid all these publicized projects, Roman Catholic women seeking to change the Church's law that forbids the ordination of women have repeatedly asked "When is he going to get around to that issue?" The only hint Francis has given is his "informal" response that the issue has already been settled. Many who are aware of this response mentally reconstruct it, knowing that the corpus of legislation called Canon Law is formulated by human beings and has been changed many times in two millennia. They suggest that a more accurate statement on his part would have been "It has already been settled *for now*." So is he positioning himself as the kindly, "feel-good" leader or is he being necessarily shrewd? In either case, Pope Francis is, if anything, an *unsettling* leader, often catching co-workers, Church members, and observers by surprise with his words or deeds. This may seem peripheral, perhaps just the natural outgrowth of his personality and spirituality—or it may be the careful strategy of a skilled administrator, keeping those around him on their toes and out of excessively well-worn ruts. After all, one constructive principle regarding social change we ought not lose sight of is that starting with what seems minor and stands a strong chance of success may allow one the latitude to build on that success over and over again with increasingly more complex projects until one has reached a more substantive goal. So far that seems to be Pope Francis' strategy.

A year after Francis was elected, on April 27, 2014, he canonized Popes John XXIII and John Paul II, offering through the canonization of these two men—whose papal leadership styles, theologies, and personalities differed so radically from one another—an intentional statement of the Church's essential unity, despite the differences among the Church's members, clergy, theologians, and even saints.

Other Individuals

In addition to the years of very public turnover in the Church's official leadership, there were some smaller, more personal developments during and after the same period. The Quixote Center, the first and longest home of the women's ordination movement, suffered from the death of Bill Callahan in July 2010 after an extended illness. In addition, following a period of pain, confusion, and reorganization, the iconic property was sold in 2011 and the center moved its reduced staff and redefined goals to a nearby attractive, modern, and modest office building. Dolly Pomerleau, long-time guide and animator in activities and research surrounding justice for women, changed her work schedule at the Quixote Center to part-time status. In April 2014 the third member of the U.S. movement's founding trio, Maureen Fiedler, moved her office to the campus of American University, from which she had long been broadcasting her successful weekly radio program *Faith Matters*.

The women's ordination movement and, more specifically, the membership-based Women's Ordination Conference, were born only a few years apart, and both remain alive today. But their members, too, have followed similar developmental lifespans. Close in time to Bill Callahan's death and the Quixote Center's relocation, the two women who established the first office of the organization, Rosalie Muschal-Reinhardt and Ada Maria Isasi-Diaz, also passed away in 2013 and 2012 respectively. In the same period of time, two publicly supportive bishops, Howard Hubbard (Albany, New York) and Matthew Clark (Rochester, New York) reached retirement age and left their structural leadership positions in the Roman Catholic Church.

In October 2012, Roy Bourgeois, M.M., was excommunicated from the Church and dismissed from the priesthood and his Maryknoll community of forty years. A relative latecomer to the community of activists favoring women's ordination—an alliance that originated in his longstanding commitments to eradicate poverty in Viet Nam and other countries as well as national leadership in the U.S. peace movement—Bourgeois was penalized for his participation in the 2008 ordination of a woman (Janice Sevre Duszynska) and in the Eucharistic liturgy surrounding it.

Organizations

Brothers and Sisters in Christ (BASIC) merged with We Are Church Ireland in March 2012. In their website statement, they indicated that the decision reflected the desire to make a more effective use of resources, not only to achieve their goals, but for the work of other similar groups. (That decision reveals a similar philosophy to *Wir Sind Kirche* in Germany/Austria, which works for the multifaceted reform of the Roman Catholic Church.) The Women's Ordination Worldwide (WOW) international conference is to be held in Philadelphia in the fall of 2015. (Since WOW's founding in 1996, this will be its third international gathering, following successful meetings in Dublin and Ottawa.) The national Women's Ordination Conference (WOC) has maintained both stability and its energetic creativity under the consistent leadership of Erin Saiz Hanna. The *Pink Smoke Over the Vatican* initiative allowed for the wide distribution of the video of the same name.

Organizations enjoying loose but amicable relationships with WOC continue, especially the Young Feminist Network (YFN), South-East Pennsylvania WOC, and RAPPORT whose membership has continued to decline in numbers, but not in the strength of its convictions or commitments. In its summer 2014 newsletter Saiz-Hanna noted that two major changes had recently developed: two new staff members were hired (one to be based full-time in Rome), and WOC's new office location had been leased in the same building as the New Ways Ministry center. The co-founder and long-time Executive Director of FutureChurch, Christine Schenk, CSJ, has retired from that position and is developing her writing ministry, with lectures and a regularly published national column.

Roman Catholic Women Priests (RCWP) consistently receives much print and other publicity, and grows at differing rates in the different parts of the U.S. church. They are forging a new-old model of priesthood that will provide a gold mine of research input for decades to come.

Developing Issues

Ordination of women to *the permanent diaconate becomes ever a more mainstream* concept and desire among laity. The stimuli changing peoples' thinking on the matter are several. More and more Catholics have experienced the ministries of male deacons in parishes, understand that they are not ordained to the priesthood, have learned that female deacons were prevalent for several centuries in the early church, and wonder why women today cannot take on the same role. As the numbers of able-bodied male priests decline, there is increased need for pastoral services, some of which even very competent lay leaders are not allowed to do. The "people in the pews" are thus deprived of the richness of sacramental life which is their right.

The increasing world-wide awareness of long-standing *oppression and violence* (physical, religious, economic, psychological) toward women and girls prompts church-goers to examine their local faith communities for evidences of similar treatment. Often they find both systemic (barring women from ordination) and personal oppression.

Papal and episcopal *authority and infallibility* are increasingly in public conversation, from the pages of the *New York Times* to idle conversations among friends, with the subjects ranging from the pope to the local bishop to one's own pastor. Anything and anyone is validly subject to scrutiny by Catholics and non-Catholics alike, with the concrete applications of the notions of authority and infallibility drawing the most attention.

Impact of the book

Most authors hope that their research and writing will affect some good. Thus far, my topic has fit nicely into several lecture series planned to celebrate the 50th anniversary of the gathering of Vatican Council II, though that coincidence of timing was not my intent in writing. Those who attend such a lecture, or read the book itself, seem pleasantly surprised to learn of the many highly qualified women and men, clergy and hierarchy included, who have contributed positively to the movement. Each day during the writing process I was conscious of my own limitations and hoped that others would come after me to examine more fully the several aspects of the story. Now and into the future, I hope this work will be of value in distinguishing fact from legend and will thus heal anger and division among members of the Roman Catholic Church concerning the ordination of women to the permanent diaconate and the priesthood.

Mary Jeremy Daigler
August 2014

Appendix A

Acronyms Appearing in the Text and Footnotes

AFAMP	*Amicale des Femmes Aspirant [sic] au Ministère Presbytérale*
AWAPM	Association of Women Aspiring to Priestly Ministry
BASIC	Brothers and Sisters in Christ
BBC	British Broadcasting Corporation
BTFWR	Baltimore Task Force on Women and Religion
CLSA	Canon Law Society of America
CMSW	Conference of Major Superiors of Women (predecessor of Leadership Conference of Women Religious)
COR	Catholic Organizations for Renewal
CTA	Call To Action
CTSA	Catholic Theological Society of America
DM	Deaconess Movement
ERA	Equal Rights Amendment
IFCA	International Federation of Catholic Alumnae
IFUW	International Federation of University Women
LCWR	Leadership Conference of Women Religious
MUA	Marquette University Archives
NAWR	National Assembly of Women Religious

NBSC	National Black Sisters Conference
NCCB	National Conference of Catholic Bishops (until 2001)
NCCW	National Council of Catholic Women
NCR	*National Catholic Reporter*
NWNC	*New Women, New Church*
NWP	National Women's Party
PFE	Priests for Equality
QC	Quixote Center
QCA	Quixote Center Archives
RAPPORT	Renewed and Priestly People: Ordination Reconsidered Today
RCC	Roman Catholic Church
RCWP	Roman Catholic Women Priests
SCA	Smith College Archives (Sophia Smith Collection)
SEPA-WOC	Southeast Pennsylvania Women's Ordination Conference
SJA	St. Joan's Alliance
SJIA	St. Joan's International Alliance
UNDA	University of Notre Dame Archives (Indiana)
UNESCO	United Nations Educational, Scientific and Cultural Organization
USCCB	United States Catholic Conference of Bishops (official name as of 2001)
WATER	Women's Alliance for Theology, Ethics and Ritual
WCC	World Council of Churches
WCTU	Women's Christian Temperance Union
WOC	Women's Ordination Conference (U.S.)
WOW	Women's Ordination Worldwide
WSK	*Wir Sind Kirche*
YFN	Young Feminist Network (of the Women's Ordination Conference)

In the Catholic tradition, initials immediately after a person's name usually indicate either their academic degrees or the religious order or community to which they belong.

Appendix B

Dedication Ceremony of Mary Lynch and Aileen Murphy

B: This morning we are here in the presence of you Bishop [Maurice J.] Dingman, celebrating the presence of Christ, in order to dedicate our lives in a special way.

M: Realizing that God can be encountered only through the activity of His Church, making this personal relationship with God essential[ly] communal, we hereby acknowledge this association.

A: We pronounce this publicly in anticipation of an increase in personal perfection through Christ, in the hope that Christ will respond by giving Himself more fully to us.

M: Conscious of the fact that there will be a need for spiritual strength in terms of patience, openness to the Spirit, perseverance, and trust in one another, we beseech your spiritual support.

A: Knowing that it is the commitment in love that gives personal and fundamental meaning to this promise, and not the activity as such, we ask for special blessings as we undertake this involvement in the building of the character of this new community.

M: We promise faithfulness to this commitment and understand that it entails a life of poverty, chastity and obedience. Thus being clearly united to God our prayer will constantly be for the graces of discernment of external events and internal inspirations in order to formulate the divine actions taking place in a human context.

A: Out of respect for your earthly guidance in this promise we ask that you expect an accountability from us as we proceed into this intensification of our spiritual life. We place our years of knowledge and experience at your call.

B: The source of our Mission is the Holy Spirit. He gives it; he keeps it alive. Our trust in the Spirit will be our continual guide. Our minds and hearts are open. We will live in the Spirit. This union fulfills the purpose of our creation.

May this dedication prepare our minds and hearts for the inspiration of the Holy Spirit.

Pronounced in the Bishop's Chapel, August 12, 1974

Author's note: M = Mary Lynch, A = Aileen Murphy, and B = unnamed third woman, who changed her mind the day before the ceremony.

Appendix C

Text of Theresa Kane's Welcome to Pope John Paul II

October 7, 1979

In the name of the religious women gathered in this Shrine dedicated to Mary, I greet you, Your Holiness Pope John Paul II. It is an honor, a privilege and an awesome responsibility to express in a few moments the sentiments of women present at this shrine dedicated to Mary the patroness of the United States and the Mother of all humankind. It is appropriate that a woman's voice be heard in this shrine and I call upon Mary to direct what is in my heart and on my lips during these moments of greeting.

I welcome you sincerely; I extend greetings of profound respect, esteem and affection from women religious throughout the country. With the sentiments expressed by Elizabeth when visited by Mary, our hearts too leap with joy as we welcome you—you who have been called the Pope of the people. As I welcome you today, I am mindful of the countless number of women religious who have dedicated their lives to the church in this country in the past. The lives of many valiant women who were the catalysts of growth for the United States Church continue to serve as heroines of inspiration to us as we too struggle to be women of courage and hope during these times.

Women religious in the United States entered into renewal efforts in an obedient response to the call of Vatican II. We have experienced both joy and suffering in our efforts. As a result of such renewal women religious approach the next decade with a renewed identity and a deep sense of our responsibilities to, with and in the Church.

Your Holiness, the women of this country have been inspired by your spirit of courage. We thank you for exemplifying such courage in speaking to us so directly about our responsibilities to the poor and oppressed throughout the world. We who live in the United States, one of the wealthiest nations of the earth, need to become ever more conscious of the suffering that is present among so many of our brothers and sisters, recognizing that systemic injustices are serious moral and social issues that need to be confronted courageously. We pledge ourselves in solidarity with you in your efforts to respond to the cry of the poor.

As I share this privileged moment with you, Your Holiness, I urge you to be mindful of the intense suffering and pain which is part of the life of many women in the United States. I call upon you to listen with compassion and to hear the call of women who comprise half of humankind. As women we have heard the powerful messages of our Church addressing the dignity and reverence for all persons. As women we have pondered upon these words. Our contemplation leads us to state that the Church in its struggle to be faithful to its call for reverence and dignity for all persons must respond by providing the possibility of women as persons being included in all ministries of our Church. I urge you, Your Holiness, to be open to and respond to the voices coming from the women in this country who are desirous of serving in and through the Church as fully participating members.

Finally, I assure you, Pope John Paul, of the prayers, support and fidelity of the women religious in this country as you continue to challenge us to be women of holiness for the sake of the Kingdom. With these few words from the joyous, hope-filled prayer, the *Magnificat*, we call upon Mary to be your continued source of inspiration, courage and hope: "May your whole being proclaim and magnify the Lord; may your spirit always rejoice in God your Savior; the Lord who is mighty has done great things for you; holy is God's name."

Appendix D

Family Tree of the U.S. Women's Ordination Movement

AD 100–820	Christian women were ordained in Mediterranean lands.
1911	The Catholic Women's Suffrage Association (St. Joan's Alliance) was founded in England by May Kendall and Gabrielle Jeffery.
1931	Several individual American women became members of the UK branch of St. Joan's Alliance, and its name changed to include "International."
1943	A St. Joan's Alliance U.S. branch was established by Dorothy Shipley Granger for the civil rights of women.
1965	The U.S. members of St. Joan's International Alliance formed a U.S. branch/chapter for the rights of women in the church, especially ordination.
1970	The Deaconess Movement in the United States was sparked by Jeanne Barnes's letter, published in the *National Catholic Reporter*.
1974	The Association of Women Aspiring to the Priestly Ministry, Belgian/French in origin, was brought to the United States by Mary B. Lynch.
1975	The founding of an activist organization in the United States was mandated by participants in the first U.S. national gathering (in Detroit, Michigan) of women supporting ordination.

1976   The Women's Ordination Conference was founded by William Callahan, Maureen Fiedler, and Dolores Pomerleau to fulfill the 1975 mandate of the Detroit conference.

1996   Women's Ordination Worldwide: International Federation of Catholic Women's Ordination Organizations was initiated by Andrea Johnson.

2002   The Roman Catholic Women Priests movement was organized in Germany/Austria by Christine Mayr Lumetzberger and Gisela Forster.

Appendix E

Archival Collections Visited, 2007–2010

Baltimore Task Force on Women and Religion Archives (Julia Heaps, Margaret M. Murphy, and Thekla Rice Collections), Baltimore, Maryland [c/o Mary Jeremy Daigler]

Marquette University Department of Special Collections and University Archives, Milwaukee, Wisconsin

Quixote Center Archives, Mount Rainier, Maryland

RAPPORT Archives, Baltimore, Maryland [c/o Mary Jeremy Daigler]

Smith College Archives (Sophia Smith Collection), Northampton, Massachusetts

Temple University Archives (Special Collections: "Women and Church"), Philadelphia, Pennsylvania

University of Notre Dame Archives, South Bend, Indiana

Bibliography

Bailey, Marie R., ed. *The Bulletin.* Garden City, NY: St. Joan's International Alliance United States Section, June–Sept. 1986.

Briggs, Kenneth. *Double Crossed.* New York: Doubleday Publishers, 2006.

Buchanan, Rene Smith. "RAPPORT: A Project of the Women's Ordination Conference." *New Women, New Church* 1 (Spring 1999): 3.

Carter, Barbara B. "Saint Joan's Quincentenary." *Commonweal* (Oct. 14, 1931): 597–99.

Cunningham, Agnes. "The Role of Women in Ecclesial Ministry." Washington, DC: United States Catholic Conference Committee on Women in Society and the Church, 1976.

Daigler, Mary Jeremy. *Through the Windows: The Work of Higher Education among the Sisters of Mercy of the Americas.* Scranton, PA: University of Scranton Press, 2001.

Daly, Mary. *The Church and the Second Sex.* New York: Harper and Row Publishers, 1968.

D'Antonio, William V. "American Catholics Today: Glimpsing the Future." Unpublished lecture delivered at St. Ignatius Church, New York, 2010.

D'Antonio, William V., James D. Davison, Dean R. Hoge, and Mary L. Gautier. *American Catholics Today: New Realities of Their Faith and Their Church.* Lanham, MD: Sheed and Ward Publishers, 2007.

Dolan, Jay P. *The American Catholic Experience: From Colonial Times to the Present.* Notre Dame, IN: University of Notre Dame Press, 1978.

Dwyer, Maureen, ed. *Proceedings of the Second Conference on Women's Ordination: New Women, New Church, New Priestly Ministry.* Rochester, NY: Kirkwood Press, 1980.

Egan, Robert J. "Why Not? Scripture, History & Women's Ordination." *Commonweal* (April 11, 2008): 17–27.

Eliasova, Magdalena. "Davidek of Czechoslovakia." *New Women, New Church* (Fall 1999): 8.

Farians, Elizabeth. "Struggle for Women's Rights in the Catholic Church." *Women's Studies Abstracts* (Spring 1973): 1–4.

Farians, Elizabeth J. *Autobiography.* www.cincinnati.earthsave.org/elizabeth/htm.

Fiedler, Maureen, and Linda Rabben. *Rome Has Spoken: Forgotten Papal Statements and How They Have Changed through the Centuries.* New York: Crossroad Publishing, 1998.

Flood, Marie Walter. *The Place of Women in the Ministerial Offices of the Church, as Witnessed by Ecclesial Tradition and Rites of Ordination.* Ottawa: National Library of Canada, 1976.

Foley, Nadine. "The Canonical Implications of Ordaining Women to the Permanent Diaconate." Silver Spring, MD: Leadership Conference of Women Religious, 1996.

Ford, Josephine Massingberd. "The Order for the Ordination of a Deaconess." *Review for Religious* 33 (1974).

Gardiner, Anne Marie, ed. *Women in Catholic Priesthood: Proceedings of the Detroit Ordination Conference.* New York: Paulist Press, 1976.

Garry, Laurie Wright. *The Women's Ordination Conference (1975–1994): An Introduction to a Movement.* Unpublished doctoral dissertation. Marquette University, Milwaukee, WI, 2000.

Halter, Deborah. *The Papal "No": A Comprehensive Guide to the Vatican's Rejection of Women's Ordination.* New York: Crossroad Publishing, 2004.

Henold, Mary J. *Catholic and Feminist: The Surprising History of the American Catholic Feminist Movement.* Chapel Hill: University of North Carolina Press, 2008.

Hunt, Evelyn. "Historic Collaborative Group Sponsors Boston Conference." *New Women, New Church* 31, no. 3 (Summer 2008): 7.

Irvin, Dorothy. *The Archaeology of Women's Traditional Ministries in the Church 100 to 820 A.D.* St. Paul, MN: Privately published, 2007.

Isasi-Diaz, Ada Maria. *La Lucha Continues: Mujerista Theology.* New York: Orbis Books, 2004.

Kalven, Janet. "Fifteen Years of Ferment." *Monthly Review* 36, no. 3 (July–Aug. 1984): 73–80.

———. *Women Breaking Boundaries: A Grail Journey, 1940–1995.* New York: State University of New York Press, 1999.

Kenneally, James J. "A Question of Equality." In *American Catholic Women.* Edited by Karen Kennelly. New York: Macmillan, 1989, 125–51.

———. "Women Divided: The Catholic Struggle for an Equal Rights Amendment, 1923–1945." *Catholic Historical Review* 75 (April 1989): 249–63.

———. *The History of American Catholic Women.* New York: Crossroad Publishing, 1990.

Kennelly, Karen, ed. *American Catholic Women: A Historical Exploration.* New York: Macmillan, 1989.

Klemesrud, Judy. "Feminist Organization Is Fighting 'Oppression' in the Catholic Church." *New York Times* (Dec. 1, 1973), 28.

Lauer, Rosemary. "Women and the Church." *Commonweal* (Dec. 20, 1963): 8–10.

Lindley, Susan Hill. *"You Have Stept Out of Your Place": A History of Women and Religion in America.* Louisville, KY: Westminster John Knox Press, 1996.

Lippett, Christa. "Davidek: Mad or a Genius?" *Tablet* (March 8, 2003).

Macy, Gary. "The Ordination of Women in the Early Middle Ages." *Theological Studies* (Sept. 2000).

Maguire, Daniel C. "Sex, Ethics, and One Billion Adolescents." Religious Consultation on Population, Reproductive Health and Ethics. www.religiousconsultation.org/sex,_ethics_&_one_billion_adolescents.htm.

McBrien, Richard. "Institutional and Ministerial Implications of the New Ecclesiology." In *Proceedings of the Second Conference on the Ordination of Roman Catholic Women.* Edited by Maureen Dwyer. Nov. 1978, Baltimore, MD.

McCarthy, Eamonn, ed. *Now Is the Time (Proceedings of First International WOW Conference).* Dublin, Ireland: Privately published, 2002.

McCormick, Richard A. *The Critical Calling.* Washington, DC: Georgetown University Press, 1989.

McEnroy, Carmel. *Guests in Their Own House: The Women of Vatican II.* New York: Crossroad Publishing, 1996.

McEwan, Dorothea. *Cymbals and Silences: Echoes from the First European Women's Synod.* Translated by Aileen Derieg. London: Sophia Press, 1997.

McGrath, Albertus Magnus. *What a Modern Catholic Believes about Women.* Chicago: Thomas More Press, 1972.

McKenna, Mary Lawrence. *Women of the Church: Role and Renewal.* New York: P. J. Kennedy & Sons, 1967.

McNamara, Jo Ann. *Sisters in Arms: Catholic Nuns through Two Millennia.* Cambridge, MA: Harvard University Press, 1996.

Morris, Joan. *The Lady Was a Bishop: The Hidden History of Women with Clerical Ordination and the Jurisdiction of Bishops.* New York: Macmillan, 1973.

———. *Pope John VII—An English Woman: Alias Pope Joan.* London: Vrai Publishers, 1985.

Neal, Marie Augusta. *Catholic Sisters in Transition: From the 1960s to the 1980s.* Wilmington, DE: Michael Glazier Publisher, 1984.

———. *From Nuns to Sisters: An Expanding Vocation.* Mystic, CT: Twenty-Third Publications, 1990.

———. *A Report on the National Profile of the Third Sisters' Survey.* Boston: Emmanuel College Press, 1991.

Neu, Diann. "Our Name Is Church: The Experience of the Catholic-Christian Feminist Liturgies." *Concilium: An International Journal for Theology,* 1982.

O'Connor, Frances Bernard. *Like Bread, Their Voices Rise: Global Women Challenge the Church.* Notre Dame, IN: Ave Maria Press, 1993.

Pelzer, Ann Marie. "A History of the St. Joan's International Alliance." In *The Journal of the St. Joan's International Alliance.* Translated by Francois Awre. Brussels: Privately published, 1992.

Pontifical Biblical Commission. "Can Women Be Priests?" *Origins* 6 (1976).

Raming, Ida. *The Exclusion of Women from the Priesthood: Divine Law or Sex Discrimination?* Translated by Norman R. Adams. Metuchen, NJ: Scarecrow Press, 1976.

Ratigan, Virginia Kaib, and Arlene Anderson Swidler, eds. *A New Phoebe: Perspectives on Roman Catholic Women and the Permanent Diaconate.* Kansas City, MO: Sheed and Ward, 1990.

Roman Catholic Women Priests. www.romancatholicwomenpriests.org.

Ronan, Marian. "Ethical Challenges Confronting the Roman Catholic Women's Ordination Movement in the Twenty-First Century." *Journal of Feminist Studies in Religion* 23, no. 2 (Fall 2007): 149–69.

Ruether, Rosemary Radford, and Rosemary Skinner Keller, eds. *In Our Own Voices: Four Centuries of Women's Religious Writings,* vols. 1–3. San Francisco: Harper Collins Publishers, 1995–1997.

Ruffing, Janet, ed. and trans. *Elizabeth Leseur: Selected Writings.* Mahwah, NJ: Paulist Press, 2005.

Schenk, Christine. "Women Deacons: Why Now?" *Focus on Future Church* 12, no. 4 (2005).

Schneiders, Sandra Marie. *Finding the Treasure: Locating the Catholic Religious Life in a New Ecclesial and Cultural Context.* Malhwah, NJ: Paulist Press, 2000.

Steinfels, Peter. *A People Adrift: The Crisis of the Roman Catholic Church in America.* New York: Simon & Schuster Publishers, 2003.

Swidler, Arlene Anderson. *Woman in a Man's Church.* Malhwah, NJ: Paulist Press, 1973.

Swidler, Arlene Anderson, and Leonard Swidler. *Women Priests: A Catholic Commentary on the Vatican Declaration.* New York: Paulist Press, 1977.

Swidler, Leonard. "Jesus Was a Feminist." *Catholic World* (Jan. 1971): 171–83.

Thompson, Margaret. "Pressures by and on a Marginal Group—Or, Are Catholic Feminists Either?" Paper delivered at the Meeting of the American Political Science Association, Washington, DC, 1986.

Walch, Timothy. *Parish School.* New York: Crossroad Publishing, 1996.

Wijngaards, John. *Did Christ Rule Out Women Priests?* London: McCrimmons Publishers, 1977.

———. *The Ordination of Women in the Catholic Church: Unmasking a Cuckoo's Egg Tradition.* New York: Continuum Publishers, 2001.

Winter, Miriam Therese. *Out of the Depths: The Story of Ludmila Javorova, Ordained Woman Priest.* New York: Crossroad Publishing, 2001.

Wittberg, Patricia. *Creating a Future for Religious Life: A Sociological Perspective.* Malhwah, NJ: Paulist Press, 1991.

———. *From Piety to Professionalism—And Back? Transformations of Organized Religious Virtuosity.* Lanham, MD: Rowman & Littlefield, 2006.

Women's Ordination Conference. *Proceedings of the Fourth Women's Ordination Conference: "Discipleship of Equals: Breaking Bread, Doing Justice."* Fairfax, VA: Women's Ordination Conference, 1980.

Zagano, Phyllis. *Holy Saturday: An Argument for the Restoration of the Female Diaconate in the Catholic Church.* New York: Crossroad Publishing, 2000.

———. "Catholic Women Deacons: Present Tense." *Worship* (Sept. 2003): 386–408.
———. "Newsnotes: They've Got a Little List." *Tablet* (Oct. 15, 2008): 19.
———. "Inching towards a Yes." *Tablet* (Jan. 9, 2010): 10–11.

Index

About the Author

Mary Jeremy Daigler has worked for many years in Catholic higher education as teacher and administrator, and more recently in health care where she worked in development and in pastoral care. Her educational background includes an MA in Latin and Greek from Johns Hopkins University, an MA in linguistics from Indiana University, and an M. Div. and doctorate in ministry from Andover Newton Theological School, Massachusetts. Her research and writing includes a book on Catholic higher education, *Through the Windows* (2001), as well as articles and reviews. A Sister of Mercy, she has served on national and regional boards and leadership committees for higher education and for church-related matters. Currently she enjoys visiting scholar status at Mount Saint Agnes Theological Center for Women in Baltimore, Maryland.